Slash/Mulch Systems

Slash/Mulch Systems

Sustainable Methods for Tropical Agriculture

H. David Thurston

Practical
ACTION
PUBLISHING

Practical Action Publishing Ltd
27a Albert Street, Rugby, CV21 2SG, Warwickshire, UK
www.practicalactionpublishing.org

© Intermediate Technology Publications Ltd 1997

First published 1997

Reprinted by Practical Action Publishing
Rugby, Warwickshire UK

ISBN 9781853393402

A catalogue record for this book is available from the British Library.

Since 1974, Practical Action Publishing has published and
disseminated books and information in support of international
development work throughout the world. Practical Action Publishing
is a trading name of Practical Action Publishing Ltd (Company Reg.
No. 1159018), the wholly owned publishing company of Practical
Action. Practical Action Publishing trades only in support of its
parent charity objectives and any profits are covenanted back to
Practical Action (Charity Reg. No. 247257, Group VAT Registration
No. 880 9924 76).

To my wife and children:
Betty, Jeffrey, Joseph, and David

Contents

Tables and Figures

Preface

I hope to accomplish several things with this book. I have described some of the many slash/mulch systems used around the world, formulated some principles for the use or adaptation of slash/mulch practices, and have attempted to show that the use of mulching and slash/mulch systems constitutes some of the most ecologically sound agricultural systems that traditional farmers have developed over the centuries. Many of these systems can be successfully adopted by resource-poor farmers in tropical regions.

The lack of key words for slash/mulch practices has been a formidable constraint to accessing information for the book. Only a few authors have used the words *slash/mulch* or *slash and mulch* in the past, and only rarely do anthropologists (who are among the few who do write about indigenous slash/mulch systems) use the words *slash and mulch*.

Unfortunately, much of the literature on indigenous slash/mulch systems is unpublished or located in obscure foreign language publications and is difficult to access, which restricted the scope of the book. Some information on cover crops, green manures, and "modern" slash/mulch systems, such as alley cropping, is included, but the reader is referred to other publications for a more comprehensive treatment of these subjects. Various mulching practices are also discussed. One author suggested that "God invented [mulch] simply by deciding to have the leaves fall off the trees once a year" (Stout 1970). Although this indicates a temperate bias for God, it describes an important worldwide source of mulch.

Common and scientific names for plants follow Purseglove (1968, 1972), while common names for diseases and scientific names for pathogens, with few exceptions, follow Holliday (1989).

The diminishing use of organic fertilizers is a major agricultural problem worldwide. Inorganic fertilizers are much easier to transport and apply, and they give quick results. Properly applied, the principles used in slash/mulch systems, especially where legume green manures are included, can significantly reduce environmental degradation and the demand for inorganic fertilizers while increasing crop yields and improving the quality of life for many resource-poor farmers.

The writing, typing, and checking of references was done by the author, and I am solely responsible for any errors.

H. David Thurston

Acknowledgments

The support of the Department of Plant Pathology and the International Agriculture Program of Cornell University, Ithaca, New York, is acknowledged. The help, suggestions, and insights of Lucy Fisher have been especially important in finalizing the book. Special acknowledgment should go to José J. Galindo who, while doing his Ph.D. thesis in Costa Rica on the *frijol tapado* system, recognized and recorded the knowledge and understanding of the Costa Rican farmers relative to this remarkable slash/mulch system. José's work was ultimately responsible for my first serious interest in slash/mulch systems.

I also wish to express gratitude for help, advice, and suggestions to: George Abawi, Mario Ardón Mejia, Stephen Beckerman, Daniel Buckles, Roland Bunch, Malcolm Cairns, Hans Carlier, Mario De la Cruz, Billie DeWalt, Barbara Dotson-Brooner, Eric Fernandes, Milton Flores, Nges Fultang, José J. Galindo, Paul Holliday, Donald Kass, Steve Kearl, Rodrigo Rodriguez-Kabana, Martha Rosemeyer, Edward Ruddell, Kenneth Schlather, Tom Scott, Margaret Smith, Thomas Solomon, Charles Staver, Christine Stockwell, Dan Taylor, Bernard Triomphe, Aberlardo Viana, Gene Wilken, and Anthony Young.

H.D.T.

1

Introduction

Slash/mulch agricultural systems are characterized by the slashing or cutting of vegetation in situ to produce a mulch for an agricultural crop rather than discarding or burning it as is often the case in traditional shifting cultivation systems.

Why might a book on slash/mulch practices be worthwhile among the steady tide of treatises on improving agriculture? While it will take the remainder of the book to do justice to this question, there are several major reasons for documenting this frequently neglected subject. First, slash/mulch practices benefit the environment by providing an alternative to destructive slash-and-burn practices, by reducing shifting cultivation through shortening required fallow lengths, and by restoring degraded soils through the addition of organic matter. Most slash/mulch practices reduce erosion significantly. The reduced fallow length that allows farmers to grow the same amount of crops on less land is especially important for resource-poor farmers who have decreasing access to arable land. Slash/mulch systems generally increase and/or stabilize yields which, in addition to improving family welfare, addresses equity issues by allowing resource-poor farmers to compete more effectively with larger commercial farmers. The systems also are often useful in disease, insects, and weed management.

It is significant that most of the agricultural systems described in this book were developed by traditional farmers; not scientists, development entities, or governments. These mulch-based systems have spread through farmer-to-farmer interactions and efforts, and only recently have NGOs (non-governmental organizations), extension agencies, and agricultural scientists "discovered" some of the systems. Many are still relatively "undiscovered." The only slash/mulch system "designed" or named by scientists, the alley cropping system, has had limited acceptance by farmers, and where alley-cropping was most successful a similar system (Garrity 1993, Metzner 1982) had been used for decades.

As you might have guessed by now, this book is not necessarily aimed at improving "modern" or "high input" agriculture; rather, it is primarily targeted at those individuals and groups interested in assisting indigenous, traditional, and other small-scale farmers with limited access to resources to improve the sustainability of their farming systems and to achieve food security.

The information on the following pages has been gleaned from a number of diverse and often unusual sources--from the chronicles of missionaries to Africa in the 1800's to articles published by international research centers and universities. Much of the information I have found on slash/mulch systems comes from anthropological studies. Most of these studies contain detailed descriptions of the history, family relationships, community life, sources of subsistence, sexual practices, clothing, weaving, religion and housing, but oddly enough, only occasionally are more than a few pages of these studies devoted to descriptions of the agricultural systems that are the primary source of sustenance for many indigenous groups.

Other important sources of information have been NGO staff who have worked (often peripherally) with slash/mulch systems which have yet to be described fully in the scientific literature. Ironically, the majority of adaptive research on slash/mulch systems continues to be done by farmers themselves, and unfortunately, few of the results actually find their way into print. There is also a growing number of researchers who have begun to systematically study slash/mulch practices, primarily those related to cover crops or green manures. However, farmers and researchers must eventually forge closer ties in order to set a research agenda that will be able to address the real issues that small farmers are dealing with in adapting their agricultural systems. Until this occurs, anyone attempting to study slash/mulch and other evolving traditional agroecosystems will be faced by substantial knowledge gaps in the literature.

In the context of this book, indigenous farmers are peoples native to an area who continue to use the accumulated knowledge of traditional agriculture transmitted by their ancestors. Indigenous knowledge is local knowledge particular to a given culture or society. The term "traditional" is usually associated with primitive agricultural systems or preindustrial peasant agriculture. Traditional farming usually is based on agriculture that has been practiced for many generations. The accumulated knowledge on agriculture is considerable; according to archeologists, humans began crop production perhaps 10,000 years ago.

Many, but obviously not all, small-scale farmers practice traditional farming. Farmers who have been resettled from mountainous areas to the lowlands or forced from fertile lowlands into marginal upland areas by population pressure may, in fact, have few traditional practices that can be successfully transferred to their new environments. Other farmers have willingly given up their traditional farming practices over the past few decades in response to the green revolution's promise of increased production.

Small-scale farmers constitute an undeniably important element in the agriculture of developing countries, and in this context "small" is generally synonymous with resource-poor. Poverty and lack of food security characterize the lives of a large sector of rural populations in developing countries who often have few resources beyond the labor of their families. Interestingly, the majority of resource-poor farmers in many developing countries are women.

Although figures vary somewhat, the following are typical. According to the National Research Council (1982), "Half of the world's population is engaged in agriculture, the vast majority in the tropics and subtropics." Goodell (1984) wrote that small farmers till 65% of the world's arable land, and Todaro (1977) stated that 70% of the world's poor live in rural areas and engage primarily in subsistence agriculture. Wood and Lenné (1993) noted: "Approximately 60% of global agriculture is cultivated by subsistence farmers using traditional methods and provides approximately 15-20% of the world's food." The Rockefeller Foundation Annual Report for 1993 (1994) noted that: "Sixty-one percent of the developing world's population participates in agricultural work for sustenance."

Increasing population pressure, associated environmental degradation, changes in land tenure patterns, and harsh socio-economic conditions are forcing many farmers to adapt their traditional farming systems in order to survive. The sustainability of agricultural production in the tropics, particularly within farming systems of resource-poor farmers, continues to erode as these changes take place, the average farm size decreases, and farmers are forced onto increasingly marginal lands by worsening socio-economic and political conditions. In conjunction with the associated increase in rural poverty, these changes result in reduced yield stability and fallow length, which in turn have led to field abandonment and irreparable environmental degradation. Accompanying problems include reduction in soil fertility which is exacerbated by soil erosion, loss of organic matter, nutrient leaching, and sometimes an increase in weeds, diseases, insects, and other pests. The slash/mulch practices outlined in this book may offer insights for farmers trying to adopt their farming systems to changing conditions.

Limited access to reliable information, examples of successful low input agricultural practices, and, in some cases, lack of access to capital, have made it difficult for traditional farmers to fine-tune their farming systems to keep up with the needs of a rapidly changing future. While technologically advanced agriculture does have a role in the amelioration of world hunger and poverty, it is imperative that agricultural practices of traditional farmers be thoroughly understood prior to any attempt to initiate changes. Building upon traditional systems using more participatory processes rather than attempting to replace them with high-input agriculture in large, top-down projects is more likely to succeed in improving the sustainability of small-scale farming systems. Slash/mulch systems throughout the tropics provide useful examples that we can learn from in our attempts to unravel the secrets of environmentally sound agricultural sustainability that can guarantee food security for small farmers throughout the tropics.

The underlying problems of subsistence and poverty of marginalized farmers will ultimately need to be addressed by more process-oriented, participatory development that can encourage land tenure security, community capacity building, and finally, empowerment of disadvantaged populations (including women). However, we cannot wait for the root problems of rural poverty to be dealt with fully before working together with farmers to begin developing appropriate agricultural production systems that can improve yield stability and conserve (or enhance) the resource base of marginal lands without costly inputs. Many of the slash/mulch systems discussed on the following pages can provide a point of departure for those embarking on such a quest.

Traditional Farming Practices

Traditional practices often provide effective and sustainable means of agricultural production; disease management is a case in point. Not only traditional practices, but cultivars (landraces) developed by traditional farmers have had profound effects on "modern agriculture," and most of our present practices and cultivars evolved from these ancient techniques and plant materials. However, traditional systems are in danger of being lost as agriculture modernizes. Therefore, those practices should be studied carefully and conserved before they disappear. Scientists are becoming increasingly aware of the value of traditional and indigenous knowledge in agriculture. Unfortunately, at the same time that this is happening, much of this traditional knowledge is disappearing forever.

Specialization has contributed greatly to the improvement of agriculture, but disciplines often over-specialize and concentrate on only one or a few aspects of agriculture and agricultural development. I have been fortunate to have been exposed to a wide variety of disciplines in the last several decades, and this book results from that broad exposure. Thus, I have become more of a generalist than a specialist and believe that a broad, multi-disciplinary approach is needed if progress is to be made in improving the agriculture of resource-poor farmers in the tropics.

During recent decades the value of the education that United States universities has provided students from developing countries has been steadily declining in its relevance to the problems these students will face when they return to their homes. It is not surprising that much of their education is inappropriate, since it is taking place in our society where only 2-3% of the population is actually living on farms. In contrast, when these professionals from developing countries return they are rejoining societies where 30, 40, or even 80% of populations are engaged in agriculture. Furthermore, most developing countries are in tropical, not temperate, ecosystems, and, although the principles of agricultural utilization of ecosystems may be the same as those in temperate zones, they must be applied using considerably different management systems in the tropics in order to produce the desired results.

Small-scale traditional farmers are not always interested in the highest yields, but rather are more concerned with attaining stable, reliable yields. They tend to minimize risks, seldom taking chances that may lead to hunger, starvation, or losing their land. Most of the decisions of small farmers are rational and many are innovative. Small farmers will adopt agricultural innovations that are sound and without undue risk. However, most agricultural projects are still primarily concerned with increasing food and fiber production; this is often inappropriate if their goal is to meet the needs of the intended beneficiaries. It is no longer news that adoption of unmodified technologies from temperate regions often lead to failure. Part of the reason for this is that North American temperate agricultural systems are relatively simple monocultural cropping systems when compared to the diverse traditional agricultural systems found in most tropical developing countries. Therefore, North American temperate agricultural systems make better subjects for reductionist studies than do the complex traditional systems of tropical developing countries where it is often difficult to isolate a single variable. Thus, the latter are often not considered appropriate subjects for "scientific" inquiry.

Wolf (1986) described the effect that negative attitudes in the scientific community towards traditional agriculture have had on agricultural research.

> Agricultural research has been needlessly hindered for two decades by pejorative attitudes toward traditional farming. Some scientists assumed that because peasant farmers produced low grain yields, their practices had little relevance to twentieth-century agriculture. Until recently, few researchers recognized the ecological and agronomic strengths of traditional practices that had allowed farmers over the centuries to maintain the land's fertility. In pursuit of higher productivity, many agriculturalists overlooked the need for long-term sustainability.

The world seems to be headed toward increasing technological domination, thus we need to stop and take stock of our current research agenda. Finding a way to integrate the needs of the majority of the world's farmers into it seems like a wise choice to make.

Environmental Problems

Many believe that the greatest threat to the world's environment is poverty. When poor people become desperate they often sacrifice their natural resources in order to survive. This leads to ever greater poverty and damaged natural resources become less productive. However, there are a variety of reasons for the deterioration of the world's environment. Along with logging, slash-and-burn systems have been repeatedly criticized as a major cause of environmental degradation and loss of tropical forests in tropical developing countries. Because of dramatic population increases in tropical developing countries, slash-and-burn agriculture has become a major cause of tropical deforestation and is responsible for the destruction of millions of hectares of tropical forests every year. According to Garrity and Khan (1994) "slash-and-burn agriculture (shifting cultivation) accounts for about 50 to 75% of the 17 million hectares of tropical moist forest currently destroyed every year." Many in developing countries are landless, and some migrate to tropical areas and attempt to survive by slash-and-burn agriculture, which is not only unsustainable but accelerates forest destruction. Deforestation rates have increased greatly in recent decades and are believed to cause a significant amount of global warming and much of the loss of the genetic diversity of flora and fauna. Deforestation has also lowered watershed stability in many mountainous tropical areas.

Slash-and-burn systems can also result in loss of soil nutrients, deteriorating soil structure, and serious weed infestations. A major problem with many slash-and-burn systems is the invasion of weeds, especially undesirable grasses such as *Imperata cylindrica*. Farmers spend an inordinate amount of time in weed control. Kasasian (1971) suggested that more human effort is devoted to weed control than any other single human activity. Farmers in Nigeria, most engaged in slash-and-burn agriculture, may spend up to half of their time in weed control (Moody 1975), although herbicides account for about 70 percent of all pesticides used worldwide on major field crops (Gogerty 1994). Weeds are a major cause of the abandonment of slash-and-burn plots after a few years. Repeated burning tends to keep fallows in grass, and such grasslands are difficult or impossible to cultivate, especially at lower elevations. *I. cylindrica* var. *major* is a fire climax species and often remains indefinitely in areas where there is burning every dry season (Denoon and Snowdon 1980). While it is important to remember that slash-and-burn systems are generally sustainable at low population levels, increasing populations in virtually every country on earth has caused slash-and-burn agriculture to become an environmentally destructive practice. Slash/mulch systems can significantly reduce the need to slash-and-burn, thereby reducing damage to the world's ever decreasing forest resources.

Changes in agricultural systems account for part of the deterioration of the world's environment. For example, before World War II most agriculture in the United States was essentially a crop and livestock system. Long rotations were common, usually included legumes, and, in addition, large quantities of animal manure were applied to the soil. In much of the United States today, the crop and livestock system has given way to cash crop systems in which rotations, if practiced, are of short duration and fertilizers are inorganic. An Amish farmer in New York described this system to me as "mining the soil." Livestock and animal manures have almost disappeared from most farms. Many believe that the cash crop system is not a sustainable model in the long term and is inappropriate for most developing countries. In today's world a study of successful systems is especially important as petroleum, water, and other resources are becoming scarce.

The diminishing use of organic fertilizers is a major agricultural problem worldwide, even in countries such as China with a long history of using organic matter in agriculture. Inorganic fertilizers are much easier to transport and apply, and they give quick results. However, the National Academy of Sciences (1979) noted "optimum yields are obtained by complementing mineral fertilizers with organic manures." Although organic manures and composts give significant quantities of nutrients to crops, they also magnify the contribution of small amounts of inorganic fertilizers (Wolf 1986). The numerous long-term benefits of organic matter in agriculture are often overlooked. Lathwell (1990) describes the problem with fertilizer:

> Despite its advantages, fertilizer alone may not be the answer to every farm's soil-fertility problems. While fertilizer nitrogen has been widely used in industrialized nations, its availability is limited in the developing world. Manufacturing nitrogen requires large amounts of energy, especially from fossil fuels, and many developing countries have neither the energy reserves nor the means with which to purchase energy inputs. Shipping costs and distribution problems also can preclude the use of fertilizer. In addition, concerns over the environmental consequences of fertilizer use, including water pollution with nitrate, have prompted a search for alternatives to fertilizer nitrogen in some parts of the world.

Ayanlaja and Sanwo (1991) describe the tremendous importance of organic matter to tropical soils:

> Soil organic matter is the key to successful and sustained productivity of soils of the tropics. This is because soil organic matter positively affects structure, aggregation, porosity, microbial activity, pore size distribution and water retention capacity of the soil. Furthermore, soil organic matter is the major nutrient storage site for the low-activity-clay soils of the tropics and so affect nutrient retention capacity, availability and mobility of macro- and micro-nutrients. It increases the water use efficiency, and therefore attenuates runoff and erosion and consequently the productivity of the soil.

Many farmers in developing countries simply do not have the resources needed to purchase the petroleum and fertilizer needed for a "modern" and highly productive agriculture. One encouraging alternative is the use of green manures which generally involve legumes that are able to fix large quantities of atmospheric nitrogen. The nutrients produced by decomposing mulches in slash/mulch systems, especially those produced from leguminous plants, are another source of nutrients. In addition to producing nutrients, slash/mulch systems reduce erosion, aid in weed control, and have numerous other benefits.

Properly applied, the principles used in slash/mulch systems, especially where legume green manures are included, can significantly reduce environmental degradation and the demand for inorganic fertilizers while increasing crop yields and improving the quality of life for many resource-poor farmers.

The use of cover crops and green manures is spreading rapidly, especially in tropical developing countries (Van der Heide and Hairiah 1989). For example, Bunch (personal communication--Roland Bunch) noted in 1994 that in the last few years, some fifty organizations in Mexico and Central America have begun working with green manures for villager use.

One caution is indicated. Individuals working in development should keep in mind that a number of plants have been introduced in the past with the best of intentions by well meaning people, but subsequently their introductions became environmental disasters and caused serious losses to agriculture. The introduction of kudzu, johnson grass, floating water hyacinth, and crabgrass into the U. S A. are good examples of environmental disasters. The adaptation, invasiveness, and competitiveness of new introductions should be considered and tested before wide-scale introductions are made.

Quality of Life in Developing Countries

Pertinent to the the meaning of the "quality of life," in 1992 I visited a *Save the Children* project in the slums of Tegucigalpa, Honduras, as part of a Cornell University class on agriculture in the tropics. Honduras is one of the poorest countries in Latin America. Poverty indicators are an infant mortality rate of over 47 deaths/1,000 live births and unemployment of 15% with an estimated 20-40% unemployment. Tegucigalpa's slums are on steep hillsides and most of the homes might be described as shacks. I was part of a small group that visited a young woman who appeared to be about twenty-five to thirty years of age. She and her family lived in a hut with a dirt floor made of scrap lumber, cardboard, plastic, and pieces of flattened tin. The home had no chimney and smoke was coming out the door as she talked to us. There was no running water in the entire slum settlement. Water was brought in by trucks and sold by the bucket at a high price. As much as 25% of the income of those living in such slums may be spent on purchasing water (Flynn 1992). The young woman scratched constantly at what were perhaps insect bites. She had four children with her in the hut and all were significantly unwashed. The woman said she had lived in Tegucigalpa for several years. Asked where she came from, she said she lived on a farm in the *campo*(countryside), but because of successive severe droughts she and her family came close to starvation, so they moved to Tegucigalpa and this slum. When we asked how living was in

Tegucigalpa, she said it was much better than living in the *campo*. Here, if her children got sick, she could take them to a free medical clinic. There were no doctors or clinics in the *campo*. There were schools here that her children could go to, so they could learn to read and write and get an education! There were no schools for her children when they lived on the farm. It was obvious that she was pregnant, and we asked if she thought she might have more children. Her answer was "*Si Dios quiere*." If God wills. The misery and suffering that this woman and her family endures is typical of the situation of displaced farm families that are flocking to large cities all over the developing world. Whether knowledge by this woman and her family of the *abonera* system utilizing slashed velvetbeans and maize that has been so successful in raising yields in many areas of Honduras would have enabled them to make a decent living and remain on their farm in spite of the drought is obviously speculation; however, such knowledge might have made an significant, positive difference in the quality of their lives.

Shifting Cultivation Systems

Shifting cultivation has been defined by Conklin (1961) as follows:

> As any continuing agricultural system in which impermanent clearings are cropped for shorter periods in years than they are fallowed.

Using the above definition nearly all slash-and-burn and some slash/mulch systems fall into the category of shifting agriculture.

Shifting cultivation has traditionally been disapproved of by governments as well as international development organizations. In 1957, the staff of the FAO (Food and Agriculture Organization of the United Nations) staff wrote: "shifting cultivation is the custom of clearing (forest or grass-woodland) and of abandoning them as soon as the soil is exhausted." FAO's attitude towards shifting agriculture during this period was highly negative. For example, in the same article they added:

> Shifting cultivation is not only a backward type of agricultural practice. It is also a backward stage of culture in general. In all respects it corresponds to the Neolithic period through which humanity passed between the years 13,000 and 3,000 B.C., considering that the substitution of iron tools for polished stone has made no substantial difference in the way of life.

FAO was so opposed to shifting agriculture that it began a campaign to "overcome" shifting cultivation (FAO 1957). Many scientists, environmental organizations, and politicians in developed and developing countries have continued to be highly critical of the practice, particularly the "notorious" slash-and-burn practices. Although slash-and-burn agriculture has been severely maligned as destructive in many quarters, Greenland (1975) noted: "In the majority of lowland areas of the humid tropics it has been a stable system, providing a limited number of people living on sufficient land as a continuing method of food production, requiring little in terms of inputs." In their recent book on shifting agriculture Peters and Neuenschwander (1988) wrote:

> Increased population pressure and exploitation of tropical forests affect the practice of shifting cultivation. Millions have turned to the ancient system out of necessity, and its inherent sustainability is succumbing to these pressures. This study is a tribute to the system, but a condemnation of its misuse.

I would agree with the above remarks of Peters and Neuenschwander. Without population pressure shifting agriculture systems were remarkably productive and sustainable for centuries.

Slash-and-Burn Systems

In 1957 Conklin gave an exceptionally brief definition of the slash-and-burn agricultural system as follows:

> Any agricultural system in which fields are cleared by firing and are cropped discontinuously.

There is an extensive literature on the numerous slash-and-burn systems used throughout the tropics. For example, over 30 years ago, Conklin (1961) listed over 1,200 references to slash-and-burn in his comprehensive review of shifting cultivation systems, but listed in the same article only two references to the slash/mulch system. Unfortunately, references to slash/mulch systems do not appear to have increased significantly since then while several books have been written on slash-and-burn systems (FAO 1973, Nye and Greenland 1960, Peters and Neuenschwander 1988, Spencer 1966) among others.

The practice of slash-and-burn agriculture consists of clearing plots from the forest and allowing the cut vegetation to dry, then burning, and finally planting crops in the ashes. Plots are used for several years and then are gradually abandoned to natural vegetation for fallow periods of up to 20 or more years. Most languages used in the tropics have a word that describes slash-and-burn agriculture. For example, the terms *swidden* and *milpa* also refer to "slash-and-burn" agriculture, but in Central America and Mexico the Spanish term *milpa* also signifies a maize field.

Slash-and-burn agriculture is far more important than most people realize. Dove (1983) states: "According to recent estimates, swidden agriculture is practiced by 240 to 300 million people on nearly one-half of the land area in the tropics." Other estimates ranged from 200 to 500 million slash-and-burn cultivators (Myers 1988). Slash-and-burn agriculture is most commonly practiced today in tropical areas, but has extended in the past into subtropical and temperate zones. Ancient farmers in Europe practiced slash-and-burn agriculture, and the system was still practiced in northern Europe and Russia in the 1800s. Pre-European Indian groups in northern North America commonly used the slash-and-burn system.

Neither the lowland humid tropics nor the tropical uplands have proven to be highly productive as one might expect, due in large measure to difficulties in maintaining soil fertility, regulating moisture, and managing pests. Slash-and-burn agriculture has been developed in order to provide for people's needs by taking advantage of available land, labor, and other resources Over centuries, traditional farmers developed slash-and-burn agriculture systems as a solution to soil depletion problems and as a method for managing pests. Unfortunately the system, due to the lengthy fallow period generally required, often requires as much as 15-30 hectares to feed one person. On steep slopes or under great population pressure, where the number of people the land has to support becomes so great that the fallow periods are greatly reduced, the system can become destructive.

Burning, as well as fallowing, rotation, polycropping, wide spacing, diversity, and shading, are practices that reduce losses from disease and other pests in slash-and-burn agriculture. In addition, the clearing of small plots permits easy migration of biological control agents, such as insect parasites and predators, from the surrounding forest.

Posey (1985) noted that in the Amazon fields are not necessarily "abandoned" after two or three years; rather, the old fields often continued to bear produce of some crops for years. The Kayapó Indians that he studied in Brazil returned for sweet potatoes for four to five years, yams (*Dioscorea* spp.) and taro (*Colocasia esculenta*) for five to six years, cassava (*Manihot esculenta*) for four to six years, and papaya for five or more years. Bananas continued bearing for 15-20 years. Thus, as crops are harvested from the slash-and-burn plots long after natural vegetation begins to return, fallow is often incomplete in the slash-and-burn system. This aspect of the slash-and-burn system is often ignored or overlooked.

Although farmers such as the Kayapó, do return to harvest some crops, it is interesting to note the various reasons given for generally abandoning slash-and-burn plots after a few seasons. Many agronomists would suggest that the nutrients supplied by the ash from burning are exhausted by crops and weeds and thus lack of nutrients cause abandonment. Numerous authors cite weed infestations as the primary cause for abandoning slash-and-burn plots. Plots are often abandoned because labor to weed outweighs labor required to clear a new plot. Wellman (1972) asserted that plant pathogens such as *Pythium* spp. might be responsible for the need to leave land fallow after slash-and-burn cultivation in the tropics. Baars (1993) noted that burning destroys mycorrhizae and suggested the following hypothetical scenario for the role of mycorrhizae in slash-and-burn agriculture:

> Burning of tropical rainforests for agricultural purposes reduces mycorrhizal population. Food crops subsequently only marginally form symbiosis with mycorrhizae forming fungi during the 1st and 2nd year of cropping and obtain their nutrient needs directly from the soil and the ash produced at burning. As available nutrient and organic matter status declines, pH drops. Effective mycorrhizal populations which developed symbiosis with crop plants during this period suffer from heavy metal toxicity. Nutrient transfer and in particular P, is stopped. Mycorrhizae with enhanced toxicity resistance, which can survive lower pH regimes, become selective and favour symbiosis with successional fallow vegetation. This is a survival mechanism in order to restore natural vegetation.

In most cases low yields caused by weed infestations are the primary cause of abandonment in most slash-and-burn plots. Loss of nutrients, pathogens, insects, nematodes, lack of mycorrhizae and other causes together or separately also help to explain abandonment. Essentially, it is the long fallow required which causes the slash-and-burn system to become destructive except at low population densities. This has fueled the search for finding sustainable alternatives to slash-and-burn.

One such initiative is the alternative slash-and-burn program managed by ICRAF (International Centre for Research in Agroforestry) The Alternatives to Slash-and-Burn (ASB) Programme (Garrity and Kahn 1994) is a global initiative designed to formulate a research and development strategy that will provide workable alternatives to unsustainable slash-and-burn agriculture worldwide. The program involves a consortium of several international research centers and national research systems as well as local and international non-governmental organizations. Research on the biophysical and socioeconomic aspects of slash-and burn, which are being conducted at selected benchmark sites in Africa, Latin America, and Asia by a multidisciplinary team from the ASB consortium, provides the basis for developing and disseminating alternative sustainable production systems for the affected areas. One of the objectives of the program's research strategy is to develop research tools for socioeconomic and biophysical research and to test and validate the alternative technologies and policies developed. The methodologies and the presentation of data need to be standardized for all benchmark sites. As part of the regional characterization, the programme is developing a georeferenced database on the socioeconomic and biophysical factors, and this requires uniform data collection and presentation. Using the Geographic Information System (GIS) will assist in diagnosis and also in determining how data can be extrapolated to other agroecological zones and farming systems. By using similar methods and standardizing the presentation of data, results can be compared and extrapolated across sites and regions. Recommendations can be extended from sites to regions and the world.

A research methodology workshop was convened in 1993 in Bogor, Indonesia, so that ASB consortium scientists could review and establish common and standardized research methodologies that could be used at the different benchmark sites. During the workshop, the scientists carried out a field exercise in West Sumatra, Indonesia, using a "hands-on" approach to test some of the methodologies for biophysical and socioeconomic characterization. Given the diversity of disciplines, the different scales of operation and the variation in biophysical and socioeconomic environments of the research sites, a common research methodology is necessary to make the initiative truly global. As the ASB programme is focused on a highly interactive resource system, the research methodology developed on land-use systems must be one that is acceptable to the multidisciplinary team involved. This will ensure that the environmentally oriented technologies designed are linked with socioeconomic policies that will provide incentives for such technologies and disincentives against further deforestation.

Slash/Mulch Systems

Slash/mulch agricultural systems can be defined as those in which vegetation is slashed or cut *in situ* to produce a mulch that is subsequently used for an agricultural crop.

There are no key words for slash/mulch in any data base I have found. Nevertheless, a search of the literature discloses innumerable variations of slash/mulch systems and practices ranging from the slash/mulch systems in tropical forests, where it is too wet to burn, to the *frijol tapado* systems, coppicing and pruning trees to produce a mulch, the new alley cropping systems, the *popal* system, the riverbank *sajal* system, and the velvetbean/maize system.

Some slash/mulch systems can be considered as a type of *shifting* agriculture, but most are distinctly different from the slash-and-burn systems. Slash/mulch systems are often overlooked or mistaken for slash-and-burn systems. In comparison to slash-and-burn systems few references can be found regarding slash/mulch systems, but such systems are probably far more important, especially in the hot, humid tropics, than most authorities realize.

Some farmer systems combine a slash/mulch practice with a slash-and-burn practice. Certain farmers, after producing a mulch by slashing, may subsequently burn or partially burn the mulch *in situ*. Or, they may burn collected mulch for application to or for incorporation into their fields.

An interesting paragraph on the origin of common beans (*Phaseolus vulgaris*) was written by Reed (1977) as follows:

> Although direct archaeological evidence is as yet lacking that tropical gardening and/or slash-and-burn agriculture were being practiced prior to the beginning of the Recent (period), or even during the Recent, indirect evidence suggests that such cultivation must have been occurring. For instance, domestic common beans, Phaseolus have been found in the Andean highlands as early as 7680 + or - 280 B. P. (before present)(Kaplan, Lynch, and Smith 1973) but the natural habitat of the wild ancestral beans is at a lower altitude on the eastern side of the Andes; cultivation, presumably in a garden, must have proceeded for several hundred years, at least, before the fully domesticated form was achieved and acclimatized to the higher altitude of the Callejón de Huayla, where it was found.

Although it is speculation, is it possible that the "tropical gardening" referred to above might have been a slash/mulch system similar to the *frijol tapado* systems previously described. In fact, several variations of

16

slash and mulch practices continue to be used at lower altitudes on the eastern side of the Andes in Colombia, Ecuador, and Peru today (Hiraoka and Yamamoto 1980, Kramer 1977, Peck 1990, Powell 1992, Vickers 1989, Whitten 1976). It makes more sense that, rather than going directly to more complicated cultivation practices, the first activity of ancient farmers was to broadcast seeds (in this case beans) into brush, cut the brush, and harvest the resulting yield. This would constitute a *frijol tapado* practice. It is also significant that slash/mulch practices are still used at lower altitudes on the eastern side of the Andes and in Peru.

For example, Mestanza I. (1994) described a system called *Haragan Chacra* similar to *frijol tapado* that is used in tropical regions of the Peruvian region of Ucayali. The name for the system comes from the relatively easy management of the bean crop after planting and the complete lack of care required during the cropping cycle. For the *Haragan Chacra* practice the farmer identifies a certain type of vegetation which consists mainly of *Cecropia* spp. trees. According to Mestanza I. *Cecropia* trees have has a high calcium requirement, and the soils where they are found have a pH close to neutral. Mestanza I. wrote:

> The farmer then cuts or slashes the undergrowth, an operation known as "roza". After slashing, the farmer sows, broadcasting 20 kilos of seed, trying to achieve a fairly uniform distribution. Finally, the large trees are felled. This concludes the planting operation. After this, the farmer leaves the plot alone, only returning when the crop is ready for harvest. Under this system, yields reach 500 to 600 kg/ha.

Hiraoka and Yamamoto (1980) describe the extensive use of related, slash/mulch practices in the eastern lowlands of the Amazon in Ecuador and Colombia. The slash/mulch agricultural systems currently used in these tropical areas are based upon the practices of indigenous Indians.

I believe that the principles guiding slash/mulch systems around the world incorporate valuable lessons for those interested in truly sustainable agriculture that is environmentally sound. As previously mentioned, under today's high population pressures, slash-and-burn systems are contributing to land degradation and the destruction of the fragile ecosystems of the tropics, especially in mountainous areas. Highlands and mountainous areas are highly sensitive to environmental degradation and vast areas are found in many tropical countries. For example, in Latin America and the Caribbean, Young (1991) noted that steep slopes and highlands make up 48% of the total area of the Andes; 78% of the total area of Central America; and 67% of the total area of selected Caribbean countries (Dominican Republic, Haiti, Jamaica, and Puerto Rico). Garrity (1993) noted that from 60 to more than 90% of the total land area of Southeast Asia is in uplands. It is in such fragile areas that principles of the slash/mulch system can make their greatest contribution. The use of mulches to reduce erosion is becoming acknowledged as the most effective strategy for reducing soil erosion on steep hillsides. A guiding principle of most slash/mulch systems is the production of mulches that protect the soil.

It is generally accepted that slash-and-burn farmers burn in order to obtain nutrients for their crops from the ash produced by burning. Jordan (1989) agreed that this is true; however, from studies made near San Carlos, Venezuela, in an Amazon rain forest, he concluded: "but it is the decomposing unburned slash on top of the soil that appears to sustain the fertility of the soil over the three-year cultivation cycle, after the ash has dissolved." This information gives an indication of the additional importance of nutrients provided by decomposing slash in tropical agroecosystems.

The experience of the farmers in different parts of the world with slash/mulch systems can be of great value to other farmers in faraway countries or continents. In addition to the centuries of traditional farmer experience with slash/mulch systems, there are also recent innovations made by both farmers and investigators working with the systems, as is the case with the increasing use of the velvetbean in Central America and Mexico. Slash/mulch systems, as is the case with the *frijol tapado* (covered beans) systems, have been used for centuries by farmers in the humid tropics, especially where burning is difficult or impossible. A study of the principles used in traditional and indigenous slash/mulch systems could well provide important lessons for improving the sustainability and productivity of agriculture in developing countries.

The author helped organize a Mulch-Based Agriculture Group at Cornell University, Ithaca, New York in 1994. "Mulch-based agriculture" includes systems in which green manures, cover crops, or agroforestry species contribute to a mulch or litter layer of vegetative biomass which is left on the the soil or partially incorporated. Emphasis is given to slash/mulch systems, mulch-based agriculture on marginal lands, and farming systems in transition from shifting to sedentary agriculture. Information, a data base, and pictures of various mulch-based agricultural systems, such as *frijol tapado* in Central America and the velvet bean/maize system can be found on the World Wide Web at the following URL:

http://ppathw3.cals.cornell.edu/mba_project/no_image.html

2

Mulching

The term *mulching* means different things to different people. It has been simply defined as an "application of a *covering* layer of material to the soil surface" (Rowe-Dutton 1957) or "any *covering* placed over the soil surface to modify soil physical properties, create favorable environments for root development and nutrient uptake, and reduce soil erosion and degradation" (Wilson and Akapa 1983). *Covering* seems to be a key word in most definitions. Lal (1987) defined "mulch" as "a layer of dissimilar material separating the soil surface from the atmosphere." In 1990 Lal further defined "mulch tillage" or "stubble mulch farming "as a tillage system that ensures a maximum retention of crop residue on the soil surface." In the following chapter, however, mulch refers to organic mulches and not to those derived from rock, plastic, or other inorganic materials.

Terms Used Relative to Mulching

There seem to be a large number of terms used relative to mulching, but they are not used consistently by all authorities. Some authors (Gindrat 1979 and Wilken 1987) distinguish between crop residues, which are developed *in situ*, and mulches, which include fresh and dried plant material and composts brought to the field. However, it should be noted that crop residues are frequently used as mulches. The no-tillage and minimum-tillage systems which have become so popular in recent years (Akobundu 1983, Lal 1981, Phillips 1980) make use of mulches (crop residues) left on the soil. Palti (1981) distinguishes between organic amendments (incorporated into the soil) and mulches (what is spread or left, i.e. stubble; on the soil surface).

Some authors refer to "live mulches" (Akobundu 1984, 1993, Karunairajan 1982). Live mulches are cover crops intercropped with the crop of interest for their mulch value. They are used to suppress weeds, control erosion, enhance fertility, and improve water infiltration of soils. Diver and Sullivan (1992) noted:

> In annual cropping systems, a legume might be overseeded as a living mulch into a grain crop. Or, a legume may be grown as a planting bed for vegetables that are transplanted into tilled or chemically killed strips in the legume stand. In perennial systems, sods of grasses, legumes, or grass-legume mixes are interplanted as living mulches between rows of berries or orchard trees.

Akobundu (1993) defined a live mulch as:

> a crop production technique in which a food crop is planted directly into a living, established cover crop without tillage or destruction of the fallow vegetation.

To add to the confusion, the terms cover crops and green manures are also used in different ways by different authors. Both cover crops and green manures are sometimes slashed to produce a mulch. Traditionally, the term "green manures" has referred to plants, such as various legumes, which were turned under or incorporated into the soil in order to enrich the soil, but in recent years the term is used more loosely, and green manure may sometimes refer to plants whose vegetation may be applied as a mulch to the soil, either slashed and fresh, or after the plant has dried up. Pieters (1927) in his comprehensive treatment of green manures stated: "Green manuring is the practice of enriching the soil by turning under undecomposed plant material (except crop residues) either in place or brought from a distance." He further stated: "A cover crop is one planted for the purpose of covering and protecting the soil." The Soil Science Society of America (1987) defined green manure as plant material incorporated into the soil while green or at maturity for soil improvement. Cover crops are those used to cover and protect the soil surface, although they may be turned under as green manures. Further, the term cover crop also refers to crops grown between orchard trees or on fields between cropping seasons to protect the land from leaching and erosion (Martin 1975).

Leguminous cover crops or green manures are especially valuable because of the substantial amounts of nitrogen many of them can fix and are often referred to as "legume green manures." The nitrogen available from legumes depends on the total biomass produced and on the amount of nitrogen in the plant tissue. Lathwell (1990) commented:

> Under favorable conditions large quantities of N can be fixed by legume green manure crops. First, legumes must be adapted to prevailing climatic conditions. Genetic diversity ensures that some legume species will be adapted to existing climatic conditions. Second, suitable soil conditions favoring dry matter accumulation are required to achieve maximum N fixation. Obtaining cultural information on the species best suited for a particular climate is a huge task, and often only limited information is available.

In addition to the nitrogen leguminous cover crops fix, legume and non-legume cover crops accumulate and cycle phosphorus, potassium, calcium, magnesium, sulfur, and other important plant nutrients.

Information on the common and scientific names, sources, and performance of hundreds of leguminous cover crops is available (Duke 1981, De Sornay 1916, Evans et al. 1983, Flores 1994, Monegat 1991, Pieters 1927, Sarrantonio 1991, Rodale Institute 1992).

Clearly considerable confusion occurs in the terminology used for mulches, cover crops, and green manures. This confusion presents an opportunity for entities concerned with these practices and plant materials to use their prestige to bring about order and a more consistent usage among the many groups and individuals working in this area.

Materials Used as Mulches

The list of materials used as mulches by traditional farmers is very long. Cereal straw and stalks are perhaps the most commonly used mulches, but other examples are crop debris, sawdust, leaves, grass, maize stover, manure, weeds, reeds, Spanish moss, gravel, and various aquatic plants. A sand and stone mulch is extensively used in some dry areas of China (Gale et al. 1993). According to Stigter (1984) materials used by traditional farmers in Tanzania include:

> Tree leaves, dried or green banana leaves, grass and straw are commonly used. In addition, use is made of chopped maize stalks and stems, inter-cropping residues, pruning remains, weeded grass and other weed residues, tree branches, cut-down trees, ash, animal dung and household rubbish. He also mentions the use of shed leaves, grazing and other

grasses, creeping plants, and short intercropped plants. Acland (1971) reported the use of various grasses, banana trash, sisal waste, coffee pulp, wheat straw, sawdust, and wood shavings for mulching coffee in East Africa. Writing in West Africa, Ayanlaja and Sanwo (1991) listed palms, oil mill slurry, maize cobs, cacao pod husks, urban refuse and compost, sugarcane baggase and filter cake, and water hyacinth as materials used for mulching.

Slashed weeds are commonly used as a mulch in tropical agriculture. For example the *frijol tapado* systems in Central America uses slashed weeds to produce a mulch. Japanese colonists, who have farmed in the Amazon of Brazil south of Belem since 1920, have developed productive farming systems that generally require large amounts of both organic and chemical fertilizers (Subler and Uhl 1990). In addition to leguminous cover crops they also use weeds as a source of organic matter. Subler and Uhl wrote: "Weeds are normally cut and left in place or piled as mulches, recycling nutrients previously removed from the soil." Alcorn (1990). describing the slash-and-burn system of the Huastec Maya in Mexico, noted:

Rotting tree roots also release nutrients for crops during the cropping phase of these systems. In the milpa system, stumps begin to sprout even as maize leaves emerge. Weeding is done only once, when the maize is six weeks old, and is accomplished by cutting new growth off near ground level. The slash is used to mulch the maize plants.

In modern or commercial agriculture, the list of materials used as mulches becomes longer and includes manufactured products such as various plastic materials, aluminum foil, asphalt paper, glass wool, and paper. Stones such as pebbles, chipped or crushed rock of varying sizes, shapes, and colors are commonly used as decorative mulches in the USA. Such mulches can reduce evaporation (Kemper et al. 1994). In most cases these inorganic mulches are beyond the scope of this book.

Mulching Practices and Soil Erosion

Soil erosion is a major environmental problem throughout the developing world. The problem is increasing rapidly, not only because more land is being cleared, but because farmers are being forced onto steeper, more fragile lands as arable land on gentle slopes becomes unavailable. Soil losses of hundreds of tons per hectare per year are

Swaify et al. 1982). The use of various soil covers, especially mulches, to reduce erosion is becoming recognized as one of the most effective strategies for reducing soil erosion on steep hillsides.

Lal (1975) and Sanchez (1976) have reviewed the work on mulching practices in the tropics, and Nair (1984) has discussed their use in agroforestry systems. Large quantities of mulch are used for some crops. For instance, in India two applications totalling 50 tons/ha of a mulch consisting of green leaves are used in ginger production (Pruthi 1993). Mulches were once commonly used in coffee culture in East Africa, but the practice has declined, primarily because of labor costs. Large quantities of grass and banana trash were commonly carried to the coffee plantations (Haarer 1962, Wellman 1961). Discussing mulches for coffee, Wellman (1961) noted that during dry seasons mulches provided sufficient soil moisture so that coffee roots could obtain nutrients otherwise unavailable without them. He also noted: "I was told in Africa, by researchers and farmers alike, that fertilizers applied to mulch grass, and this mixture then used as mulch, was more profitable than fertilizer applied directly to the soils of their coffee shambas." This information is similar to that obtained by Rosemeyer and Schlather in Costa Rica showing that the efficiency of phosphorus fertilizer can be greatly increased by applying it to a mulch.

In Nigeria, Okigbo and Lal (1982) tested 22 different mulch treatments and found that a rice hull mulch increased maize yields by 0.7 t/ha and cassava yields by 12 t/ha. They also observed: "As mulches minimize soil erosion, crop yield can be sustained without requiring a bush fallow rotation." On uncropped land at IITA (International Institute of Tropical Agriculture), Nigeria, with a 61 mm rainfall, Lal (1977) made a study of mulch rate on water runoff and soil loss. On land without mulch there was 50% water runoff and 4.83 tons/ha of soil was lost. Two tons/ha of mulch had a 19.7% runoff and a 2.48 tons/ha soil loss. Four tons/ha of mulch had a 8% runoff and a 0.52 tons/ha soil loss. Six tons/ha had only 1.2% water runoff and 0.05 tons/ha of soil was lost. Garrity (1993) cited Panningbatan who found in the Philippines that soil loss was reduced by over two-thirds by a vegetative barrier, but "the maintenance of crop residues on the soil surface reduced soil loss by more than 95%." Griggs (1995) reported the following dramatic figures from the Philippines:

> On mungbean and maize plots with slopes of between 14 and 21%, the planting of hedgerows and the use of hedge clippings and crop residues as mulch cut annual soil loss from 105 to just 5 t/ha.

A study by Nill and Nill (1993) in southern Cameroon on the effect of mulch on rates of soil loss gave the following results:

> The influence of different rates of Guinea grass (*Panicum maximum* Jacq.) mulch on runoff and soil loss was investigated under simulated rainfall conditions and the decomposition of the mulch was monitored over one cropping season. With 20% and 60% cover, runoff was reduced by 30% and 60%, respectively, compared with the control; this was the result of reduced surface sealing and thus higher infiltration of the covered plots. Compared with the uncovered plot, soil loss was 12% with 20% cover and almost negligible with 60% cover. There was no runoff or soil loss with 100% cover. Between 1.5 t/ha and 13.0 t/ha of fresh biomass were required to provide between 20 and 100% cover. Up to 60% cover, the cover effect increased linearly. Above 60%, the cover effect was reduced because of the overlapping of the mulch material. Decomposition during one cropping season reduced the 60, 80 and 100% cover treatments to 15, 15 and 50%, respectively, and the 20% and 40% cover treatments to only 5%. Lower than average daily rainfall was accompanied by higher rates of decomposition.

Barreto (1994) described experiments initiated by CIMMYT in Central America for on-farm testing of crop management factors and erosion control practices under a various maize-legume cropping systems. All legume species tested (*Canavalia ensiformis, Vigna unguiculata* and *Mucuna* spp.) reduced maize yields somewhat compared to sole maize; however, " the results indicate that it is possible to obtain between 40-50% average soil cover over the maize cycle with all legumes provided that both crops are seeded simultaneously." Thus, erosion can be significantly reduced with maize-legume systems. Barreto (1994) wrote:

> Crop residue mulch is often cited as an important ingredient of improved farming-cropping systems; however, procuring the necessary amount of biomass for adequate soil protection throughout the year presents serious practical implementation problems in dry-land environments. In addition, limitations to annual crop biomass production imposed by temperature and moisture regime, topography, soil, crop management, cropping system, etc. all hinder implementation of conservation tillage systems for sloping soils as residue-loading rates are generally insufficient to form a protective mulch over the soil surface year round. It is evident that biomass production in low yielding environments determines whether sufficient residue is available to form mulch. This is particularly relevant where crop residues are grazed or destroyed by fire.

However, the use of mulches is one of the most effective ways that erosion can be reduced on steep hillsides. Low biomass production availability due to climatic and edaphic conditions, grazing and both intentional and unintentional burning are among the reasons that mulch based systems have been difficult to adapt to drier climates. Thus, the use of various soil covers, especially mulches, in very dry environments has not been as successful as their use in wetter environments. For example, Garrity (1993) wrote:

> The practice of retaining surface residues through conservation tillage systems is wholly unexploited in Southeast Asia upland farming systems, yet its ecological value is nowhere as profound in reducing erosion than on tropical sloping uplands.

Research is needed on the identification, utilization, and management of crop residues, mulches, green manures and cover crops in dry environments where many of the poorest farmers are found in tropical countries. It is clear that the use of mulches often constitute the most effective and inexpensive methods of reducing soil erosion, one of the world's major environmental problems.

Positive Effects of Mulches

Some of the positive effects of mulches include:

1. Decreases evaporation of soil moisture, thus conserving moisture and protecting against drought (exception--living green mulches) (Adams 1966, Ayanlaja and Sanwo 1991, Buckles et al. 1994, Buckles 1995, Lal 1975, Lal 1977, Moreno and Sánchez 1994, Russell 1973, Wilk 1985, 1991, Wilson and Akapa 1983).

2. Increases infiltration (water absorption) rates (Ayanlaja and Sanwo 1991, Lal 1975, 1987, Pieters 1927).

3. Reduces erosion and water runoff by maintaining soil cover (Adams 1966, Akobundu 1993, Ayanlaja and Sanwo 1991, Barreto 1994, Buckles et al. 1994, Buckles 1995, Bunch 1994, COPROALDE.CEDECO 1991, El-Swaify et al. 1982, Griggs 1995, Lal 1975, 1977, 1987, Moreno and Sánchez 1994, Nill and Nill 1993, Russell 1973).

4.   Reduces soil temperatures (Cook et al. 1978, Lal 1975, 1987, Russell 1973, Sanchez 1976).

5.   Increases earthworm populations and activity (Cairns 1994, Fragoso et al. 1993, Lal 1987, Mulongoy and Akobundu 1992).

6.   Increases soil organic matter (Ayanlaja and Sanwo 1991, Bunch 1990, 1994, Cook et al. 1978, Harwood and Plucknett 1981, Lal 1975, McCalla and Plucknett 1981, Pieters 1927, Sanchez 1976).

7.   Increases soil nutrients, especially nitrogen from leguminous plants (Ayanlaja and Sanwo 1991, Barreto 1994, Buckles et al. 1994, Buckles 1995, Lathwell 1990, Moreno and Sánchez 1994, Pieters 1927, Russell 1973, Wellman 1961).

8.   Improves soil tilth (Cairns 1994, Lal 1975, Pieters 1927, Russell 1973).

9.   Protects seedlings and young plants from the impact of rain, hail, and the wind (Cairns 1994, DeWalt and DeWalt 1984, Thurston 1992).

10.   Protects seedlings and young plants from birds and other animals. Hans Carlier (personal communication) describes the use of *titepati* (*Artemisia vulgaris*) leaves in newly planted vegetable seedbeds near Pokhara, Nepal. Women cover the seedbeds with freshly cut *titepati* leaves to avoid damage from birds and domestic fowl and to prevent the young plants from drying out. Children reportedly also leave seedbeds covered with *titpati* alone as the leaves smell and taste bad.

11. Reduces rain splashing, which is an important means of dissemination for numerous bacterial and fungal pathogens (Burdon and Chivers 1982, Fitt and McCartney 1986, Moreno and Sánchez 1994, Moreno and Mora 1984, Galindo et al. 1983a, 1983b).

12. Encourages suppressiveness of soils to soil-borne pathogens, such as fungi and nematodes, in some cases (Abawi and Thurston 1994, Bunch 1994, Muller and Gooch 1982, Rodriguez-Kabana et al. 1987, 1992a, 1992b).

13. Aids in weed management by outcompeting and shading (Akobundu 1993, Bunch 1990, Cairns 1994, De la Cruz 1994, Flores 1989, Lal 1975, Lorenz and Errington 1991, Russell 1973).

14. Reduces labor (Bunch 1990, 1994, Kramer 1977, Pachico and Borbon 1987). There is generally much less labor involved in mulching than in the incorporation of plant material. Nevertheless, the cost and labor involved in mulching will vary greatly, depending on the plant material used and, if crop residues produced *in situ* are not used, depending on the distance plant material has to be transported (Thurston 1992).

15. Usually increases crop yields over time (Agboola and Udom 1967, Lal 1975, 1987, Nill and Nill 1993, Okigbo and Lal 1982, Pereira and Jones 1954).

Probably the major value of mulches is their ability to prevent soil erosion and simultaneously improve soils and increase crop productivity. Losses from soil erosion worldwide are alarming, and the welfare of future generations is seriously compromised if erosion is not halted. The denuded hills of Madagascar, Haiti, Honduras, and the Philippines testify to the tragedy of unchecked soil erosion. In many cases the use of mulches is a practicable option for significantly reducing today's rampant soil erosion.

Negative Effects of Mulches

Unfortunately, the effects of mulches are not entirely positive; some of their potential drawbacks are as follows:

1. Mulches may provide a good environment for the multiplication and survival of slugs, which sometimes cause serious losses to crops such as beans when mulched (Andrews 1987, Bunch 1994). In Costa Rica the same slugs that attack beans also vector a serious human nematode pathogen (Beaver et al. 1984, Rizzo et al. 1994).

2. Various pests such as mice, rats, rabbits and snakes may also find thick mulches an attractive habitat (Buckles et al. 1994, Bunch 1990, 1994, Cairns 1994, DeWalt and DeWalt 1984, Wilk 1985). In Central America the poisonous fer-de-lance snake has been found in mulches, although Roland Bunch (personal communication) reported that farmers in northern Honduras, where the fer-de-lance is common, use velvetbean mulches and had reported no problems.

3. Mulches may also provide nutrition and a suitable environment for certain plant pathogens (Abawi and Thurston 1994, Cook et al. 1978, Moreno and Sánchez 1994, Mora and Moreno 1984, Palti 1981).

Moreno and Sánchez 1994, Mora and Moreno 1984, Palti 1981).

4. Mulches may increase the populations of some insects (Andrews 1987, Cook et al. 1978, Crowe 1964). For example, leaf miners (*Leucoptera meyricki* and *L. caffenia*) have become major pests in areas east of the Rift valley in Kenya since 1954 due in part to the general use of mulching, which initially greatly increased coffee yields. Crowe wrote: "Mature caterpillars landing on mulched soil are less likely to be desiccated or captured by predaceous ants than those landing on bare soil." The second reason for the populations change was the increased use of copper fungicides. The reasons for this are not known, but Wellman (1961) made the same observation relative to the use of copper in Latin America. Crowe added that it was interesting to note that although the use of mulches increased leaf miner populations, their use also led to a decline in coffee thrips, probably due to the cooling effect of the mulches on soil.

5. The effect of mulches incorporated into the soil on the C/N ratio is important, as soluble soil nitrogen may be locked up in the microorganisms decomposing the organic material. This may cause a serious nitrogen deficiency, and even make some crops more susceptible to soil-borne pathogens (Jordan 1989).

6. In some cases mulching results in the loss of nitrogen through volatilization as ammonia from decomposing plant material. In Brazil, Costa et al. (1990) found that 45% of the N applied as a velvetbean mulch was not recovered after 178 days. Had the material been incorporated into the soil losses would have been much less.

7. Although labor is actually reduced in many mulch-based systems, in some cases labor costs may increase. A major problems with the use of mulches is that large quantities of material are often needed and if material has to be brought in from sources outside of the field, as was done in China for centuries, there is a tremendous cost in human labor (Thurston 1992).

Incorporation Versus Mulching

Incorporation into the soil by plowing or other means of turning under cover crops or green manures, especially leguminous cover crops, minimizes volatilization of nitrogen (N). The rate of volatilization depends on various environmental factors, such as temperature and the carbon/nitrogen (C/N) ratio of the decomposing material. In Brazilian experiments, the treatment in which mucuna was incorporated into the soil "had a net inorganic N accumulation 60% higher than the treatment with mucuna (*Mucuna aterrima*) placed on the surface after 178 days" (Costa et al. 1990).

Incorporation of cover crops or green manures can also make future tillage operations less difficult, especially those made with animals or by human labor. Many small farmers in the tropics use no-till systems and hand tools such as a planting stick, and, in such cases, a mulch would cause few problems. The considerable labor needed to incorporate plant material into the soil often makes the operation impossible or extremely difficult for resource-poor farmers. In drier areas with extremely poor soils, however, the effort may well be justified by the increase in yield. The decision of whether to mulch or incorporate will depend on agronomic as well as labor and socio-economic considerations.

3

Slash/Mulch Systems
in the Americas

Slash/Mulch Systems Described by Spanish Chroniclers

Indian tribes living centuries or millennia ago in the humid tropical forests of the Americas were likely the first to develop the Latin American slash/mulch systems. There are numerous areas in the tropics where it is so wet that it is impossible to burn, and thus over time a systems were developed by indigenous groups that utilized decomposing mulch as a nutrient source. Patiño (1965) in his book *Historia de la Actividad Agropecuaria en America Equinoccial* included several excellent descriptions of the system and listed numerous early Spanish chroniclers who described the use of the slash/mulch systems for various crops soon after their arrival in the Americas. Patiño noted that the system can be used in virgin forests, but areas that have been previously slashed and mulched and subsequently left in fallow for several years were preferred.

In the 1500's Pedro Cieza de León in his book *Cronica General de Peru* (cited by Patiño 1965) described an Indian practice in the Chocó Province of Colombia: "on hillsides they cut the vegetation and plant their roots and other food crops into it." In 1577 Miguel Cabello de Balboa (1945) reported a native practice in the province of Esmeraldas on the Pacific coast of Ecuador as follows: "they do no more than broadcast maize seed in the hillsides and cut the vegetation over it and collect the harvest: one hundred to one." The above are surely early descriptions of the slash/mulch system. In 1722 the traveler Francisco Coreal (cited by Patiño 1965) noted that the Indians near Buenaventura used the slash/mulch system. Later, in 1780 the Spanish Captain Juan Jiménez

Donozo visited the Atrato River in Western Colombia and made the following description of the slash/mulch system of the Indians:

> They do no more than broadcast (the maize seed) in the brush or forest, which, because of the high moisture, is impenetrable, and later they cut the brush, in such a way that the leaves begin to rot and the branches dry and thus this material serves as a mulch through which the maize germinates.

Patiño cited other descriptions of the slash/mulch system (called *tapado* in Spanish), from various locations on the Pacific coast of Colombia and also from Panama and Costa Rica. After its introduction to the Americas by the Spanish, rice was also planted in the *tapado* system. I found no firm evidence in the literature on how long the slash/mulch system had been used. Nevertheless, the widespread use of the system in hot, humid lowland areas at the time the Spanish first arrived indicates that it probably had been used for many generations by various Indian groups.

Slash/Mulch Systems of the Pacific Coasts
of South and North America

Francisco José de Caldas in 1801 (as cited by Patiño 1965), wrote the following:

> In those places where it rains continuously such as in the Province of Chocó, and the entire west coast of the country, they don't burn; but the excessive humidity combined with great heat makes the land there very fertile. They plant in these areas without another operation except to cut the small bushes and trees, broadcasting at the same time the grain, after which they cut the vegetation covering the already germinating maize. The nutrients which should be utilized by the forest are instead utilized in the maize planting.

The Chocó of Colombia, has an extremely wet climate and records some of the highest rainfall in the world. Numerous authors have described or recorded the presence of the slash/mulch system in the Chocó: Anon (1982), Archer (1937), Ceron Solarte (1986), Eder (1963), Lotero Villa (1977), Patiño (1956, 1962, 1965), Roberts et al. (1957), Torres de Arauz (1966), Valencia-C. (1983), West (1957) and Whitten (1974).

A comprehensive account of the Pacific lowlands region is given by Robert C. West (1957). His study was made from 1951-1954 under the auspices of the office of Naval Research, Washington, D.C. The region is between 1° and 8° north of the equator and consists of the lowland Pacific coast from Darien in Panama through the province of Chocó in Colombia and extending into the province of Esmeraldas in Ecuador. This Pacific lowland region is one of the wettest areas of the world with average annual rainfall totals ranging from 120 to over 400 inches (3-10 meters). Humidity usually fluctuates between 80-95 percent. Most of the area is covered by a dense tropical rainforest. Quibdó, located in the Province of Chocó, Colombia, receives an astonishing 10 meters of rain annually.

The city of Buenaventura in Colombia is on the Pacific coast of Colombia. My first visit to Buenaventura was for several days in 1954 during the "dry" season, and, although the days were clear with bright sunshine, an extremely heavy rainfall lasted all night. West (1957) describes such a rainfall pattern as common for the area and gave the following description of the slash/mulch system:

> Throughout most of the Pacific lowlands, however, the heavy precipitation and lack of a dry season precludes the effective use of fire. Instead a peculiar system, which might be called "slash-mulch" cultivation, of probable Indian origin, has evolved. Seeds are broadcast and rhizomes and cuttings are planted in an uncleared plot; then the bush is cut; decay of cut vegetable matter is rapid, forming a thick mulch through which the sprouts from the seed and cuttings appear within a week or ten days. Weeds are surprisingly few, and the crops grow rapidly, the decaying mulch affording sufficient fertilizer even on infertile hillside soils.

The Chocó region is only sparsely populated by Indians and today, eighty-five percent of the population consists of the descendants of black slaves brought to the area by the Spanish in the 17th and 18th centuries to work in gold mining. The black population has since lost much of its African heritage and has adopted Indian and Spanish customs and ways of life. Many black farmers practice a slash/mulch agriculture adapted from the practices of the now disappearing indigenous Indian populations. The cutting or slashing of vegetation for a slash/mulch plot in the Chocó by the black population was a community affair or kind of "minga" with a line of ten or fifteen men and women working together to cut the brush with their machetes. The minga is a cooperative labor group common among Andean Indian groups, but not among the Indians of the Chocó. West (1957) described the practice as follows:

The institution as practiced by the modern Pacific lowland Negroes contains many African elements, such as chanting, which involves a lead singer and chorus, beer drinking during progress of work, and feasting at the end of the day. According to local inhabitants, the *minga*, one of the few African cultural survivals of the Pacific lowland Negro, is rapidly disappearing as a social institution.

The machete is the primary tool used in slash/mulch cultivation. West writes: "the steel machete, is used to cut the bush, to dig holes for planting rhizomes and cuttings, to weed, and to harvest plantain, bananas and other fruit." Not only maize, but also cassava, bananas, and plantains were planted in the Chocó using the slash/mulch system (West 1957). After planting, the bush is cut down and the shoots emerge through the rotting mulch.

A primitive race of maize variously called *chococito* or *maiz indio*, especially adapted to the slash/mulch system, is commonly planted in Ecuador, Colombia, and Panama according to Patiño (1956, 1962). Patiño (1962) made observations on the slash/mulch system and *chococito* maize in the Pacific lowlands region from 1945 to 1955 in studies made under the auspices of the Rockefeller Foundation and the National Research Council of the U.S.A. He noted that *chococito* maize seed is generally broadcast--not planted--on the Pacific coasts of Panama, along the coast of Colombia, and in the provinces of Esmeraldas and Pinchincha in Ecuador. This race of maize grows from sea level to almost 1,700 meters elevation. However, at the highest elevations it is planted with a digging stick (*espeque*) and is not broadcast.

Patiño noted that few references were found regarding the slash/mulch system, and that many writers, even when describing agriculture in the Chocó, ignored or overlooked the system. This has also been my experience in researching the literature; not only on the Chocó, but also in Africa and Asia. For example, the interesting book by W. F. Sharp (1976) entitled *Slavery on the Spanish Frontier: the Colombian Chocó, 1680-1810* makes no mention of the slash/mulch system, although agriculture was a major activity of most of the people in the region during that time period.

Most of the slash/mulch fields in the Chocó are near streams or rivers because rivers are the major means of transportation in this extremely wet region. Patiño (1962) gave the most complete description of the system of slash/mulch for maize of any of the authors found. He described the system of broadcasting and cutting (slashing) of the vegetation with machetes. After broadcasting, the maize seed was covered with a mulch 5-50 cm thick, but germinated rapidly and broke through the mulch. No further care was given to the crop until close to harvest and, as Patiño wrote, after planting the field was "abandoned to luck." Near maturity, the crop was protected from animals and birds, usually by children. The maize matured after 4 to 5 months. Ears with insect damage were consumed immediately as *choclo* (green ears harvested and consumed before maturity), and only sound ears were placed into storage. West (1957) noted that the harvested ears of maize were hung on the rafters of farmer's houses near the cooking fires where the smoke and heat thoroughly dried the maize, thus preventing damage from fungi and insects.

Roberts et al. (1957) and Timothy et al. (1963) called the *chococito* race of maize used in the slash/mulch system *"chococeño,"* although, according to Patiño (1962), the race should probably have been called *chococito*. Roberts et al. considered *chococito* to be a product of the hybridization of maize with *Tripsacum* spp. These authors also wrote that *chococito* was confined almost exclusively to the humid regions of the Colombian and Ecuadorian Pacific coast. Roberts et al. suggested that *chococito* must have a most uncommon "rusticity," as it is grown without any cultural care except to broadcast it into bush, which is subsequently cut over it. Timothy et al. (1963) also described *"chococeño"* extending from its center of distribution in Colombia into the humid forests of the northern Ecuadorian province of Esmeraldas.

Another description of the the slash/mulch culture in the Chocó was made by the Swedish anthropologist Sven-Erik Isacsson (1985). He worked in the upper Atrato river basin near Quibdo, Colombia, where rain occurs almost 300 days per year. Isacsson made most of his observations during a five months period when he lived with a family group of Emberá Indians. Subsequently, he made other visits to the same area during the period 1969-1975. The Indians in this area use a slash/mulch agricultural system. Isacsson noted that their cultivated fields for maize ranged from 0.09 to 1.28 hectares with an average field size of 0.49 hectares. According to his informants a fallow of two years after harvest was considered sufficient time so that another crop could be planted, but some fields were held in fallow for up to 15 years. Two crops were often planted the same year. The Indian's main crop was maize, and they had six different types: *maiz colorado, maiz negro, maiz amarillo, maiz capio amarillo,* a variant of *maiz amarillo* with large grains and cobs, and *maiz blanco*. At the time of planting, a sower (*regador*), carrying the seed grain in a basket over his shoulder, broadcast handfuls of grain into the bush to be cut. Three or four individuals called *socoladores* followed the regador cutting the bush, consisting of small trees, vines, and bushes, over the broadcast seed. The cut vegetation was left to decay over the maize seed forming a mulch. No subsequent weeding was made, but the crop was subsequently protected from rodents and parrots. After 2-3 months, some of the maize was harvested green as *choclo*, and, after about four months, the rest of the maize was mature. The grain was stored in the husk in the attic of the Indian's houses where smoke and heat conserved the grain and reduced insect damage. It is interesting that far away in North America, in 1621, Captain John Smith of the Virginia colony discovered what the local Indians already knew, i.e. that maize dried in the husk and subsequently stored in the husk has much less insect and fungus damage than shelled maize (Weatherwax 1951).

Isacsson (1985) recorded 14 different types of bananas and plantains cultivated in the slash/mulch system by the Emerá Indians. The size of fields used for plantains and bananas averaged 0.44 hectares. Plantains were by far the most important of the *Musa* species used. *Musa* corms were spaced 1.5 meters apart and were planted in holes made with a digging stick. After planting, forest vegetation was slashed over the planted corms and the decaying bush produced a mulch. The slash/mulch practice for sugar cane was different from that used for maize or plantains in that the vegetation was chopped up more finely into small pieces before the cane was planted in holes. Isacsson wrote that at one time cassava was an important crop in the slash/mulch system, but due to crop damage, primarily by domestic pigs, little cassava was grown in the area he studied.

Paganini (1970) describes the use of the slash/mulch system in parts of the Darien province of Panama.

> In certain parts of the Darien, however, particularly those areas settled by Colombiano refugees and Nonameño Indians, a "slash-mulch" cultivation is practiced. Slash-mulch was first reported by West as being the predominant system in the Pacific Lowlands of Colombia. Paganini added: The practitioners of the slash-mulch system, however, do not used that term as a descriptive title to their peculiar activity. Planting in *tierra cruda* is their way of differentiating the slash and mulch from the slash-and-burn, the latter being called planting in *tierra quemada*.

Panamanian farmers noted that their *tierra cruda* (slash/mulch) plots suffered far less from insect attacks than slash-and-burn plots. Snedaker and Gamble (1969) also reported the use of the slash/mulch practice in the Darien province and wrote that the fallow period in Panama varied from four to six years. Snedaker and Gamble had samples of slash analyzed for their concentration of mineral nutrients. Gamble et al. (1967) also noted the use of the slash/mulch practice by farmers in Panama and Colombia.

The slash/mulch practice has not always been seen as a valuable farming systems. In his book *Living Poor: A Peace Corps Chronicle* Moritz Thomsen (1969) describes his negative reaction, as a Peace Corps volunteer, to the slash/mulch system. He worked and lived in a small village in the province of Esmeraldas on the Pacific Coast of Ecuador where the common system of agriculture was the slash/mulch system. When Thomsen first encountered the slashed debris produced, he suggested that the local farmers should burn the three feet of dead weeds and branches they had cut in their slash/mulch plot, rather than planting in the mulch. Thomsen's reacted to the slash/mulch system as follows (pages 192-194):

> The ground was three feet deep in dead weeds and branches. Wai came up with an ax and felled the timber. Our first hectare, but what a mess. It was the custom to plant corn on ground thus cleared, but it seemed obvious that the yields would be minimal, and I refused to let them do it. "We'll have to burn first," I insisted, talking to the socios out in the field, where we stood in a drizzle of rain. "It is hardly our custom to burn wet brush," they told me sarcastically. "This is not the United States," Ramon told me. "This is the way we do it; you should have a little more respect for our customs." "But that's the only reason I'm here," I told him, "to destroy your crazy customs."

Unfortunately, Thomsen was able to convince the farmers to burn, and later, under his direction, his "*socios*" cleared 20 hectares of land and even obtained a tractor for plowing the land. Because of drought, heavy rains, roving animals, and insects, the maize that was planted on the cleared land produced little yield. In order to control the insects Thomsen wrote: "We sprayed with DDT, Aldrin, Malathion, Dipterex, Chlordane, BHC, and Parathion." Such an obvious overkill insecticide treatment would be characterized by many today as nothing but a horror story. The tractor was later abandoned as impractical for the area. Although Thomsen undoubtedly had the best of intentions, his book provides a arresting story of how agricultural ideas from the temperate zone are often inappropriate to traditional agriculture in the tropics.

Another description of an Indian group's farming system was given by Eder (1963) who described the slash/mulch system of a Noanamá Indian group in the Río Siguirisúa Valley of the Colombian Chocó. After cutting the lighter understory of the forest they broadcast seeds or planted roots in holes prepared with a digging stick. Three to four weeks later the trees were felled over their plots. He noted that women did the primary preparation and planting of the plot, but men felled the trees. The *"minga"* or communal work group common to the Chocó black population in their slash/mulch system was not used by the Noanamá.

Another description of a slash/mulch system was given by Finegan (1981) who described the system in a study he made 70 km inland from the city of Tumaco on the hot, wet Pacific coast of Colombia near the border with Ecuador. His studies were in a lowland area populated by black subsistence farmers. Finegan suggested that the techniques used were probably modified from the original systems practiced by the vanished indigenous populations. The study area was between Barbacoas, with a rainfall of 7.6 m (300 inches) per year, and El Mira, with a rainfall of 3.5 m (140 inches) per year. Because of the excessive rainfall, the farmers in the area commonly slashed vegetation consisting of small trees, vines, and bushes, but could not burn it. Maize, cassava, sugar cane, beans, various fruit species, trees for wood, taro (*Colocasia esculenta*), sweet potatoes, yams (*Dioscorea* spp.), and tannier (*Xanthosoma* spp.) were crops planted in this polyculture system.

Four plant layers were identified in the subsistence plots: ground level, second level, middle level, and overstory. The ground level consisted of crops less than two meters in height, such as cassava, beans and maize. The second level consisted of taller perennials such as bananas and plantains. In the middle level fruit trees and palms dominated and reached nine meters or more. The top or overstory level consisted of timber species and, perhaps, tall fruit trees. After the first few years of harvests, the economic importance of the lower levels became minor as weeds took over. Finegan (1981) noted that farmers also utilized various plants as "site indicators" for determining the degree of soil fertility, drainage conditions, and the amount of shade present in a potential slash/burn field. They also knew of certain plants that indicated when land was ready for replanting.

Cerón Solarte (1986) described the slash/mulch system of the Awa-Kwaiker Indians who occupy an area at an elevation of 500-1,500 meters in the foothills of the Andes near the lowland area described above by Finegan. The area is mainly in the province of Nariño in Colombia, but also extends into neighboring Ecuador. In their slash/mulch system (called locally *tumba y pudre* in Spanish) *chococito* maize was the most important crop in the system. Maize seed was broadcast after slashing the vegetation which consisted of small trees and bushes. Larger trees were cut into the slash/mulch plots after the maize germinated. Crops grown in the system were plantains, sugar cane, cassava, and beans.

Slash/Mulch Systems of the Amazon Basin

The agricultural system of the indigenous Ecuadorian Jungle Quichua Indians is a complex slash/mulch system. This ethnic group, also know as the Canelos Quichuas, live in the hot, humid tropical forests east of the Andes near the town of Puyo and are neighbors of the Jivaro Indians. Whitten (1976) has written a engaging book on these people and includes interesting details regarding their agriculture. The most important crop of the Canelos Quichua is cassava. When a *chagra* (slash/mulch plot) is cleared for cassava planting, members of a family work together clearing vines, brush, and small bushes down to the surface roots "making the jungle mulch and humus covering the soil as clean as possible." Plots are generally one half to two hectares in size. Excess plant materials are transferred to the edge of the plot to be used later as mulch. Trees in the plot are cut down selectively with axes; a variety of useful trees, including many palms are left growing to provide wood, fiber, fruit, and the delicious *palmito* (heart-of-palm). Logs and trunks of felled trees remained in the plots.

Whitten described the planting of cassava in the *chagra*, but noted that other plants such as *achiote* (*Bixa orellana*), *chirimoya* (*Annona squamosa*), palms, and rubber were also often planted. He noted "Women also scatter beans around the *chagra* at this time, though such beans are not often used for food. Rather they are used to fix nitrogen in the soil, prolonging the utility of this newly planted *chagra* space." The species of bean used was not identified by Whitten. Once the cassava is harvested a second cassava planting is made in the same plot, and at this time plantains and bananas are also planted in the *chagra*. More beans and various cucurbits are also planted. After harvesting the second crop of cassava a new, contiguous section of forest is cleared for a new cassava *chagra*. Depending on the soil, availability of land, and other factors, *chagras* are moved outward from the original planting from three to five miles over a period of twelve to twenty years. Whitten wrote that at the tail end of this long territory some of the land:

> for the manioc-cycling chagra is used for such crops as plantains, bananas, maize, and *naranjilla* (*Solanum quitoense*). Maize and *naranjilla* seeds are simply broadcast into the remaining bush; then the second-growth brush and vines are again cut and partially cleared. Snakebite in such brush clearing is much more frequent, since the palm viper and bushmaster fall or fling themselves from over the heads of the machete wielders. The meticulous ground-level cleaning associated with manioc is not undertaken. Instead, compost-mulch from the *chagra* edge is spread over the area, together with the brush cut down on top of the seeds. This slash-

mulch cultivation is much the same as the one used in the wet Pacific Littoral. The *naranjilla* plants are frequently transplanted to get better spacing, but are weeded only to maintain pathways to the ripening fruits.

Other plants found in the *chagras* are semi-wild cherry tomatoes, peppers, tobacco, taro (*Colocasia esculenta*), sweet potatoes and datura plants. Datura plants (the species was not given) are used as hallucinatory drugs to produce visions. Jicama beans (yam beans - *Pachrrhizus erosus*) are also planted. Although the yam bean pods are poisonous, they produce a large, sweet white root which is eaten raw. Various lilies and anthuriums are left to grow, and the lily bulbs and new anthurium leaves are harvested for food and medicine. The variety of crops grown in the chagras, the fallow periods between plantings, and the numerous benefits from the use of mulches together appear to have produced a stable, sustainable system of agriculture for the Canelos Quichuas. Hudelson (1987) also mentions the use of the slash/mulch system by the Quichuas in the Amazon forest of Ecuador.

Hiraoka and Yamamoto (1980) described the extensive use of a slash/mulch practice which is a variation of the widespread shifting cultivation practiced in the eastern lowlands of the Amazon basin. They noted that these slash-mulch systems are prevalent in the eastern lowlands of Ecuador and Colombia. The systems are distinguished by the fact that the felled vegetation is not burned. Their studies of agricultural development in the Eastern Amazonian lowlands took place from 1975 to 1977. The area is populated primarily by colonists who probably developed the slash/mulch systems based on practices of indigenous Indians. Hiraoka and Yamamoto noted that the slashed vegetation serves as a mulch and, as it decomposes, nutrients become available for the plants cultivated in the system. There is no dry season in the area, thus the system is an adaptation to a wet environment that has no distinct dry season. Four processes (*socola, plantio, tumba* and *chapeo*) constitute the practice. *Socola* is the slashing or cutting of the brush consisting of small trees, vines, and bushes and may begin at any time of the year. The planting of seed or cuttings, called *plantio*, takes place 5-10 days after *socola. Tumba*, the next stage, was described as follows:

> When sprouts appear, the remaining vegetation, excepting economically useful types, is removed. In the *tumba*, as this phase is known, between 20 and 30 percent of the seedlings are crushed or covered by the felled vegetation, but enough plantings survive to provide harvests.

If weeds are a problem there may be one or two weedings (*chapeo*) before the harvest of annual crops. A large number of crops are planted in the fields in the Lago Agrio area, and Hiraoka and Yamamoto (1987) suggested that the farmers of the area practice a "true polyculture." Annuals include rice, maize, and sweet potatoes while semiperennials consist of yams (*Dioscorea* spp.), *papa mandi*, plantains, bananas, and cassava. Perennials include tree or shrub crops such as coffee, cacao, *chonta, achiote* (*Bixa orellana*), and various citrus species. The canopy produced by the semiperennials and perennials eventually takes over the plots after the harvest of the annual crops. Hiraoka and Yamamoto concluded that the system is sound from both a human and an ecological perspective and ideal both for the physical environment and the settlers. The mixture of annuals, semiperennials, and perennials extends the life of the plots; the canopy produced by semiperennials and perennials protects the soil from direct sunlight; the mulch reduces erosion, provides organic matter, reduces runoff of rain, and provides nutrients to the crops. They concluded that the slash/mulch system appears to be sustainable and should slow rates of deforestation in the Amazon, given a stable population of low-density.

Peck (1990) gives a brief description of the slash/mulch system of the Napo Quichua that live in the Napo province of Ecuador in the Amazon basin. Rainfall in the area is reported to be 3,100 mm annually and there is no distinct dry season. The agricultural system used by the Quichua is called a *chacra* system and uses slash/mulch practices such as those described by Hiraoka and Yamamoto (1980) and Whitten (1976).

Another description of the use of the slash/mulch practice in Ecuador was given by Powell (1992). In 1984, the Ecuadorian Ministry of Agriculture, with technical assistance from USAID and the Peace Corps, initiated a six year agroforestry demonstration project in the northeastern Amazon region of Ecuador. Virgin forests in the area had been opened to settlers due to oil exploration and drilling plus a governmental land grant program. Because of the high rainfall (3,000 to 4,000 mm/year) and the absence of a dry season, settlers adopted the slash/mulch system of the indigenous Indian groups in the area. They planted numerous food crops in the system such as maize, bananas, plantains, and cassava in addition to cash crops such as coffee and pasture for cattle. The slash/mulch practice begins with the harvest of valuable timber trees that are used for housing construction or sold as lumber. Powell wrote:

Most of the forest canopy is removed once seeds have germinated and small plants become established. Trees are felled in a criss-cross pattern to minimize the number that fall directly on the ground and damage crops.

Very large trees and trees of known economic importance are sometimes left as partial shade. Valuable trees are later harvested and sold whenever quick cash is needed. Corn is harvested in 3-4 months. A general cleaning during the harvest eliminates weeds competing with the bananas, plantains, cassava, and coffee seedlings. Farmers also cut-up trees and branches from the previous felling that are suspended above the ground. The organic material is left to decompose and mulch crops. Damaged coffee seedlings, bananas, and plantains are replanted and a second rotation of corn is sometimes planted. Banana and cassava are first harvested in 9-12 months, and coffee in 1.5-2 years. The bananas and cassava are gradually eliminated as the coffee reaches full production. Many farmers practiced agroforestry by leaving timber trees in their coffee plantations or pastures.

Attempts to establish trees in mature coffee plantations and cattle pastures have usually failed, although a few wealthy farmers by numerous replantings and the use of protective stakes around the tree seedlings, were able to establish trees. Powell (1992) noted:

Farmers and project personnel together determined that the best time to establish trees in a coffee plantation or pasture is during the initial stage of the slash-and mulch cycle when food crops, and coffee seedlings or pasture grasses are planted. Tree seedlings benefit from overstory shade provided to new crops, from weedings to release crops, and from mulch. High survival rates minimize replanting. Trees grow for 1.5-2 years before initial coffee production, and 9 to 12 months in new pastures before cattle are introduced.

Charles Staver (personal communication) described the use of both the slash-and-burn and the slash/mulch system in the Guanare River basin of Venezuela for both maize and beans. Beckerman (1987) also mentions the use of the slash/mulch practice in the Amazon.

The few descriptions above are probably little more than a tantalizing sample of the slash/mulch systems that probably exist in the vast area encompassed by the Amazon basin. It is likely that many slash/mulch systems have never been described, that they have been mistaken for the far more common slash-and-burn systems, or that they are part of a combined slash/mulch and slash-and-burn system.

A Slash/Mulch System on Riverbanks in Belize

Wilk (1985, 1991) described a slash/mulch system used by the Kekchi Maya Indians on riverbanks in Southern Belize. The expressive name for the system in Spanish is *matahambre* (kills hunger) and in Kekchi *sak'ecuaj* (sun cornfield). During the dry season the floodplains of the major rivers become dry enough for cultivation. Such fields on the riverbanks, which have enough slope to drain, and have been previously cleared and burned, subsequently produce a secondary vegetation called *sajal* in Kekchi and *vega* in Spanish. *Sajal* vegetation consists of low shrubs, vines, and various leafy plants. Wilk writes:

> The *sajal* vegetation is slashed at the roots, chopped up, and spread to form a springy mat of decaying matter, into which corn is dibbled. This mulch protects the soil from erosion during the wet season flooding and helps conserve soil moisture during the dry season.

Maize is generally the only crop grown; however, because *sak'ecuaj* fields are held in long-term tenure, a few fruit trees or sugar cane may be grown in the fields also. Little weeding is necessary, and the *sajal* is allowed to grow with the maize, as the *sajal* vegetation shades out undesirable weeds. The main pests of the *sak'ecuaj* fields observed by Wilk were rats, birds, and coatimundi. Slashed fields must be planted promptly, or weeds will outgrow and reduce the yields of the maize. Wilk estimated the labor used (man-hours/hectare) as: 205 for clearing and mulching, 78 for planting, 21 for weeding, 56 for guarding, 58 for harvesting, and 30 for transporting the harvest. Maize yield varied widely with an average yield in the study area of 839 kg/ha. The minimum yield recorded was 234 kg/ha and the maximum was 1943 kg/ha. If additional labor in care and weeding is allocated to *sak'ecuaj* fields they will produce a higher yield. Primarily due to longer fallow periods, yields from slash-and-burn maize fields (*milpas*) in nearby areas were generally higher than yields from the *sak'ecuaj* system.

Why then do the Kekchi continue to use the *sak'ecuaj* system if yields are lower? Table 3.1 illuminating the reason is given by Wilk and illustrates the long-term value of the riverbank *sak'ecuaj* system.

Riverbank fields can be reused for a number of years. Wilk found "the average is 5.2 consecutive years of use followed by an average 2.8 years of fallow." He found one field that had been in use continuously for 12 years. In contrast wet season *milpas* (using the slash-and-burn system) were abandoned after a single crop because of weed problems. The *matahambre* system is obviously less destructive to the environment

TABLE 3.1. Yield in Shelled Maize in Wet and Dry Season Farming

Measure	High forest (milpa)	Low forest (milpa)	Dry season (riverbank)
Yield in kg/ha	1,865	1,274	839
Yield in kg/man-hour	2.33	2.61	1.83
Yield in total kg/ha over 25 years of plot use	1, 875	1,633	13,446

Source: Adapted from Wilk (1985).

than the slash-and-burn system. Wilk (1985) suggested that riverbank *sak'ecuaj* fields can be sustained for many years because the soils appear to be more fertile than hill soils, the *sajal* vegetation prevents the invasion of grasses, and the decaying mulch improves soil texture and provides nutrients to the crops.

The *matahambre* system of the Kekchi Maya Indians is an excellent example of an ingenious indigenous riverbank system which appears to be sustainable and which is a combination of slash-and-burn and slash/mulch practices. The system also produces acceptable yields of maize over the long-term, manages weeds, and is less destructive to the environment than systems which rely entirely on slash-and-burn practices.

Frijol Tapado (Covered Beans) Systems

The *frijol tapado* system (Figure 3.3) is an example of a system that is easily managed, requires few outside inputs, is sustainable, causes little or no damage to the environment, and provides a stable source of food to its users. Traditional farmers in many areas of Central America grow beans (*Phaseolus vulgaris*) using a slash/mulch system called in Spanish "*frijol tapado*," which in English means "covered beans." When the Spanish first arrived in Costa Rica, they found the Indians of the area producing beans with the *frijol tapado* system (Araya and González

1994). Beans were so important that they were included in the tribute collected by Spanish governors. Maize is also grown in a similar system called "*maiz tapado*" (Moreno and Sánchez 1994).

Today, most *frijol tapado* fields are small, varying between 0.04 and 2.17 ha with a mean of 0.48 ha (Araya and Gonzalez 1994). In 1992 about 65% of the beans in Costa Rica were produced in *frijol tapado* fields (Arias and Amador 1991), but as recently as 1981 over 80% of the beans were still produced by the *frijol tapado* system (Rosemeyer et al. 1989). The *frijol tapado* practice consists of broadcasting bean seeds into carefully selected weeds, then cutting and chopping the weeds with a machete so the broadcasted bean seeds are covered with a mulch of weeds (Alfaro and Waaijenberg 1992, Araya and Gonzalez 1987, Araya and Gonzalez 1994, Arias and Amador 1991, Cavallini 1972, Galindo et al. 1982, Jimenez 1978, Patiño 1965, Rosemeyer 1994, Skutch 1950, Von Platen et al. 1982, Von Platen 1985).

Until recently very little research was done on the *frijol tapado* system. Araya and Gonzalez (1994) suggest the following factors to explain the lack of research:

1. The belief that it was an unsophisticated, peasant system that could not be improved (Jimenez 1978).
2. Difficult access to the production areas, due to location and topography.
3. Agricultural practices such as weed and disease control and mineral nutrition changes were difficult to carry out or would alter the system.
4. The economic situation of farmers using this system was a limiting factor for acquiring inputs and transporting them to the cultivation site.
5. The belief that the system depended on a transition from forest areas to pasture.

Importance of Weeds in the Frijol Tapado *System*

Weeds are of significant importance in the *frijol tapado* system, and farmers take them into account from the moment the land for planting is chosen. Fields selected for *tapado* are generally occupied by broadleaf weeds and certain grasses, which will not regrow rapidly after they are cut. However, there are some "serious" weeds (in the negative sense of the term) that can compete with beans for light, nutrients, space, and moisture. Shenk (1994) wrote the following regarding weeds and site selection:

Through visits and discussions with farmers in several regions of Costa Rica, we concluded that low plant population was a key factor limiting productivity of frijol tapado, despite broadcasting about 45 kg/ha of seed. When establishing frijol tapado, farmers applied ecological and agronomic principles by choosing sites with the least aggressive weeds possible, combined with the use of indeterminate (climbing type) beans which tend to grow above elongating weeds. However, this need to avoid sites with aggressive weeds, often limited the area available for this planting system.

Perhaps "weeds" is not the proper term to use when discussing the *frijol tapado* system. We all have a notion about what constitutes a weed, but sometimes it is difficult to decide what a weed is. Crop plants can become weeds when they appear where they are not wanted. "Weeds," if used for food then are transformed into useful "crop" plants. Weeds also may help in some instances to control wind and water erosion and can serve as food for wild and domesticated animals. Chacón and Gliessman (1982) wrote that traditional farmers in Tabasco, Mexico, did not have a word for "weed" in their vocabulary, but instead used a concept of "good" and "bad" plants (*mal y buen monte*). Furthermore, the same plant could be either good or bad depending on where and when it was found.

Some species of weeds are considered beneficial in the *frijol tapado* system. The development of various weed species is used by traditional farmers as an indication of soil fertility in choosing sites for *frijol tapado* plantings. Weeds indicating good soil fertility in *frijol tapado* areas listed by De la Cruz (1994) were *Melanthera aspera, Calea urticfolia, Elephantopus scaber, Sida rombifolia, Phytolaca* spp. and *Piper* spp. Conversely, *Pteridium aquilinum* indicated poor soils. Also, the density and dominance of certain species provides an indication of how long the land has been fallow (Araya and Gonzalez 1987). De la Cruz (1994) wrote:

> Some of the criteria used by the farmer to decide that a particular (weed) species is beneficial to the slash/mulch system are: it should be soft-stemmed (not woody) and easy to cut. The shoots of some types of shrubs form supports for beans. Cutting (slashing) should produce an even, good quality cover. The majority of species that are easy to cut belong to the family Compositae. These plants have little woody tissue even when well-developed which makes cutting and chopping in the field much easier.

Some of the weeds farmers prefer for the *frijol tapado* system and that are recognized as easy to manage are: *Calea urticfolia, Viquiera guatemalensis, Melanthera aspera, Montanoa hibiscifolia, Verbesina tonduzzi,*

Guitite armistus, and *Millinis minutiflora* (De la Cruz 1994). Araya and Gonzalez, (1987) noted:

> Weed preference also depends on the type of bean that is going to be sown. For example if the bean is an aggressive climbing variety, a site will be selected which has certain shrubs which, when they resprout, can act as a trellis for the bean crop. This encourages the development of the crop and allows a greater sowing density.

De la Cruz listed the following plant species as particularly harmful to the *frijol tapado* system: *Pteridium aquilinum, Serjania* spp., *Heliconia latispatha, Hypawhenia rufa, Imperata contracta, Zeugites pittieri, Antharaxon hispidus, Commelina diffusa, Bidens pilosa, Panicum pilosum, Asclepias curasavica, Urera* spp., and *Rottboellia cochinchinensis.*

It is remarkable that farmers that have never been in contact on two widely separated continents have both noticed the deleterious effect of a weed species on crops, especially beans. According to Stauder (1971), the Majangir tribe in Ethiopia avoids sites for planting crops where the weed *Bidens pilosa* (hairy beggar's tick or black Spanish needle) dominates. On an entirely different continent, de la Cruz (1994) cites *B. pilosa* as a weed species in Costa Rica that is "especially harmful to the slash/mulch system for bean production." It is also further interesting that *B. pilosa* has been shown to be allelopathic to beans by several investigators (Campbell 1982, Rosado-May F. et al. 1986, Stevens and Tang 1987, Stevens and Tang 1991). Extracts from *B. pilosa* inhibit the growth of beans (*Phaseolus vulgaris*) and and other crop species. Rosado-May F. et al. (1986) noted that farmers avoid *B. pilosa*, as it it also allelopathic to maize.

Vegetation or weeds that produce a low cover that can easily be overtaken or overgrown by the bean crop are preferred. It was observed that the bean variety Talamanca had the sort of a competitive growth habit that facilitated weed management in the *frijol tapado* system. Regarding the possible use of herbicides in the *frijol tapado* system, De la Cruz (1994) concluded:

> The use of chemical control in the system must be carefully analyzed. Obstacles to using herbicides in the system may include not only economic and socio-cultural factors but also ecological aspects related to plant management. Use of herbicides or other weed control that gives rise to the dominance of a few weed species would be contrary to the fundamental basis of the slash/ mulch system.

Schelhas (1991) studied the *frijol tapado* system near the Braulio Carrillo National Park in Costa Rica. He reported:

> In San Ramon, where there is little forest clearing and underutilized land is rare, it is not uncommon for landholders to reserve 3/4 to 1 and 1/2 hectares of land in *charral* (a fallow area) for planting beans. The reserved area is generally divided in half, with beans being cultivated in each half in alternate years. Annual cultivation results in grass invasion, and the two year system tends to result in a weedy to woody fallow although grass invasion may still occur. If soil quality goes down or weeds invade, another area may be sought out. Several landowners report continuous cultivation in alternate years for 10 or more years.

The above observations highlight the broad and comprehensive knowledge that traditional *frijol tapado* farmers must have of their farming system to make it successful and productive. Further, as Chacón and Gliessman (1982) noted, some traditional farmers in Latin America do not used the word "weed", but rather describe "good" and "bad" plants (*mal y buen monte*). Their attitude towards plants is quite different than that of farmers in most so-called developed nations. Modern agriculture could benefit from the important principles relative to weed management gained over centuries by the traditional farmers of the Americas.

Role of the Mulch in the Frijol Tapado System

The quality of the mulch produced by slashing vegetation often determines the success of the planting (Figure 3.1). The mulch must not be so thick that it can inhibit bean germination and growth. Also, as the mulch decomposes it produces most of the the nutrients the beans need to produce a good crop. The bean root-mulch layer mimics a natural forest root-litter mat in which a nutrient cycling process takes place. A semi-determinate type of bean, between a bush and a climbing bean, is planted. The beans grow through the mulch and eventually their foliage covers the mulch. Skutch (1950) succinctly described the practice:

> The bean seed is broadcast through the low, dense vegetation, which is then cut down with machetes and chopped up (*picado*) so that it lies close to the ground. The bean vines sprout up through the mulch of stems and leaves, finally covering them over. No cultivation of the crop is necessary or feasible.

The mulch produced by the *frijol tapado* practice is also important in managing bean diseases which are disseminated by rain splash. Web blight, a destructive disease of beans and other legumes worldwide, is effectively managed by farmers who use the traditional practice of *frijol tapado*, even in areas where climate is optimal for web blight development. The mulch prevents soil-splashing, which was found in a Costa Rican study by Galindo et al. (1983a, 1983b) to be the most important source of inoculum of the fungus *Thanatephorus cucumeris* causing a severe bean disease called web blight. In Nicaragua, Tapia Barquero and Camacho Henriquez (1988) reported less web blight (*T. cucumeris*), bacterial blight (*Xanthomonas campestris* pv. *phaseoli*), angular leaf blight (*Isariopsis griseola*), and Entyloma leaf smut (*Entyloma petuniae*) in beans that were mulched. Prevention of soil-splashing doubtless accounts for the reduction in disease reported.

Yields of the Frijol Tapado *System*

In the absence of web blight, the yields from fields under the *frijol tapado* system are generally lower than those from fields planted in drilled rows with clean cultivation. When measured in farmer's *frijol tapado* fields in the Acosta area of Costa Rica, yields averaged 528 kg/ha, while in Puriscal they were 463 kg/ha (Von Platen et al. 1982). In a study of Costa Rican *frijol tapado* farmers Araya and Gonzalez (1994) classified farmers into three groups and found yields to vary widely as illustrated below:

> Yields between 0 and 450 kg/ha; yield below the national average, 37.5% of the farmers fell within this grouping, the most frequent class being between 0 and 300 kg/ha (34.4%). Between 450 and 1050 kg/ha; 46.8% of farmers fell in this group with the mode between 600 and 750 kg/ha. Between 1,050 and 1,800 kg/ha corresponding to 15.6% of farmers.

Some scientists have negatively characterized the *frijol tapado* system as "primitive" (Jimenez 1978, Van Schoonhoven and Voysest 1989), and some agronomists in Latin America have opposed continuation of the system. For example, Jimenez (1978) suggested that there should be a change from a strong dependence on the rather "primitive" system of production called *frijol tapado* towards a more modern technology suitable for the mechanized growing of beans. Nevertheless, in the early 1990s in Costa Rica well over half of the beans produced were still grown by the *frijol tapado* system (Arias and Amador 1991).

A major advantage of the systems is erosion prevention on steep slopes where *frijol tapado* is most common. An evaluation of the *frijol tapado* system by Araya and Gonzalez (1994) also suggested the following advantages:

1. The resultant population dynamics from two or more fallow years reduces the population of weeds and favors the development of herbaceous plants and shrubs which have a long recovery period after cutting.
2. Appropriate soil fertility for sowing beans is maintained without agricultural inputs.
3. The lessened demand for labor allows the farmer to get on with other tasks.
4. Improved bean varieties are not required. The native varieties have been selected for this system either by natural or human selection pressure over thousands of years and tolerate the pathogen variability and climatic conditions prevalent in the growing area.
5. This situation allows in-situ conservation of native bean species.

According to Araya and Gonzalez (1994) practices which might be effective in improvement of the *frijol tapado* system are small-scale production of pathogen free seed, pelletization of seed with *Rhizobium phaseoli* inoculum, and fertilization with phosphorus. They suggested that the most serious problems for the continuation of the *frijol tapado* system were:

1. The reduction of the agricultural frontier and the need for more intensive land use.
2. Politicians and professionals working in environmental conservation programs or agricultural extension programs are ignorant of the merits and advantages of this system.

Frijol Tapado *System Versus the* Espequeado *System*

Pachico and Borbon (1987) noted that bean yields in Costa Rica from the 1950s to the 1970s were low; around 400 kg/ha. They noted that the main system for growing beans during this time was the *frijol tapado* system. With the explosive population growth in Costa Rica that peaked in 1950 there was a need and a demand for more beans than the *frijol tapado* system was producing. Pachico and Borbon (1987) described the technology changes that subsequently occurred among small farm bean producers. They observed that the *frijol tapado* system combined the advantages of low labor and capital investments in addition to erosion, weed, and disease control. They added that addition of inputs such as chemical fertilizer or pesticides to the *frijol tapado* system, characterized as marginal intensification management, did little to improve yields.

As land became an increasingly scarce resource compared to labor, efforts were made by the Costa Rican government through the Ministry of Agriculture (MAG), the University of Costa Rica, and CIAT (International Center for Tropical Agriculture) to introduce improved bean varieties, clean seed, and a more intensive system of bean production in which beans were planted with a digging stick (*espequeado*). According to Pachico and Borbon 82% of the farmers using the *espequeado* system used fertilizer, 71% sprayed for insect or disease control, and all controlled weeds. The *espequeado* system spread rapidly after 1978. The *espequeado* system required more capital and labor than than *frijol tapado*, but it produced greater yields. Also, less time was needed for fallow than the *frijol tapado* system. Improved bean varieties yielded more than the old varieties in the *espequeado* systems (1103 kg/ha compared to 719 kg/ha) while in the *frijol tapado* system little yield increase occurred. Pachico and Borbon (1987) noted a widespread adoption of the new system in Costa Rica.

The relative importance and yields of different bean production systems in Costa Rica are given in Table 3.2.

TABLE 3.2. Importance of the Principal Bean Production Systems in Costa Rica in 1991

System	% of farms	Farm area (ha)	Yield (kg/ha)	% of area in C. Rica
Tapado	54	1.0	400	61
Espequeado	39	2.0	700	13
Semi-mechanized	7	7.5	1.300	26

Source: Adapted from Alfaro and Waaijenberg (1992).

Subsequent studies have not been as positive about the advantages of the *espequeado* system. Rosemeyer 1994, Rosemeyer et al. (1989), and Whalen (1990) described later studies of the *frijol tapado* system in the

Coto Brus area of Costa Rica. Farmers of the area broadcast beans into
secondary vegetation and then slashed the vegetation leaving a mulch
covering the soil that is 15-20 cm thick. The investigators compared two
systems for planting beans; the high input system called *espequeado*,
which consists of planting with a digging stick, and the *frijol tapado*
system. Planting generally goes on without fallow in the *espequeado*
system year after year, whereas in the *frijol tapado* system in the Coto
Brus area beans are planted in the same plot for 2-3 years and later the
plot is fallowed for 1-2 years. Different levels of fertilizer were applied to
both systems (0, 160, 325, 650, 975, and 1,300 kg/ha). Rosemeyer et al.
(1989) reported that the mulched *tapado* without fertilizer gave yields
significantly higher than those of the *espequeado* system (without
fertilizer) in both years. Augmenting the *frijol tapado* system with
moderate amounts of fertilizer increased yields significantly and, in
comparison with the *espequeado* system, used much lower amounts of
fertilizer per unit of production. Yields from the *espequeado* system,
when fertilizer was applied at commercial rates (650 kg/ha), were more
than double those from *frijol tapado*. Regarding her studies of the *frijol
tapado* system in Costa Rica Rosemeyer (1994) concluded:

> Beyond the current controversy concerning a definition of sustainability,
> the question remains of finding the optimum point between high yield
> (needed to feed the present population) and the need to maintain basic
> sources of natural resources intact. Application of fertilizer to the
> slash/mulch system at levels half those recommended for the sown
> system results in much higher production levels (double in the second
> year) than found in the sown system using the complete application.
> Where beans are produced on steep slopes, increasing the productivity of
> the slash/mulch system through additions of P, fallow period enrichment
> with leguminous species or more effective symbiosis, can prolong their
> use as a method of soil conservation. This system protects soil from
> erosion, an important factor considering that 70% of bean production in
> Central America is carried out on hill slopes. It may be that components
> from traditional systems can be incorporated into the design of profitable
> and sustainable agroecosystems.

Bellows (1994) also compared the advantages and disadvantages of
the *espequeado* and *frijol tapado* systems. She conducted socioeconomic
surveys with both *frijol tapado* farmers and *frijol espeque* farmers and
also conducted on-farm experiments comparing *frijol tapado*, *frijol
espeque*, and *labranza zero* (no till). Bellows' (1992) informants reported
that *frijol tapado* was usually planted on land that had been fallowed for
9 months to 5 years, with 3-4 year fallows being the most common.

Farms were divided into 3 or 4 lots and each year, *frijol espeque* was planted in one lot while the others remained in fallow. She noted that *frijol tapado* might be practiced on the same lot every year if land was scarce. It is obvious, from the several observations on fallow length, that fallow periods for the *frijol tapado* system depend on numerous factors such as land availability, slope of land, rainfall, soil type, land tenure, traditions, and the composition of the vegetation.

From the results of her studies in Costa Rica Bellows (1992) wrote:

> The use of agrochemicals in *frijol espeque* (*espequeado* system) allows farmers to use their land more intensively. Despite the potentially higher yields of *frijol espeque*, *frijol tapado* can provide almost three times the returns on capital investments compared to *frijol espeque* (income/cost=10.60 for *tapado* versus 3.76 for *espeque*) when the opportunity value for land is low. A high, competitive, opportunity value for labor during the period of bean growth also favors *frijol tapado* over *frijol espeque*. No labor inputs are used for *frijol tapado* during the period between planting and harvesting.

Bellow's studies help explain why bean producers in Costa Rica continue to use the *frijol tapado* system, especially in areas where off-farm activities such as coffee harvest provide farmers with a secure source of income during the period of bean growth. Bellows (1994) also concluded that the no-till system used in conjunction with a fallow mulch was both environmentally stable and productive. She noted however, that the *frijol tapado* system depends on the ability of land owners to fallow their land and that tenant farmers would probably be discouraged from using the system since a combination of burning and *frijol espeque* would give them higher yields. Farmers continue to use *frijol tapado* "because it fits a distinct agronomic and socioeconomic niche."

First National Campesino Meeting on Frijol Tapado

In 1991 a group of *campesinos* near San Ignacio de Acosta, Costa Rica held the *Primer Encuentro Nacional Campesino de Frijol Tapado* (The First National Campesino Meeting on Covered Beans) (COPROALDE-CEDECO 1991). The report of their meeting provided important information and insights relative to the system and the impressive amount of knowledge needed to use the system successfully. Twenty six *frijol tapado* farmers met for three days and exchanged information on the system. Yields in the San Ignacio de Acosta area from *frijol tapado* varied from 100 to 1,400 kg/ha. A summary of the characteristics of the system in different regions of Costa Rica was made which included the source, varieties, and amount of seed used for planting, size of fields, field orientation towards the sun, major problems, length of fallow period, storage practices, labor costs and requirements, costs of production, time of planting, land tenure, pests, and "good" and "bad" plants found in *frijol tapado* fields. Some of the conclusions and recommendations of the *Primer Encuentro Nacional Campesino de Frijol Tapado* were as follows (COPROALDE.CEDECO 1991):

1. The practice takes advantage of organic matter for nutrients and the mulch reduces the incidence of some insects and diseases.
2. The mulch produced by the practice reduces erosion on extremely steep slopes.
3. The beans produced are an "organic" food as chemicals are rarely used in the *frijol tapado* system.
4. Aspects of the system that could be improved are: selection of clean seed, supplemental fertilization with phosphorus, better prices for beans through more efficient marketing.
5. Strengthening of campesino organizations to improve opportunities for credit, better prices, and marketing.
6. Negotiations with land owners should be made to reduce the land being converted to animal pastures.

I visited the San Ignacio de Acosta area in October 1992 and was impressed by the extremely steep slopes that were used for *frijol tapado* in the area. The farmers said that they knew from their parents and grandparents that the *frijol tapado* fields in the area had been used for well over a century. Nevertheless, I saw no evidence of serious erosion in the area.

Occurrence of the Frijol Tapado *System in Latin America*

The *frijol tapado* system is found in other countries of Central America such as El Salvador (Mercado et al. 1994), Guatemala, and Nicaragua (Rava 1991, Tapia 1987). In Honduras the *tapado* system is also used for maize and sorghum (DeWalt and DeWalt 1984). In Spanish the name for *frijol tapado* in Honduras is *sembrado en crudo* (Personal communication–Martha Rosemeyer). In northern Guatemala almost half of the growers used the *tapado* system for beans in the years 1985-1986 with yields averaging 700 kg/ha (personal communication--Aberlardo Viana). Nicaraguan yields are about 500 kg/ha, but 100 kg/ha of seed are required for planting (Rava 1991). In 1987 Tapia (1987) reported that 28% of the total area planted to beans in Nicaragua consisted of *frijol tapado* plantings.

Mestanza Iberico (1994) describes a system similar to *frijol tapado* used in Peru in tropical regions of the department of Ucayali. The system is called in Spanish *"Haragan Chacra."* The name comes from the relatively easy management of the bean crop after planting and the complete lack of care required during the cropping cycle.

> This farming method is practiced exclusively in highland areas and for this reason the farmer needs to identify a certain type of vegetation which has mainly *Cecropia* spp. trees. This species has a high calcium requirement and soils where it grows have a pH close to neutral. The farmer then cuts or slashes the undergrowth, an operation known as *"roza."* After slashing, the farmer sows, broadcasting 20 kilos of seed, trying to achieve a fairly uniform distribution. Finally, the large trees are felled. This concludes the planting operation. After this, the farmer leaves the plot alone, only returning when the crop is ready for harvest. Under this system, yields reach 500 to 600 kg/ha.

After harvesting the bean crop, the slashed litter left on the fields is often burned and maize may be planted as a monoculture or in association with pasture grasses. After the maize harvest, pasture is usually established in the area. Mestanza Iberico noted that weed problems were minimal because the cover given by the cut grass does not allow early weed development.

No other references were found to *frijol tapado* systems in other areas of Latin America. Nevertheless, it is likely that some exist that have not been described in the available literature. The *maize tapado* system found in the Chocó of the Pacific coast of South America (page 30) is similar in many respects to *frijol tapado*.

Web Blight of Beans

Web blight of common beans is caused by the fungus *Thanatephorus cucumeris* (asexual stage--*Rhizoctonia solani*). The disease has been described in detail by Schwartz and Galvez (1980) and Thurston (1984). In the humid lowlands of the tropics, web blight is possibly the single most destructive disease of beans. Beans are traditionally grown in cooler, temperate areas in Latin America, but because of population pressures, farmers migrate from high-altitude to low-altitude areas and often take beans with them. In warm and humid tropical areas *T. cucumeris* can cause rapid defoliation of beans and sometimes complete crop failure. For example, in 1980, an epidemic of web blight occurred in the Guanacaste region in the northern part of Costa Rica, resulting in a 90% reduction in bean yields (Galindo 1982). This severe loss occurred on beans planted in drilled rows with clean cultivation. As with many tropical diseases, precise information on yield losses is difficult to obtain, but the disease has been characterized as severe in Mexico (Crispin and Gallegos 1963), Costa Rica (Echandi 1965), and elsewhere in Latin America (Cardenas-A. 1989, Schwartz and Galvez 1980).

The main sources of inocula that can initiate infection are mycelial fragments and sclerotia (fungal resting bodies). Basidiospores (airborne sexual spores produced by Basidiomycete fungi) can also cause infection (Cardenas-A. 1989, Echandi 1965, Galindo et al. 1983). The study by Galindo et al. (1983) found sclerotia and fungus mycelia free in soil or in the form of colonized debris to be the main source of inoculum in the hot, humid areas of Costa Rica. Inoculation of beans occurred mainly by splashing of rain drops containing infested soil. Large numbers of small sclerotia were produced on rain-splashed soil and debris adhering to bean tissues and on detached tissues on the soil surface. These sclerotia provide new sources of inoculum, which again can be splashed on to beans. Weber (1939) suggested that sclerotia may also be disseminated by wind.

In the study by Galindo (1982) in Esparza, Costa Rica, infections caused by basidiospores were observed as previously reported by Echandi (1965). However, the lesions observed were not numerous, remained restricted in size, and apparently caused little damage. Studies by Galindo et al. (1983a, 1983b, 1994) on management of web blight by mulching indicated that in the area of Costa Rica where they conducted their research, and during that time period, basidiospores played a minor role in disease spread. Cardenas-A. (1989) studied web blight of beans in Colombia and found that at higher, cooler elevations basidiospores did play an important role in disease epidemiology. Mulching was of no value in management of the disease under the conditions of his experiments (in Darien, Colombia, 1,400 meters above sea level). Cardenas reported that the maximum and minimum temperatures there were 23.6° and 16.5° C, while Galindo (1982) reported that the maximum and minimum temperatures in his study area (Esparza, Costa Rica) were 30° and 20° C, respectively. Rainfall was also much higher in the experimental site in Costa Rica. These climatic differences probably help to explain the different results obtained. This is a striking example of the need for site-specific studies when using mulching as a plant disease management practice.

The *frijol tapado* system was compared in experiments in Costa Rica with another mulch system (a 2.5-cm thick layer of rice husks, a cheap by-product commonly found in the area) using both web blight susceptible and tolerant bean cultivars (Galindo et al. 1983b). Bean yields were increased significantly by mulching with rice husks or by *frijol tapado* as seen in Table 3.3.

TABLE 3.3. Effect of Mulch Treatments on Bean Yield of Two Cultivars Planted in Two Web-Blight-Infested Fields in Costa Rica in 1980

	Bean seed yield (kg/ha)			
	Experimental field		Commercial field	
Mulch Treatment	Porillo 7	Mexico 27	Porillo 70	Mexico 27
None (clean cultivation)	0	0	273	217
Frijol tapado	-	-	637	534
Rice husks	655	587	835	679

Source: Galindo, J. J., G. S. Abawi, H. D. Thurston and G. Galvez. 1982. "Tapado", controlling web blight of beans on small farms in Central America. N.Y. Food and Life Science 14(3):21-25. p. 25.

Rice husks and *frijol tapado* were equally effective in avoiding splashing of infested soil and in managing web blight (Figure 3.2), and both treatments gave better control of web blight than the fungicide pentachloronitrobenzene (PCNB). PCNB is a highly effective chemical against *R. solani* and can be applied as a soil or foliar treatment.

In Costa Rica *frijol tapado* fields are generally planted in hilly areas (COPROALDE-CEDECO 1991, Galindo et al. 1982, and Alfaro and Waaijenberg 1991). Bellows (1992, 1994) noted that most small-scale farmers plant beans on land with slopes of 50-70%. Waterlogged areas which occur during heavy rainfalls, and which are conducive to web blight, do not occur on steeply sloping land. Farmers select hills that receive full sunlight early in the morning, thereby drying off the dew and reducing the periods of high humidity which favor the web blight disease. Rainfall generally occurs in the afternoon.

Over 50 farmers were interviewed in Tabasco, Mexico, by Rosado May and Garcia Espinosa (1986) relative to their strategies for management of web blight of beans. In this area yield losses of up to 95% of bean production due to web blight had been recorded. The *tapado* system was used in association with maize, and farmers also increased the distance of planting for better disease management. Two farmers claimed that they saw no web blight in fields where the "good" weed *Euphorbia heterophylla* (painted leaf) had been prevalent. It was discouraging that all farmers interviewed indicated that they were expecting a chemical solution to the web blight problem.

Possible Improvements for the Frijol Tapado *System*

Alfaro (1994) and Alfaro and Waaijenberg (1992) described various field trials made by different institutions to improve the production of the *frijol tapado* system between 1978 and 1991. The focus of most studies was on the use of improved seed, increasing the seed rate per hectare, and on the addition of inorganic fertilizer. Although the results were highly variable, the authors concluded that in general the yields of the alternative practices were not superior to those used in traditional *frijol tapado* systems, that local or traditional bean cultivars produced more yield than "improved" cultivars, and that increasing the seed rate per hectare and the addition of fertilizer did not consistently produce positive results. Regarding increasing the seed rate per hectare Alfaro (1994) wrote:

> The positive effect of amount of seed on production may be related to seed quality. This is particularly true for local cultivars which generally carry diseases. Depending on the duration and conditions of storage, these seeds can show variation in germination. For this reason, as the amount of seed is increased the possibility of obtaining productive plants at harvest increases. On the basis of these results, it is recommended that regional programs be set up with the participation of local farmers, for small scale production of disease-free local varieties of seed.

Shenk (1994) suggested the following modifications of the *frijol tapado* systems that might improve yields:

1. increase bean plant populations by planting bean seed with a dibble stick or other similar apparatus.
2. use higher seeding rates.

3. apply the herbicide glyphosate to create a mulch, but delay broadcasting bean seed until treated vegetation begins to die, some seven to ten days after the glyphosate application.

It should be noted that very few farmers use herbicides in their *frijol tapado* plantings. Furthermore, the long-term consequences of herbicide use in *frijol tapado* systems are unknown and herbicide use may cause serious damage to the environment.

Positive and Negative Aspects of the Frijol Tapado *System*

Positive characteristics are as follows:

1. The system appears to be sustainable over time.
2. The system is easily managed.
3. The system can be used by extremely poor farmers in harsh environments.
4. For the farmers that practice it, the system provides a secure source of food and income that fits in well with the labor requirements off farm and other on-farm activities.
5. The *frijol tapado* system is well suited for steep slopes that normally do not permit annual crops. Most small-scale farmers plant beans on land with slopes of 50-70% (Bellows 1995).
6. The mulch and the bean crop do not leave the land bare, and thus the system can reduce or eliminate erosion.
7. The system uses few outside inputs; thus, little if any capital is required.
8. Labor costs are not high. Less labor is needed than for planting of other crops. Labor productivity is somewhat low per unit of land, but is high per work day.
9. The system--if extended--can reduce the use of the destructive aspects of the slash/burn system.
10. The system provides beneficial organic matter and nutrients for the crop.
11. The mulch conserves soil moisture and lessens high soil temperatures that can interfere with plant growth.
12. The mulch and the bean plant cover effectively prevents weeds.
13. The mulch prevents soil-splashing and thus clearly reduces losses from diseases such as web blight of beans and common bacterial blight.

60

Negative characteristics of the *frijol tapado* production system are:

1. Reported low yields when compared to conventional bean system (in the absence of web blight).
2. Slugs, diseases, and insects, and other pests may cause some losses.
3. Poisonous snakes, such as the fer-de-lance, may utilize the mulch as cover.

Alfaro (1994) suggested that more socioeconomic studies of the *frijol tapado* system are needed:

> Since the majority of studies on the slash/mulch system for beans have been agricultural in nature, there should be more socioeconomic studies of the system. This would improve understanding of the rationale used by producers in traditional practices. This is particularly important given the need to identify sustainable agricultural production systems and in the light of current economic policy which has led to substantial increases in the price of imported inputs and a reduction of credit for the production of basic grains.

A significant finding regarding the potential of *frijol tapado* and other mulch-based systems has been made by Martha Rosemeyer and Ken Schlather of Cornell University (Bunch 1995). Schlather (1996) did the research for his Ph.D thesis in Costa Rica (in cooperation with Martha Rosemeyer) investigating nutrient dynamics in the *frijol tapado* system. According to CGIAR (1995):

> An estimated 60% of bean production in developing countries suffers from low soil phosphorus availability. Fertilizer is often not available or too expensive for poor farmers. Besides the direct and drastic effect of P deficiency itself, it also appears to be the main factor limiting biological nitrogen fixation. Nitrogen fixation in common bean is lower than in many other grain legumes. Poor fixation is primarily caused by environmental constraints. Such constraints cannot be overcome by inoculation with improved Rhizobium strains.

Investigations were made into possible improvements to the system. "Improvement" in the Schlather study was defined as yield increases and increases in the number of annual bean crops before returning a field to long-term fallow. Three components of this research included (1) an agronomic survey of farmer practices in both the indigenous mulched system and the introduced, unmulched *espequeado* system, including an analysis of labor and capital costs associated with both systems; (2) P fertilizer response trials and fertilizer management trials using very modest amounts of fertilizer; and (3) investigation of the effects of certain fallow species that the farmers considered to be "good weeds" such as indicator species that farmers looked for when identifying fallowing fields for cropping.

The results of Schlather's and Rosemeyer's research suggests that P adsorption, becoming bonded to aluminum and other ions in acidic soil, a major problem in half the world's tropical soils, can be avoided in humid tropical regions by applying fertilizer P to a layer of mulch above the soil. Crop roots growing in the decomposing mulch layer above the soil absorb the added P before it is adsorbed by the soil. These results suggest that farmers in humid tropical regions can greatly increase the efficiency of P fertilizer by applying it to the mulch layer in mulched systems. These findings could have a significant impact on improving slash/mulch systems around the world.

Discussing mulches for coffee, Wellman (1961) noted that during dry seasons mulches provided sufficient soil moisture so that coffee roots could obtain nutrients otherwise unavailable without them. He also noted "I was told in Africa, by researchers and farmers alike, that fertilizers applied to mulch grass, and this mixture then used as mulch, was more profitable than fertilizer applied directly to the soils of their coffee shambas." This information is similar to that obtained by Rosemeyer and Schlather in Costa Rica showing that the efficiency of phosphorus fertilizer can be greatly increased by applying it to a mulch.

Conclusions - Frijol Tapado System

The frijol tapado system is an excellent example of a traditional system that is easily managed, sustainable over time, environmentally sound, requires low inputs, and provides a secure source of food and income that fits in well with farmers' off-farm activities. A challenge remains to modify the system to make it more productive without losing its advantages (Galindo 1994). In the absence of web blight, the yields in fields under the *frijol tapado* system are often lower than those in fields planted in drilled rows with clean cultivation. However, it should be noted that these comparisons are made in plots with differing soil and topography. For this reason, some in Central America oppose continuation of the *frijol tapado* system; however, most resource-poor farmers in Costa Rica continue to use the *frijol tapado* system to produce beans. Farmers persist in using the system because of its low risk, its small investment in labor (primarily to cut weeds), and because there is always some yield even when prolonged periods of rain produce conditions that allow *T. cucumeris* to destroy beans under the clean cultivation system. Numerous observations have been made that covered beans can be planted on steep hillsides without erosion problems. Also, once planted, *tapado* fields required little if any maintenance, so farmers can safely leave a planting while they depart to harvest coffee or engage in other off-farm activities. *Tapado* fields require less labor and, although they have a low productivity per land unit, they have a high return on a labor per work-day basis. Furthermore, because of the mulch produced, the *tapado* beans suffer less from possible prolonged droughts, as compared to the clean cultivation system, and thus the risk of decreasing bean harvests is reduced. Regarding risk, Gonzalez and Araya (1994) wrote:

> The risk inherent in the slash/mulch system is low from the point of view of the small investment it needs. The farmer is only risking his seed and work and not using cash since the system is endogenous. However there are great risks to production because of the variability of productivity due to weather, soils, weeds, pests (slugs) and the varieties used. The farmer knows the system well and is prepared to trust to his luck.

What is the future for the *frijol tapado* system? A similar system has been noted in Cameroon, Africa, but there is little evidence that the system is spreading to other areas. Although most of the beans in Costa Rica were once produced with the system, today a little more than half of the beans in Costa Rica are produced in *frijol tapado* systems. It is doubtful that the *frijol tapado system* will be widely adapted in other tropical areas, but the principles of the system are being adapted in the mucuna system and other mulch-based agriculture systems. These principles will be the major contribution of the systems for future generations.

Maiz Tapado System in Costa Rica

Though *frijol tapado* is widespread within Costa Rica, *maiz tapado* (covered maize in English) is relatively rare among non-indigenous Costa Ricans (personal communication--Martha Rosemeyer). The Bribris are an Indian group that live on both sides of the a rugged Talamanca mountainous reserve near the Panamanian border on the Pacific side of the country. Among their other crops are maize, beans, bananas, plantains, peach palm, squash, guava, yams, and rice. Rainfall recorded at the Bolas rainfall station on the Bribri reserve gave a 20-year average of 3623 mm (145 inches) with a four month dry season of less than 125 mm rain each month. Other sites in the Bribri reserve probably have an even higher rainfall.

Visits (personal communication--Martha Rosemeyer) made to fields in the Bribri reserve at Las Brisas (600 m elevation above sea level) and Cerro Chins at 1,400 m confirmed that *maiz tapado* among the Bribris is in common use. Maize and beans are planted separately by the Bribris using many different traditional varieties. Soils in the area were described as rocky, red clays, and possibly ultisols. Plantings were made on slopes of approximately 40%. Planting in the *maiz tapado* system is done during the *postrera* season from August to September. One farmer reported that maize could be planted into a mulch of mostly second growth vegetation, but not into ferns (*Pteridium aquilinum*) or "Calinguero" grass (*Melinis minutiflora*) vegetation.

Maize is generally planted a month or two earlier than beans so that plants are larger and stronger to withstand the high winds that occur during the December-January dry season. To plant, farmers cut passageways through the second growth vegetation, broadcast seeds into the vegetation, and then slash the vegetation on top of the seeds. Farmers said that the only difference between *maiz tapado* and *frijol tapado* is that the vegetation is not chopped up once it is on the ground as it is for beans, because maize is a "stronger" seed than bean. They said that the seed is bigger, so it has more force to penetrate the unchopped mulch layer.

Maize is harvested in January and February and is used for food and to make "chicha" (a fermented, non-distilled maize beer). Farmers in the Bribri area also use a system called *maiz espequeado* using a white seeded maize variety. *Espequeado* is a more intensive system of production in which seeds are planted with a digging stick. Most farmers in the area also plant a little *gandul* (pigeon pea or *frijol de palo--Cajanus cajan*) and cassava. Interestingly, these two crops were often planted in acid soils in old, degraded pastures with high populations of bracken fern (often an indicator of poor soils). Cassava is known to grow on very infertile soils, and thus is often the last crop planted before a fallow which restores soil fertility.

The more complex system of this indigenous Indian group in the Bribri reserve deserves more intensive studies, as they probably have a long history of agriculture and appear to have found ways to use even the most degraded areas of their reserve for food production. Comparison of yields and other characteristics of the *maiz tapado* system with other cover crop/green manure systems in Central America could increase our understanding of the potentials for adapting these systems to increase the productivity of resource-poor farmers throughout the region.

Slash/Mulch Maize and Sorghum Systems in Honduras

One of the major problems in Central America is erosion and environmental degradation of hillsides because of present or past slash-and-burn agricultural practices. This is an especially serious problem in Honduras, as about 70% of the land in Honduras is hilly with gradients of more than 25% (Melara and del Rio 1994). However, slash/mulch systems can shorten fallow periods and reduce or eliminate erosion. Near Pespire, in southern Honduras, three systems of slash/mulch have been described by DeWalt and DeWalt (1984). Although slash-and-burn practices are also common in the area, previously cropped land on hillsides is generally rested or kept in fallow for five to six years. After this amount of time the land is ready to be slashed again and is then called *en quamil*. Vegetation is slashed during the middle of the season of high rainfall and subsequently decomposes to form a mulch.

The most frequently used system of slash/mulch is based on maize culture and is called *maiz de la postrera* or *socolar*. Near the end of August weeds, vines, and small bushes are cut, but small trees are left standing. Next, maize seeds are planted into the resulting mulch with a pointed digging stick called a *bareto* or *chuzo* in Spanish. The decomposing vegetation is pushed to one side and a hole is made through the mulch into which the maize seed is planted. After the maize has germinated and grown for some time the larger trees are cut. Farmers claimed that the falling trees did little damage to the maize as long as the maize had not formed rigid stems. The maize finds it way through the maze of tree trunks and brush left in the fields. DeWalt and DeWalt (1984) estimated that 23-31 man-days of labor were needed to plant one manzana in *maiz de la postrera*.

The second system of slash/mulch described by DeWalt and DeWalt (1984) was for planting sorghum. The system is called *maicillera*. Farmers broadcast sorghum seed among the weeds, bushes, and trees which are cut the same day with a curved machete called *machete de taco*. The slashed weeds, bushes, and trees fall over the sorghum seed forming a mulch. Farmers noted that the sorghum must germinate rapidly or ants, rats, mice, or birds will consume it. Thus, if there was no rain in the next day or two after planting, farmers stopped planting *maicillera*. Labor (man-days) for the *maicillera* system was estimated at 28-42 days. Preventing bird damage took from 2-15 days of labor. *Maicillera* plantings near Pespire were generally made in July and August. As the varieties of sorghum used in southern Honduras are photosensitive, the period of flowering is the same for the harvests planted at the end of April as for those planted in September. Farmers stated that yields were the same for both dates of planting.

The third slash/mulch system described by DeWalt and DeWalt (1984) is quite similar to the second system (described above) except that the sorghum is planted in September and October and is used as a forage for animals rather than for grain. The system is called *quatera*. The system is only used by farmers who have animals. Plantings are later and plant populations are denser. The entire sorghum plant is pulled up, bundled, and fed to animals during the dry season.

Advantages listed by Honduran farmers for the above slash/mulch systems follow:

1. The whims of climate do not affect this system as much as others. Other systems often depend on precise timing of plantings and conditions too wet or too dry may cause serious problems.
2. Broadcasting seed in the *maicillera* and *quatera* systems eliminated the hard labor of planting with a digging stick.
3. The mulch produces a soil covering which hides broadcasted seed from pests.
4. The mulch is important because it prevents seed and seedlings planted on steep hillsides from being washed away by heavy rains.
5. The mulch prevents erosion on steep hillsides.
6. The slash/mulch systems provides some management of weeds and insects. Informants stated that insects were less of a problem in the rainy season because of the immense quantities of green foliage available in comparison to the dry season. As insects have access to abundant food during the rainy season they cause less damage. Weeds and other vegetation are cut initially for mulch, and later their thick, dead vegetation forms a mulch which inhibits weed growth.

In 1995, two staff members from CIDICCO (Milton Flores and Marcel Jansson) and Martha Rosemeyer (CIIFAD Mulch-based Agriculture Field Coordinator) of the Cornell University Mulch-based Agriculture Project (personal communication--Martha Rosemeyer) studied the *maicillera* systems in Honduras. They concluded that the sorghum *tapado* or *maicillera* system is alive and well and widely practiced in the southern zone of Honduras in the state of Choluteca, Aldea of Linaca, and is part of a complex sorghum/cattle-based agricultural system. The *maicillera* (sorghum/*tapado*) system is planted in June and July, and is one of five different local cropping systems that include sorghum (*Sorghum vulgare*) as follows: "*maicillera, milpa de primavera, guatera, sorgera,* and *postrera.*" The *maicillera, sorgera,* and *postrera* are mulch systems. Which cropping system is chosen in any specific year depends on the needs of the farmer and the availability of land, labor, and capital. In most of these systems the sorghum is planted with maize. The sorghum systems are integrated with cattle through the use of sorghum in three ways: (1) cattle grazing on the plant in the field after the seed head is cut, (2) the post harvest "cut and carry" of the plant to cattle in a corral, or (3) the cutting, drying, and storing of the pre-flowering plant as forage for cattle. These systems merit further study, especially in other areas where the system is practiced in Honduras.

Farmers in the areas where *maicillera* is practiced have previously used slash-and-burn practices, but now most are not burning and are leaving more trees in their *maicillera* and other fields due to effective programs of NGOs in the area. The intensive education campaign of NGOs coupled with deforestation, the decrease of potable water, and the increase in wood prices has further stimulated the interest in trees as part of farmer's cropping systems.

Traditional varieties of maize and sorghum are usually planted together in these the slash mulch systems. According to local farmers, there are two general types of sorghum. One is the *maicillo* or photoperiod sensitive types which can take 3-8 months to mature. The other type, referred to as *sorgo* consists of photoperiod insensitive introduced varieties that take three months to mature. The *sorgo* seed is generally saved from the previous year. The farmers planting maize were using *maiz grueso* which has either yellow or white seed on a purple or white cob and thus is called *tuso morado* or *tuso blanco*.

One of the primary problems, according to all the farmers interviewed, is seed predation by ants. To determine the seriousness of the problem, sorghum seeds were thrown on the ground (personal communication--Martha Rosemeyer). Within five minutes ants (both black and red types) had found the seeds and were carrying them off. Large losses and poor stands in sorghum and maize were attributed to these ants. Mixing of the seed into the soil by the person who chops and uproots the vegetation protects seed from being found by the ants.

Two materials are used to coat the sorghum seed black and thus protect seed from ants. First, the "carbon" or black powder from inside small batteries is smeared on seeds. Secondly, the residue from wood smoke residue is scraped off of cooking stoves and mixed with lard and applied to the seeds. The white sorghum seeds are blackened and this seems to make it difficult for ants to find seed in or on the soil.

The broadcasting of seeds into the vegetation using an overhand throw or broadcast takes considerable skill. The woody vegetation is cut with a hooked machete called a *pando* while the herbaceous vegetation is loosened with the blunt end of the machete and pulled up. Sorghum seeds are mixed into the soil, in contrast with *frijol tapado* where the bean seeds are broadcast into the vegetation, fall on the mulch, but seldom touch the soil.

In the *maicillera* system trees are often left in the fields. Many *maicillera* fields are on very steep slopes and farmers noted that trees were useful to hold on to when climbing up and down the inclines. Trees are especially useful during the harvest. The trees also are valuable as a source of construction materials and for firewood.

Yucatán Jack Bean and Other Mexican Slash/Mulch Systems

De Jesus Huz (1994) described the use of jack bean (*Canavalia ensiformis*) with maize in the Yucatán Peninsula of Mexico. He noted that jack bean was extremely resistant to the dry conditions in the area where he worked, which received an annual precipitation of only 600-700 mm/year. The legume provided a soil cover for two to three months of drought, thus preventing soil erosion from wind and moisture loss. Jack beans grew well in the nutrient poor, degraded soils of the region and also provided organic matter. Seed was planted in the maize rows 15-20 days after planting to avoid competition of the vines with the maize. Vines were pruned once about a month after planting. After the maize was harvested the jack beans were allowed to continue growing and to cover the ground during the dry season. Later, after many of their leaves had dropped, the jack beans were slashed, and the resulting mulch was left on the ground. Later maize was planted into the mulch either in rows or with a digging stick. According to De Jesus Huz (1992) the results have been spectacular. In an area where yields were usually about 600-1,100 kg/ha, one field planted to maize and jack bean for three years in succession yielded 2,600 kg/ha of maize.

The above work has important implications for the many semi-arid areas of the world. Most slash/mulch systems are successful only in high rainfall areas. The use of *C. ensiformis* in the above system should be investigated and considered for the many semi-arid areas with poor soils found in other areas of Latin America, Africa, and Asia.

68

Coe and Diehl (1980) describe the slash/mulch agriculture systems used near the village of Tenochtitlán, Mexico, on the Atlantic coast of the Isthmus of Tehuantepec. Farmers of the area have four distinct agricultural seasons or maize crops, as each crop has its own distinct time to plant and to harvest. There are two primary maize crops (*tapachol* and *temporal*) and two secondary ones (*chamil* and *tonamil*). Most farmers plant one or two of these crops, however, no one plants all four. Two of the crops involve the use of a slash/mulch practice.

The *tapachol* crop is planted between November and February and harvested by May or June. It can be planted on both cultivated soil types — Coatzacoalcos and Tenochtitlan — but is the only major crop put on Coatzacoalcos series soils. Field preparation for the *tapachol* involves cutting the vegetation, which is not burnt but is left to be used as a mulch.

Plots selected for a *tapachol* crop are generally planted on the previous years *temporal* fields, as the vegetation in such fields is easy to cut and provides an effective mulch without impeding weed growth. The vegetation often consists of a tall grass called *zacate camalote* (*Paspalum fasciculatum*) which sprouts in previously cultivated fields. Coe and Diehl wrote: " The dead vegetation protects the soil and plants from desiccation and provides some fertilizer as it rots." Cut vegetation is burned in both the *temporal* and the *chamil* crops. They add: "The rainy season crop is called the *temporal* or the *cosecha grande*. This is the largest crop of the year in terms of the area planted, the number of people who plant it, and the total harvest."

The *chamil* crop is planted in March on low-lying humid soils and involves cutting and burning of vegetation (Coe and Diehl 1980). Harvest is in May or June, but not many people plant *chamil* crops because "suitable land is scarce, insufficient moisture at the critical times in the growing season poses a risk, and there is always the danger of early floods." The *tonamil* crop is planted in late August or early September and harvested in November. This crop also involves slashing vegetation to produce a mulch and is planted on high, well-drained soils. The harvest is smaller and there is a greater risk of losses due to pests. Thus, the *tonamil* crop is often called the *aventurero* or risk-taker crop.

Slash/Mulch Systems Used to Establish Banana Plantations

The early systems used to establish banana plantations in the Americas seem to have been slash/mulch systems. Reynolds (1921, 1927) described the early system which banana companies used to establish new banana plantations in Central and South America and the Caribbean. First, large areas of forest land were cleared for planting. Few details were given, but Wardlaw (1929, 1961) described what he called an "extensive system." In 1961 Wardlaw wrote:

> The forest underbrush is cutlassed to allow of the staking out of the rows, and the planting holes, 15 inches in diameter and 15 inches deep, are dug at regular distances. Suckers or "bits" are planted and the forest is then felled. After some two or three months, the young banana plants begin to appear through the tangled mass of trunks, branches and twigs. As the growth of the young banana plants and the decay of the forest debris take place with astonishing rapidity under the prevailing warm, humid conditions, very soon, with periodic cutlassing of the secondary bush, especially round the young plants, an orderly plantation comes into being, and bunches of fruit may be obtained within the year.

Wardlaw noted that upkeep of the plantation was simple and consisted of slashing the forest trees and bushes, drainage, and removal of superfluous suckers. The system was extensively used initially in Latin America, but now has been replaced with a more "modern" agriculture which includes extensive drainage, tilling, liming, and maintenance of nutrients. Reynolds (1921) noted:

> The enormous amount of logs, branches, leaves and trash covers the ground like a mulch and instead of being destructive, actually establishes the most favorable conditions possible for the growth of the young banana plant. The hot humid atmosphere and the wealth of fungus and bacterial organisms cause the felled trees to undergo rapid decomposition. The twigs and smaller branches quickly rot, adding humus to the soil.

In his book on bananas, Simmonds (1966) also described the use of the slash/mulch system for establishing banana plantations. He wrote:

> Thus, in Central America, land brought into commercial banana cultivation from forest is usually surveyed, underbrushed, drained, lined out and then planted with bananas; as soon as the suckers have been planted but before the shoots have appeared above the ground, the bigger forest trees are felled. Thereafter, the only treatment is a periodic lopping of branches which are interfering with banana growth.

The above early descriptions of the establishment of banana plantations in Latin America and the Caribbean depict slash/mulch practices which probably were adapted from the traditional systems of indigenous Indian groups of the region. One of the earliest references to slash/mulch systems in Africa describes the system of slash/mulch banana plantation establishment used in Cameroon, Africa (Borel and Pélegrin 1951). The system used in the Cameroon is similar to ones described above for bananas in Central America.

Kudzu System in Peru

The University of North Carolina has conducted extensive research on soils and crops in the Amazon near Tingo Maria, Peru, during several decades. However, the results of some of the experiments of the North Carolina group in this area of Peru (Bandy and Sanchez 1981, Sanchez and Benites 1987) were not subsequently used in the region by farmers; primarily because of the considerable difficulties of marketing the product. Nevertheless, the results demonstrated the potential value of a slashed cover crop (kudzu--*Pueraria phaseoloides*) for controlling weeds and increasing crop yields in tropical areas. Bandy and Sanchez described their experiment as follows:

> An experiment was initiated in 1975 planting *Pueraria phaseoloides* land under cultivation in a way that by 1980 several plots were 5, 4, 3, 2 and 1 years of kudzu fallow. These treatments plus a natural 25-year old forest fallow were slashed and burned or slashed without burning in April 1980 and grown to a corn-rice-peanuts succession without lime or fertilizers. The 25-year old forest fallow had an excellent burn adding to the soil 12 tons dry matter/ha of ash. The kudzu fallow with considerably lower biomass averaged about 1.4 dry matter/ha of ash. Although the P, K, Mg, Cu and Zn concentrations in the kudzu a were several times higher than the forest fallow, the latter provided higher total additions of N, K, Ca, Mg, S, Mn and Fe to the soil than the kudzu fallow. Corn and rice grain yields after the forest fallow averaged 2.1 and 2.8 tons/ha respectively. When a 1 to 3 year old kudzu fallow was slashed and burned they averaged 76%, of the yields obtained by slashing and burning a 25-year old forest fallow. When same age of kudzu fallow were slashed but not burned they averaged 92% of the forest fallow yield. Keeping these soils under kudzu fallow for 1 to 3 years can approximate the initial productivity of a 25-year old forest fallow, with considerable time savings.

Regarding the weed control obtained in the experiments Sanchez and Benites (1987) noted "the one-year kudzu fallow therefore effectively suppressed weed growth in a way far superior to the herbicide combinations attempted to date." It should be recalled that kudzu can also become a weed in some areas if it escapes from cultivation. Research in Leyte, the Philippines: "found that tropical kudzu (*P. phaseoloides*) was successfully established by broadcasting seed in Imperata fallows, and it suppressed the Imperata in less than one year" (Garrity 1993). The practice was only successful when fires were controlled, as kudzu is highly flammable when dry.

One might wonder whether the slashed kudzu fallow system with its promising yields was subsequently used by farmers in the Tingo Maria area. Unfortunately, difficulties in marketing the crops grown in the kudzu system made adoption of the system uneconomical for farmers of the region. and thus the system is not in common use (personal communication—Jane Mt. Pleasant).

Hairy Vetch/Tomato System

Recently USDA researchers (Abdul-Baki, Teasdale and Prince 1992, Abdul-Baki and Teasdale 1993) reported the results of what was essentially an experimental slash/mulch agricultural system using two winter annual legumes. However, the "slashing" was completed by a high-speed flail mower. In their experiments, made at Beltsville, Maryland, two annual legumes [hairy vetch (*Vicia villosa*) and a subterranean clover (*Trifolium subterraneum*) variety "Mt. Barker"] were planted in the fall in prepared beds. In early May of the following spring the cover crops were mowed with a high-speed flail mower immediately before transplanting tomato seedlings. The seedlings were transplanted into the resulting mulch in the beds with minimal interruption of the soil or mulch cover. In 1993 they wrote:

Plants in the vetch treatment with no tillage produced a higher yield than those grown under black polyethylene, paper, or no mulch in conventional systems. Both plant mulches delayed fruit maturity by about 10 days relative to black polyethylene mulch. The proposed approach eliminates tillage, reduces the need for applying synthetic fertilizers and herbicides, and is adapted to large and small-scale tomato production in a low-input, no-tillage system. It also may be used to produce other vegetables.

According to Raver (1991), the Abdul-Baki and Teasdale treatment that used hairy vetch as mulch, averaged 45 tons of tomatoes per acre. The yield with plastic mulch was 35 tons per acre, and without mulch the yield was only 19 tons per acre. Plots mulched with hairy vetch had hardly any Colorado potato beetles (*Leptinotarsa duodecimata*), whereas beds mulched with plastic mulch were heavily infested with the beetle. Research is continuing to confirm the above results.

In 1994 Abdul-Baki and Teasdale reported that among the legumes tested (common vetch, subterranean clover, arrowleaf clover, Austrian winter pea, bigflower vetch and crimson clover), that hairy vetch was the best cover crop for the mid-Atlantic region. Hairy vetch seed was broadcast at 25 to 40 pounds of seed per acre into permanent beds that can be used for 2 to 3 years. They calculated that the vetch produced 3,000 to 5,000 pounds per acre of dry matter and fixed 100 to 200 pounds of nitrogen per acre. This amount produced enough N for a commercial crop of tomatoes without supplemental commercial fertilizer. Phosphate, potassium, and other micronutrients were also produced by the vetch. From their work they concluded:

> This no-tillage system with a winter-annual cover crop has consistently yielded greater total fruit than traditional bare soil or black polyethylene mulch treatments. It eliminates the use of preemergence herbicides, nitrogen fertilizer, and polyethylene mulches, resulting in economic savings and environmental conservation. By reducing tillage and adding a cover crop, it builds soil quality and contributes to the sustainability of production for future generations.

Abdul-Baki and Teasdale (1995) reported on comparing a conventional system for snap beans (cv. Matador) and sweet corn (cv. Silver Queen) using plowing, preemergence herbicides, and commercial fertilizer with a hairy vetch systems using reduced use of herbicides and commercial fertilizer. Sweet corn and snap bean yields in both systems were comparable.

The promising research described above illustrates that the principles of the slash/mulch practice can be applied to modern agriculture with considerable success.

4

Slash/Mulch Systems of Africa

Compared to slash/mulch systems in Latin America and Asia, the following descriptions of slash/mulch systems in Africa are, in most cases, woefully inadequate due to the lack of literature on the subject. However, this is probably not a reflection on the existence of slash/mulch agriculture, as much as a statement of the need to describe and analyze the systems currently in Africa. Below are some of the African mulch-based agricultural practices which have been described by various authors in the past.

Slash/Mulch Systems in Cameroon

An early reference to slash/mulch systems in Africa concerns a system of slash/mulch banana plantation establishment used in Cameroon, Africa (Borel and Pélegrin 1951). The system used in the Cameroon is similar to one described for bananas in Central America (Reynolds 1921, 1927). (See page 67).

In her Master of Professional Studies thesis Dotson-Brooner (1995) discussed in detail the agriculture of the Kom people. Kom is a mountainous region in the North West province of Cameroon occupied by the people of the Kom and Mbesa tribes who have traditionally been ruled by the Fon (paramount chief). Ninety percent of the Kom are farmers. The traditional knowledge regarding agriculture of these people is impressive. For example they have fourteen different names for soil types in the Kom and Mbesa languages. Dotson-Brooner noted that historically "although traditional shifting cultivation is often taken as being synonymous with slash-and burn agriculture (as it is in most areas of the world), in Kom the traditional system actually minimized the use of fire and used an alternative slash-mulch method." The following excerpt from Dotson-Brooner (1995) cites the unpublished manuscript of Nges Fultang, a local man who wrote on Kom agriculture, to illustrate the principle of prohibition of burning in former times:

> One of the most ancient values of Kom agriculture, is the fact that fire burning of bushes (the forest and areas of secondary successional growth), and farming soil, was highly prohibited. At the approach of every dry season in early days of Kom, especially between 1865 and 1945, young men with their *juju (Finii)* would come before the Fon and councilors to vow to prevent fire in the bushes and farms. This ceremony was accompanied by some rituals and feasting. At the end of the ceremony the calabashes were given to the Fon's queens. When these young men returned to their quarters the elders in the various leisure points saw to it that the Fon's orders were taken seriously. People who burnt farm land were punished by a fine of a goat and not a chicken. In those days goats were too scarce and such a penalty even forced some people to flee from their homes.

The slash-mulch method is presently used for growing both maize and beans by the Kom people. Preparation of land for dry season beans is accomplished without the use of fire, using the traditional slash-mulch method. Beans are planted approximately six weeks before the end of the rains and harvested in the dry season. The system is strikingly similar to the *frijol tapado* system of Costa Rica (see page 57).

Barbara Dotson-Brooner (personal communication) gave this description of the slash/mulch system used for beans in the forested areas of the Cameroons as follows:

> Farmers in Fundong Division, in the NW Province of Cameroon, cultivate beans. One or two months before the end of the rainy season in this area, young men begin to clear patches of forest with machetes, slashing down the undergrowth, but leaving the larger overstory trees standing. Common beans are planted directly in the ground beneath, through the mulch of downed undergrowth. By the end of October when the rains are ending, these forest farms have an almost continuous bright-green carpet of young bean plants sprouting through the moist protective layer of mulch. The trees' shade and the thick mulch combine to protect the soil from the dry season sun and allow excellent growth and production of dry beans for sale by the bucket in local markets.

Dotson-Brooner's informants gave the following description of traditional land preparation and crop-planting in the forest:

> At first, trees in the forest were cleared without using fire in an extensive way at any stage of the clearing process. Herbaceous forest understory vegetation, shrubs, and small saplings were cleared by groups of men using the machete like cutlass. Axes made from iron locally mined and smelted were used to cut down larger trees, with a few scattered trees of certain species, such as "Alang" (*Crassocephalum mannii*), and "Fewim" (*Albizia* sp.) being allowed to remain growing inside the farm.

After an area has been slashed, the dead forest vegetation is left on the soil surface to decompose for a one or more weeks.

> Once the farmers judge the place to be ready, planting is accomplished. With the use of a small cutlass or an iron planting knife (*antu*) approximately 10-15 cm in length, women make narrow holes through the mulch and into the soil. The holes are more or less randomly distributed at a spacing of about 5-10 cm. As the holes are made with the knife held in one hand, 1-3 seeds are simultaneously placed inside the hole using the other hand, until the whole plot has been planted.

Informants suggested that the *Alang* and *Fewim* trees are left inside the plots because the leaves dropped by these particular trees are "good manure" and "make the ground to be soft". Dotson-Brooner (1995) added: "In this system, not only was *Alang* merely allowed to grow naturally within the farm plot, it was also planted from cuttings, allowed to grow, then pruned to allow leaves to manure the ground."

Fultang (Unpublished Manuscript 1993) also described the slash/mulch system used for planting beans in Cameroon as follows:

> The preparation for planting of beans (as a sole cash crop) was and is usually carried out as from July to September every year. The farms were and are cleared in July and material left to rotten. During the months of August and September planting of beans is usually carried out. People who own large farms plant as much as twelve to forty-eight tins of beans. The planting is a communal activity. Men, women and children take part in the labour for no payment of any kind.

The key words in Fultang's description are "material left to rotten." Fultang's depiction obviously describes a slash/mulch practice. Leaving trees in plots as a source of organic matter for soil improvement (eg.

these particular trees are "good manure" and "make the ground to be soft.") and the use of a system almost identical to the *frijol tapado* system of Central America are especially noteworthy.

Bahuku Slash/Mulch System in Zaire

The missionary Ruth B. Fisher (1910) briefly described a slash/mulch system used by a pygmy tribal group called the Bahuku. The practice was seen in Zaire and located "In a strip of forest lying between the Semliki River and the Congo forest, and within four hours of Mboga." Fisher wrote:

> They have no means of digging up the soil , but their method of cultivation is to cut down the grass and shrubs, to fell the trees, and sow their crops of Indian corn, beans, and sweet potatoes among the stubble and roots.

The above resembles a description of a slash/mulch system as no mention was made of burning. Although a search of the literature of other pygmy groups of Zaire was made, no other references to similar slash/mulch practices were found. It would be useful to determine whether the system used by the Bahuku in the early part of this century has survived or evolved, and, if it is no longer used, what has replaced it.

Majangir Slash/Mulch System in Ethiopia

An Ethiopian tribal group called the Majangir or Majang occupy a broadleafed tropical forest at an altitude between 600 to 1,800 meters in a transitional zone between the southwestern highlands of the Ethiopian Plateau and the savannah lowlands of the Sudan-Ethiopian border. Stauder (1971) and Sutcliffe (1992) have described the subsistence agricultural system of the group, which is based on shifting cultivation of maize and sorghum, collecting honey, plus hunting and fishing. A few other plants are collected from the wild or cultivated. In addition to slash-and-burn agriculture, they have a slash/mulch practice used for sorghum and sesame. According to Sutcliffe: "The mulch sorghum fields may be third year old fields or old fields not cultivated for two to three years. Sorghum is broadcast in the middle of the rains in July and the vegetation is then cut over the seed as a mulch to suppress weeds."

The Majangir call their mulch fields *"kate."* According to Stauder, a *kate* site might be any land with secondary growth that has not grown back into forest. They prefer lush secondary growth, but avoid sites predominated with grass. Sites where the weed *Bidens pilosa* (hairy beggartick or black Spanish needle) dominates are also avoided. De la Cruz (1994) cites *Bidens pilosa* as a weed species in Costa Rica that is "especially harmful to the slash/mulch system for bean production." It is noteworthy that *B. pilosa* has been shown to be allelopathic to beans by several investigators (Campbell 1982, Rosado-May F. et al. 1986, Stevens and Tang 1987, Stevens and Tang 1991). Extracts from *B. pilosa* inhibit the growth of beans (*Phaseolus vulgaris*) and and other crop species. Rosado-May F. et al. (1986) noted that farmers avoid *B. pilosa*, as it it also allelopathic to maize.

Sesame is also produced in slash/mulch fields. Sutcliffe wrote:

> The sesame fields are smaller and are on land which has been cultivated for 5 years or more. Again seed is broadcast, the vegetation is cut as a mulch until germination, then swept up and cleared from the field. As sesame is resistant to pests and diseases it can be cultivated some distance away from the old and new fields.

Sutcliffe also described the floodplain fields of the Majangir as follows:

> The riverside field is made on flats adjoining perennial streams and is planted to maize or sorghum near or after the end of the rains and which then matures on the residual moisture. Either the fields are broadcast and mulched (during the rains) or fired and planted (after the rains).

Tanzania Sunhemp System

In Tanzania *Crotalaria ochroleuca* (crotalaria or sunhemp) is used as a green manure. A workshop on the use of crotalaria was held in Tanzania, and Tanzania's Ministry of Agriculture has approved crotalaria as a nitrogen fixing plant which can reduce the use of fertilizer (Anon 1989). Crotalaria is usually incorporated into the soil as a green manure. It is frequently intercropped with maize. However, sometimes crotalaria is used "in mulching to protect fruit trees" and is planted between bananas, citrus and coconut where it is cut to provide a mulch. Before sunhemp is cut, all pests move from fruit trees to sunhemp leaves, until these are completely eaten." The article added that in Tanzania crotalaria was useful in preventing erosion, was a palatable silage for animals, and was used for insect and nematode control. Duke (1981) reported that sunhemp hosts 20 types of plant-parasitic nematodes.

Conclusions

While the literature on African slash/mulch systems is presently too scarce to make generalizations, the examples we have support the trend that, if given a choice, shifting cultivators will often burn rather than mulch when possible. It is interesting, however, the that Kom people in Cameroon used rather severe sanctions to prevent burning in a system that has a striking resemblance to the *frijol tapado* system of bean production in Central America. It is important to document and understand traditional systems in which the trade-off between burning and mulching was weighed and the people themselves opted for mulching long ago.

With regard to more modern attempts to encourage cover crop/green manure use and other mulch-based technologies, the use of mucuna has been introduced by several research and educational institutions as well as NGOs. Its gradual spread has been noted in Benin,and Nigeria. The differing reasons given for its increasing success is further documented in chapter 8 of this book. Studying the reasons for adoption or disadoption of these newly introduced systems, as well as the traditional slash/mulch systems, and reviewing them in light of the experiences in Asia and Latin America will all be useful in determining what direction mulch-based agriculture could be headed in the future.

5

Slash/Mulch Systems of Asia and the Pacific Islands

Slash/Mulch Systems on Mentawai, Indonesia

Few references were found in the literature on the occurrence of slash/mulch systems in Asia. Conklin (1961) cites Maas (1902) as describing a slash/mulch practice on Mentawai, Indonesia, associated with taro (*Colocasia esculenta*) production. About 21,000 Mentawains and about 3,000 immigrants live on Siberut Island which is one of the Mentawai Islands of Indonesia. A recent description of a slash/mulch practice there is given by Persoon and Wiersum (1991) as follows:

> Of special interest here is the field which is cleared in the forest. Once a good site has been selected the men start to clear the undergrowth. Before they cut down the big trees they plant already shoots of various kinds of bananas, tubers and some other plants. Once this is done they cut down the trees. Trees nor leaves or branches are being burned. They are all left to rot gradually. So once the trees are cut the field looks chaotic with trunks and branches fallen over another. Gradually however the leaves wither. A few weeks after tree cutting numerous other plants (such as various species of bamboo and seedlings of fruit trees) are planted, followed often a few months later by seeds of seedlings of various kinds of fruit trees.

For the first few years the bananas, tuber crops, and other plants are harvested. Subsequently, fruit trees dominate the system and the food crops are grown elsewhere. In the following years the fruit trees continue to grow along with spontaneous secondary vegetation. Thus, the forest "regains more or less its original structure although it is a forest dominated by fruit trees." Persoon and Wiersum wrote:

> The Mentawaian way of converting primary forest into a forest of fruit trees is ecologically sound and sustainable and rather different from many other systems of shifting cultivation in Southeast Asia. By not burning the leaves and trees, and by limiting the size of fields there is almost no erosion. Also the topsoil is not disturbed. And because of the gradual decomposition process of the cut vegetation there is a slow release of nutrients.

The island's natural environment was stable for centuries because of low population intensity and the traditional religion's taboos against non-productive agriculture. Access to land was vested in the community which also controlled the rights to utilize the forest. Some small-scale logging had occurred, but in the 1970's large scale logging began. Persoon and Wiersum (1991) wrote:

> The Indonesian government claims state-ownership over the forest, granting concessions to logging companies. Also in relation to concessions for the extraction of rattan, local rights were not acknowledged. According to the Indonesian "Basic Agrarian Laws" (1960) people can only claim rights on land they actually cultivate. Primary forest is by definition excluded from that. The government may issue concessions to logging companies for exploitation of commercial timber trees on state land. The same holds true for the rattan extraction.

They add:

> The national development efforts have mainly been aimed at uprooting the "traditional way of life". The traditional religion had to be abandoned, people are being concentrated in new resettlement villages and many development activities are directed at the social and economic incorporation of the local people into the mainstream of Indonesian life.

Thus, a sustainable traditional agriculture system is disappearing and the ecology of the island is suffering severely.

Swamp Rice System in West Kalimantan, Indonesia

A Dyak group called the Kantu of West Kalimantan, Indonesia, subsist primarily on rice grown in slash-and-burn systems. Generally, slash is burned, but in one case described by Dove (1980, 1985) a slash/mulch practice is used. The swamp vegetation is grass and is usually slashed with a brush-sword after which it is dried in the sun for about five weeks and then burned. Sometimes the grass cannot be burned and then "they are mulched into the earth using brush-sword, hoe and foot."

> Seeding techniques vary according to the relative wetness of the land, and include sowing with or without dibbling, and broadcasting. Approximately one month later, the seedlings are thinned out and transplanted elsewhere in the swidden, to a uniform density of 14 plants per square meter. Seedlings for transplanting are also obtained from dry-land nurseries. An average 146 liters of threshed, un-husked grain seeds per hectare is used in planting the swamp swidden as compared to a total of 69 liters per hectare in the dry-swiddens. Planting is followed by vigilance against rice-pests and then by harvesting which begins approximately 166 days after it was planted (or 133 days after it was transplanted). Swamp swidden-yields average 2132 liters/hectare as compared to 975 liters/hectare in the dry-swiddens.

Negative aspects of this technology were described by Dove (1980):

> However, there are limits to this technology. The most important of these limits is the availability of natural swamp-land. A second limitation concerns the inability to grow anything other than rice in the swamp swiddens. The Kantu' grow 29 different food-crops, other than rice, in their dry swiddens. Only one of the food-crops, i.e. taro, can be grown in the swamp swiddens.

The high yields of the swamp swiddens were most impressive, but the return per work-day in the swamp swiddens was only slightly higher than the yields in the dry swiddens. Dove wrote that the swamp rice technology allowed the Kantu to exploit land that otherwise would not be utilized. Also, the swamp swiddens were never damaged by flooding as dry swiddens were. Fallow periods in dry swiddens averaged 5 to 20 years whereas the swamp swiddens were used for two or three years after cropping.

Indonesian Mulch-Rotation System

During a workshop Lorenz and Errington (1991) proposed a kudzu slash/mulch system for Indonesia which they called a "mulch rotation" system. Their description of the system is as follows:

> As a result of the workshop, a modified mulch rotation system was introduced on a trial basis. The system starts with a one-year fallow when a legume cover crop--*Pueraria javanica* Benth.-- is grown on land cleared of rain forest. After one year the cover crop is cut by hand and food crops are sown into the decomposing mulch. This continues for three seasons (one year) and the cover crop is again planted (as cuttings) into the last food crop--upland rice--after which the land is left under the legume cover crops fallow for a further year.

Labor was a primary constraint for the system, but since it was a no-till method, and because the mulch suppressed weeds, the labor of both tillage and weeding were reduced. The author's analysis of labor needs concluded that, although labor peaks were reduced, the system must be designed so the available labor supply matches the system's labor requirement.

Slash/Mulch Systems of Papua New Guinea

Slash/mulch practices have been recorded several times in Papua New Guinea according to Vasey (1992). Clarke (1966) reported that the people of the Nduimba basin and the Kompai people used both slash-and-burn and slash/mulch practices in New Guinea. The people known as the Kaluli of the Orogo live in a region of Papua New Guinea called the Great Papuan Plateau. Schiefflin (1975) described their swidden system in which, instead of slashing and burning vegetation before planting, they plant in the mulch produced by the slashed underbrush first and then fell trees on the top of the planting. The Kaluli live in an area covered with a dense tropical forest at elevations from 750 to 1,050 meters and with an annual rainfall of almost 5,000 mm. Many different crops are grown in the area. Their slash/mulch system was described by Schiefflin as follows:

> Bananas, breadfruit, and pandanus are grown on the slopes down the sides of a ridge and are planted in the opposite manner. The people first cut the underbrush under the canopy and then plant shoots (obtained from old gardens) with a digging stick. Then, after four or five days,

when the crop has "taken" groups of men fell the canopy on top of the crop and the tangled wreckage is left to itself. The plants soon find their way up between the fallen trunks and the garden grows normally.

Short term crops such as banana and sugar cane are planted higher on the slopes of the ridge, while breadfruit and pandanus (screw pines, *Pandanus* spp.), which take much longer to mature, are planted on lower slopes. As each crop is harvested the area is abandoned and allowed to regenerate to forest. Government officers thought the practice of felling trees on top of the crops was destructive and estimated that 40% of the crops were destroyed because of this practice. However, Schiefflin and his collaborators found that less than 5% of the crops were damaged and pointed out the several advantages of the practice. The tangle of trees and the mulch produced by the slashed vegetation protect the soil from the intense rains of the region, most of which fall in a few very heavy showers. Thus, erosion is prevented and the organic matter produced helps maintain good soil structure and fertility. The Kaluli cycle of rotation was 25-30 years. Schiefflin concluded that "It would appear that Kaluli methods of cultivation, though quite different from the highlands, produce a better diet for less work while preserving the character of the forest environment." Schiefflin mentions other systems of slash/mulch agriculture used by other tribal groups in Papua New Guinea (the Etoro people and the Onabasulu people).

The Etoro people of Papua New Guinea also live on the Great Papuan Plateau in an area with a rainfall of over 6,000 mm (263 inches). Kelly (1977) described their slash/mulch system for taro and bananas:

> In taro-banana gardens, no effort is made to create brush piles or to clear most of the garden of debris. Larger trees are felled first to form a network of trunks which will keep the bulk of the timber off the ground and prevent crop damage. The remaining trees are felled across these trunks in an irregular manner and are left untrimmed. In overall appearance, the garden resembles a section of forest recently struck by a tornado. The leaves and twigs decompose providing a gradual release of nutrients and the taro and bananas grow up through the debris.

Kelly noted that felling trees after the taro and bananas were planted minimized the time that soil was exposed to the high intensity rainfall common to the region. Rooney (cited by Denoon and Snowdon 1980) reported that on Manus, in Papua New Guinea, taro was planted amid unburned slash. Similar slash/mulch systems are found in Irian Jaya, Indonesia (Figure 5.1).

The slash/mulch systems of Papua New Guinea have several positive characteristics. These include prevention of erosion, supplying crop nutrients, better human diets for less work, and environmental conservation. Thus, the systems appear to be sustainable in the absence of high populations.

Southwest Pacific Slash/Mulch Systems

Weightman (1989) describes in considerable detail the agriculture in the island of Vanuatu in the Southwest Pacific. The root crop taro (*Colocasia esculenta*) is one of the people's most important crops. Weightman describes how slashed grass is used as a mulch along with leaves and swamp mud in raised beds for taro cultivation:

> In the coastal swamps, planting is on raised rectangular beds, surrounded by water channels dug to lower the water table and provide water circulation between them. The grass cover is not burned, but cut and used, sometimes with the addition of leaves for the subterranean mulch. Mud dug out to clear the channels is thrown onto the bed where it acts as a fertilizing agent. If the bed is used for a second or subsequent season, the turning and mulching of the soil is repeated to ensure a good yield.

Conclusions

While a variety of traditional slash/mulch systems have evolved in Asia and the Pacific over the past millennia, more recently the adoption of tree/shrub-based mulch systems (chapter 9) seems to have had more success in Southeast Asia than in Latin America. Alternatively, annual cover crop systems using mucuna and canavalia seems to have enjoyed more enthusiastic adoption in Latin America than in Asia. While the reasons for this are not entirely clear, these two regions have considerable experience to share that could undoubtedly be valuable for one another.

The literature generally supports the idea that traditional Asian slash/mulch systems have been adopted/adapted for environmental reasons and are heading toward disadoption as a result of political or population pressure. Availability of and returns on labor have also proven to be challenges in both maintaining older slash/mulch systems (as in the Kantu swamp swiddens), in the proposed kudzu slash/mulch system described by Lorenz and Errington, and in some of the hedgerow or alley cropping systems being introduced in Indonesia.

While the more traditional slash/mulch systems may need to be further adapted to meet the reduced land and labor availability, newer systems (green manure/cover crop systems using either annual or perennial species) which are being considered for introduction need to be studied more thoroughly to understand whether they in fact can provide a viable option (socioeconomically as well as agronomically) to slash-and-burn agriculture. In this regard, the connection between research and extension may need to be strengthened in order to avoid the introduction of systems or species which may in fact not be suitable for specific areas.

6

Slash/Mulch Systems That Also Include Burning

Some farmer systems combine a slash/mulch practice with a slash-and-burn practice. Certain farmers, after producing a mulch by slashing, may subsequently burn or partially burn the mulch *in situ*. Or, they may burn collected mulch for application to or for incorporation into their fields. The following paragraphs describe some of the combined practices.

Combined Slash/Mulch and Slash-and-Burn Practices in Panama

According to Beckerman (personal communication) some related indigenous cultural groups such as the Emberá and Noanamá Indians from the Colombian Chocó have moved into drier areas of Panama and are modifying their agriculture to combine slash/mulch practices with slash-and-burn practices. Beckerman noted the following from his field notes:

> Raul says that to plant corn, you fell the land in October, and scatter the seed, without burning or digging it in. Then in March you harvest it, burn the field (after a *machetazo*) and plant the corn with a *chuzo* (a digging stick). Thus two crops from same field. You can also plant plantains at the second planting.

Accordingly, the Emberá Indians initially use the slash/mulch practice, but later use a slash-and-burn practice, since it is dry enough to burn in the Panamanian region.

Combined Slash/Mulch and Slash-and-Burn
Practices in the Amazon

Some Indian groups in the Amazon basin also combine a slash/mulch practice with a slash-and-burn practice. Vickers (1989) studied the agricultural practices of the Siona and Secoya Indians of the Amazon region of eastern Ecuador. He described their practices as follows (Vickers 1978):

> In order to prepare the land for cultivation the forest must be slashed and felled. The debris is usually, but not always, burned after a period of drying during the "dry season" (November to January). Nearly all gardens are intercropped with species that have varying structural characteristics so that there is a layering effect from the subsoil to the highest level of the garden. Root crops such as manioc (*Manihot esculenta*), sweet potatoes (*Ipomoea* spp.), and malanga (*Xanthosoma* spp.), grow beneath the soil surface. Within one-two meters of the surface are maize (*Zea mays*), sugarcane (*Saccharum officinarum*), pineapples (*Ananas* spp.), and papayas (*Carica papaya*), and finally the tallest of the garden cultigens, peach palm (*Guilielma gasipaes*) and *Inga* spp. An inventory of cultigens at the village of Shushufindi revealed no fewer than 54 species and 112 native taxa of food-producing plants.

Although the Siona and Secoya customarily use a slash-and-burn system; sometimes, if they are unable to burn the slashed forest because of too much rain or other reasons, they plant in the mulch produced by slashing the forest. They also might plant in wetter months during migrations to new settlement sites when there is a need to bring new plots into production as soon a possible.

The Urarina, an Indian people of the Amazon in northern Peru have a agricultural system similar to that described above for the Siona and Secoya Indians. Their agriculture can become either slash-and-burn or slash/mulch (Kramer 1977). The understory brush is slashed, plantains are planted in the cut brush, and then trees are felled on the cut brush and plantains. Occasionally they burn the slashed brush after it dries, but at times, if there is too much rain or if there is insufficient vegetation for a good burn, they do not burn, but simply let the slashed vegetation decompose. They may also plant maize, cassava, peanuts, squash, sugar cane, taro, and sweet potatoes in their plots. Plots are generally abandoned after 2-3 harvests. Their system also effectively protects the soil from erosion. Kramer noted that the Urarina consider the system less difficult and laborious than the conventional slash-and-burn system.

Harris (1972) noted that in the upper Orinoco area of Venezuela cassava is planted among "tangled and rotting debris" by shifting cultivators rather than the thoroughly burned slash-and-burn plots used for maize. He wrote:

> Here it was observed that manioc swiddens were customarily cleared and burned very incompletely, the stem-cuttings being planted among tangled and rotting debris, whereas maize swiddens were cleared and burned more thoroughly and the seeds planted in open ground. Analysis of soil samples from manioc and maize plots revealed that, whereas in the latter organic carbon showed an expected decrease following clearance and burning, in the former it actually increased.

"Burnt Earth" in Sarawak

One of the intriguing older practices of Chinese farmers in Asia is their use of a material with the curious name "burnt earth." According to Ridley (1912) the material was widely used by Chinese farmers in tropical areas. Holliday (personal communication) suggested that the Chinese were probably among the most efficient of ancient farmers in the tropics and that their activities in the East Indies (Indonesia, Sarawak, and Sabah) may go back to the second century B. C., and perhaps even earlier. "Burnt earth" combines the preparation of a mulch by slashing tree foliage, covering and layering the mulch with soil, and slowly burning the mulch, sometimes in trenches. The final product ("burnt earth") was used as a fertilizer. Ridley (1912) gives a brief description of the preparation and use of "burnt earth" as a fertilizer for black pepper (*Piper nigrum*) on Sarawak as follows:

> Low scrub, bushes, boughs of trees and other such vegetation are cut, and partly dried by being left in the sun. A quantity is laid on the ground and covered with soil, until a good-sized pile is made. This is then ignited and allowed to smolder for some days or even weeks, until the vegetable matter is charred. After being allowed to cool it is used for manuring. This burnt earth is very suitable for such plants as vanilla and pepper, which require much potash.

The "burnt earth" was generally mixed with planting soil and each year, after harvesting, was incorporated into the soil of the mounds that the peppers were growing in.

Over the years "burnt earth", wood ashes, and various types of organic matter were added to the mounds in which the pepper plants were growing. Holliday (personal communication) noted that over the last century the use of "burnt earth" gradually declined because of the lack of sufficient trees available from the vanishing Asian forests. As the old methods of mounding with "burnt earth" declined, mounds were still used in pepper production, but a "wide variety of proprietary, organic materials were added" to the mounds, and the foot rot disease became very destructive. Foot rot was apparently never recorded during the years that "burnt earth" was commonly used. Foot rot of black pepper is caused by the fungus *Phytophthora palmivora* (Holliday 1963). Mounding would certainly reduce the severity of a pathogen like *P. palmivora*, but presumably would not completely eliminate it. Whether the use of the "burnt earth" practice in mounding prevented the pathogen from becoming serious is unknown, but it is possible that the production of suppressive soils in the mounds due to the use of "burnt earth" and organic material kept pathogens from becoming serious.

Eupatorium Inulifolium System in Sumatra

An in-depth, anthropological study of the agriculture and other aspects of the resource-poor Minangkabau farmers in West Sumatra, Indonesia, was recently published by Cairns (1994). *Eupatorium inulifolium* (called *rinju* by local farmers) is an aggressive, fast growing shrub first introduced by the Dutch into a botanical garden in Bogor, Indonesia, near the end of the nineteenth century. From that initial introduction, the plant has spread throughout many areas of Indonesia. Considered a weed by some, resource-poor farmers in a few areas have found it a valuable addition to their farming systems and have learned to exploit it in a variety of ways. *E. inulifolium* is initially herbaceous, becoming woody as it matures; dense thickets 3 meters high are common. The shrub occurs primarily in higher elevations from 200 to 1,800 meters above sea level and produces large quantities of seed that are easily dispersed by wind.

E. *inulifolium* was introduced into West Sumatra primarily to combat Imperata grass *(Imperata cylindrica)*. Cairns (1994) cited Stoutjesdijk (1935) as:

> pointing to E. *inulifolium's* fast growth and high biomass production, copious shedding of branch and leaf litter, fast fertility regeneration and reputation for invading and killing out Imperata stands, designated it as having promising agronomic potentialities and warranting closer investigation.

One of E. *inulifolium* common names is *sialak padang* which means "destroyer of Imperata fields."

Problems arose with E. *inulifolium* after its introduction by the Dutch. As the plant was an aggressive colonizer it became a serious problem in rubber plantations and cattle operations. As might be expected, it was considered a difficult to control, noxious weed by members of the population with more political power than the resource-poor farmers who practiced shifting agriculture for their livelihood. This conflict of interest between ranchers/plantation owners and shifting cultivators was generally decided in favor of those with more political power.

Cairns directed a study of three villages of Minangkabau farmers in West Sumatra. The villages were chosen to provide contrasts in altitude, topography, and age of settlement. A team of researchers interviewed farmers and also took samples of soils and vegetation in the area. E. *inulifolium* has been present in the area for about 50 years. The farmers interviewed perceived a number of positive benefits from the plant. For example, when E. *inulifolium* is present in an area, farmers indicated that this was a reliable indication of soil fertility. They stated that soil under *rinju* thickets is "black and moist", with good tilth. Thus, the presence of *rinju* indicates a good site for shifting agriculture plots. On red clay soils of poor fertility *rinju* does not do well, and cultivators noted that plants appeared to be "yellowish and unhealthy". Cairn's data from laboratory analysis of soil samples collected in different sites confirmed the farmers observations. Samples were taken from soils under Imperata grass, ferns (which were another undesirable plant-- *Pteridophyta* spp.), and E. *inulifolium*.

Cairns (1994) briefly described several systems of shifting agriculture in which resource-poor farmers utilized E. *inulifolium* as follows:

1. First, many farmers still practice slash-and-burn agriculture. He noted "Sometimes *rinju* biomass may be gathered from

other areas and added to the slash to increase intensity of the burn and volume of nutrient-rich ash produced".

Two systems of slash/mulch agriculture are used in Minangkabau:

2. The first systems is for annual crops. *Rinju* plants are slashed and their foliage is "arranged in rows, and annual crops planted between." As the slashed mulch decomposes it is gradually pushed to the base of the crop plants where it slowly releases nutrients for the crop.

3. Some farmers used *E. inulifolium* as a cover crop for perennial tree crops. They noted that *rinju* provides shade, maintains a moist micro-climate, prevents erosion and weed invasion. In these tree plantings *rinju* is slashed periodically and left as a mulch between tree rows.

4. When *rinju* plants are young and the foliage is tender, farmers slash the foliage and chop it into small pieces which are then incorporated into the soil with a hoe. Also, when potatoes are to be planted, young leaves are placed in the hole made at the time of planting along with the potato seed piece. Leaves are also collected by some farmers for incorporation as a green manure into raised beds for vegetables

Local shifting cultivators also noted that the high volumes of litter produced by stands of *E. inulifolium* was converted by termites, earthworms, insects and other soil inhabitants into a black soil rich in organic matter. Superior soil moisture retention was also discerned in soils developed under *rinju* plants. Many farmers noted the ability of *rinju* plants "to both shade out and suppress problem weeds such as Imperata during the fallow period or prevent them from becoming established in the first place." The list of uses Indonesian farmers have found for *rinju* also includes its use as a shade or nurse plant for cinnamon tree seedlings, as an insecticide (some farmers sprayed a concoction of it onto onions and peppers to kill insects), as a living fence, as firewood, as poles for vine crops, for construction, for medicine, and finally for weaning children from breast feeding. Cairns (1994) wrote:

> Probably the most novel utility of *E. inulifolium* documented by the study, some women described capitalizing on its bitter taste to wean children from breast feeding. Juice from crushed leaves is smeared on a mother's breast often enough to convince even a thirsty and insistent youngster that

his meal ticket has suddenly developed a bitter taste and it was time to look elsewhere for sustenance.

The numerous ways that Minangkabau farmers have found of utilizing E. *inulifolium* for their benefit provides further evidence of the ability of indigenous peoples to adapt to change and create ingenious solutions for their many problems.

Nonetheless, there are problems with *rinju*. It is an invasive weed under some conditions and can compete with crops and trees for soil nutrients. Controlling the plant takes time and labor. As *rinju* grows rapidly into a tall plant it may shade some crops and thus reduce yields. Although the ability of E. *inulifolium* to provide shade and a moist micro-climate can be a positive consideration for some crops, the shade and moist conditions can also provide a better environment for the development of certain insects and diseases. Furthermore, the dense thickets formed by E. *inulifolium* produce an ideal habitat for many animals such as rats, insects, and wild pigs.

Cairns (1994) concludes his study with the following statement:

> E. *inulifolium* not only performs critical ecological services within farming systems of isolated and marginalized upland communities, but its benefits are specifically targeted at the poorest strata within these village who lack financial resources to purchase inorganic fertilizers, and cannot make the transition from fallow rotation to permanent cultivation. The role E. *inulifolium* has played in enabling intensification of bush-fallow systems and mitigating pressure on forest margins in the study area suggest that its skillful management could be an important component of stabilizing farming systems on sloping highlands.

This rather isolated example of a farming system developed within the past fifty years that is providing resource-poor farmers with an adequate livelihood while simultaneously preventing soil erosion and noxious weed invasion is another illustration of the value of the lessons to be learned from slash/mulch agriculture practices developed by indigenous peoples. The development of a recent traditional system underscores the point that "traditional" does not necessarily mean "outdated" or ancient. New traditional knowledge continues to be developed or adapted by indigenous or non-indigenous farmers throughout the world. However, in order to adapt new or older traditional knowledge to a rapidly changing world, traditional systems must be studied and documented; at least with respect to socioeconomic, agronomic, and biophysical aspects. Only then can we fully realize the costs and benefits involved in adapting them to improve agricultural sustainability.

The Marceño or Popal System in Mexico

One of the most fascinating traditional systems of maize production is the *marceño* (March planting) or *popal* system (Garcia Espinosa 1980, 1987, Garcia Espinosa and Krishnamurthy 1985, Garcia Espinosa et al. 1994, Gliessman 1990). The system has probably been used in the state of Tabasco, Mexico, by the Chontales Indians since pre-Colombian times. Swamps may constitute 60% of the area of the state of Tabasco at certain times of the year. Some of the swampy areas used for the *marceño* system are naturally flooded for up to seven months of the year (Orozco-Segovia and Gliessman 1979). When the water in these swamps retreats and the swamp's surface becomes dry, a slash/mulch system is used by the Chontales Indians to plant maize.

The dominant vegetation in some swamps is *popal* grass (*Thalia geniculata*), but in other swamps grasses such as *Scleria macrophylla*, *Echinochloa cruspavonis*, and *Cyperus articulatus* are also used. In the Chontal area of Tabasco during the dry season the Chontales Indians cut the *popal* grass and allow it to dry. Local short-maturity cultivars of maize are then planted with pointed dibble sticks into the 30-40 cm layer of slashed *popal* grass in holes 10-15 cm deep. Four to six grains of maize may be placed in each hole. Other crops such as squash, cucumbers, various vegetables, and beans may also be planted into the slashed *popal* grass. When the maize seedlings begin to emerge after planting, the grass is set on fire, and, although the top leaves of the maize seedlings are scorched, the plants survive and continue to grow.

This system can be considered to be a slash/mulch system because the burning, when properly done, is superficial. Only the top layer of leaves of the slashed mulch is burned, and thus a thick mulch of the slashed popal grass remains. A superficial burn is desirable in order not only to avoid killing the maize seedlings, but also to avoid burning the mulch entirely and thus endangering the recovery of the popal grass. Some weeds and insects may be destroyed by the burning (Garcia Espinosa et al. 1994).

Weeding of herbaceous weeds and slashing of any popal grass regrowth is done with a machete about thirty days after planting. A final weeding may be made two and one-half to three months after planting at which time the maize ears are "doubled over" (*doblado* in Spanish). After the maize grains mature, traditional farmers usually bend the stalk or the ear of the maize, so the stalk or the tip of the ear hangs down.

Farmers find that by using this practice the grain is protected from rain, dries better on the plant in the sun than in storage, is less accessible to rats and birds, grain reaches such a low moisture content that storage deterioration is greatly reduced, and plants are less likely to be blown down by the wind (Thurston 1992). Fungi and insects cannot infect or infest grain when it is properly dried (Christensen and Kaufmann 1969). The final weeding also reduces access of rats to the ears as well as facilitating easier access of workers to maize within the field. Rain may cause a re-inundation of *popal* fields, but if the maize is "doubled over" it is not lost. Orozco-Segovia and Gliessman (1979) wrote that it was not unusual to observe the final maize harvest take place in canoes.

During the time soils in the system are flooded, they are under anaerobic or near-anaerobic conditions. Thus, flooding has eliminated many soil-borne pathogens and other pests. Soil profiles show a thick layer of organic matter in popal soils which may be 30 to 40 cm deep (Gliessman 1990). The high content of organic matter in popal soils may also contribute to the development of soils suppressive to plant pathogens. Evidence of biological control of soil-borne pathogens was found by Garcia Espinosa (1980, 1987, 1994) who inoculated maize soil from Tabasco that had a declining production due to soil-borne pathogens and *popal* soil, which has a 30% organic matter content. Evidence of suppression of *Pythium* spp. and *Rhizoctonia* spp. in the *popal* soils was found. Lumsden et al. (1981) found that *popal* soils were suppressive to the fungi *Pythium aphanidermatum*, *Sclerotinia rolfsii*, and *Rhizoctonia solani*, all important soil-borne pathogens.

According to Orozco-Segovia and Gliessman (1979) near Cardenas, Tabasco in 1977 yields of 4-5 t/ha of the maize cultivars *mején* and *cuarentano* were reported. Yields averaging 7 t/ha were reported in the municipality of Nacajuca, Tabasco. In contrast, average yields from conventional maize plantings were 1.3 t/ha in the state of Tabasco in 1976. Thus, the yield advantages of this traditional system are clear. The *popal* system ·uses no outside inputs except labor, whereas conventional maize is grown with fertilizer and other inputs. This traditional system is worthy of further study and efforts to determine its potential for use in other similar swampy areas of the tropics.

Sierra Leone Coppicing System

In northwest Sierra Leone, Nyerges (1989) studied the farming practices of Susu farmers residing in the Kilimi area. These farmers usually practiced "minimal cultivation" which, although it also included burning, also included coppicing and the production of a partially burned mulch. Nyerges described the Susu practice as follows:

> To summarize the features of "minimal cultivation," most villagers farm in 15 to 30 year-old fallows and fell the trees in them at one meter high. Beginning in late January, farmers first clear the smaller stems, averaging 4 cm in diameter, and leave the larger boles for later. As a result, farm sites lose their canopy not all at once but in stages, and the canopy retains some of its soil-protecting function for some time after felling begins. Indeed, some of the largest trees (ranging from from 27 to 300 cm diameter in one example) are never felled. The debris of felling completely covers the site until a partial burn takes place in April. Farmers never entirely remove this debris, and the charred tangle of stumps, stems, and branches left on farmsites may cover up to 18% of the ground surface.

Under minimal cultivation, the root masses of trees that were felled at the beginning of the swidden cycle are left undamaged by ax and fire, and the soil structure typical of the closed-canopy forest is also maintained. Nyerges noted that variation from the "minimal cultivation" practice resulted in invasion of fallow sites by grasses and vegetatively reproducing "pioneer" trees from the nearby savanna.

Tembe-Thonga Slash/Mulch System in South Africa

Taylor (1988) has described the agricultural practices and systems of the Tembe-Thonga people in Maputaland, South Africa. Among their practices is a slash/mulch system. Swampy areas in Maputaland to be cultivated with bananas are first cleared of undergrowth and then trees are felled. Subsequently, after the vegetation dries, it is usually burned, but in some cases, rather than burning, a slash/mulch practice is used as described below (Taylor 1988):

> Vegetation is not burnt and instead is left to rot. Felling of trees and vegetation is done some months before planned cultivation and some slashing of regrowth is necessary.

Taylor (personal communication) noted that slashed undergrowth was usually allowed to decompose for 3-4 months before planting. There are two alternative slash/mulch practices; either to wait until partial or total decomposition has taken place or to plant crops into a dry mulch.

Unfortunately, yield data for comparing the two variations were not available.

The Kru Slash/Mulch System of West Africa

The Kru people consist of about 1 million members living in Liberia and the Ivory Coast. Massing (1980) described the Kru cultural area and their agriculture, but had only one tantalizing reference to a Kru combined slash-and-burn and slash/mulch system as follows:

> Among the Mande, broadcasting of seed grain and tillage by hoe require a more thorough cleaning of the farm site lest a large part of the seed rice be lost. On the other hand, the Kru method i. e. planting by hoe or dibble-stick, can be effected between the debris without waste of seed grain. The differences of field preparation and planting between the We and Mande areas and the Southern area seem associated with ecological zones which crosscut the KCA (Kru Cultural Area). It is popular belief shared by many Europeans that the Kru are lazy because they do not remove debris from their fields and reburn it. But it appears that the vegetal material left on the field provides protection against the more intense rainfall in the coastal zones and, at the same time, gradually releases nutrients to the soil during a longer growing season. The longer dry season in the interior of the KCA and in the Mande area and less intense rainfall require greater exposure of seeds to rain and a maximum release of nutrients to the soil during a shorter growing period than at the coast. It is also possible that planting minimizes the danger of seed grain being washed away by heavy rains, a danger which is less serious in the interior.

The above paragraph appears to describe an agricultural system that combines slash-and-burn and slash/mulch practices, although much is left to the imagination. The reference to the European's belief the the Kru are lazy because they do not reburn is an indication of a lack of understanding of the merits of the slash/mulch agricultural system among many "western" authorities.

The Mountain Ok Taro System of Central New Guinea

Morren and Hyndman (1987) described the combined use of slash-and-burn and slash/mulch by the 28,000 members of the Mountain Ok people of a mid-altitude area of Central New Guinea. Their preferred crop is taro (*Colocasia esculenta*). The Mountain Ok have continued practicing their traditional method of shifting cultivation because their population density has remained low and their available land area is extensive. Morren and Hyndman note:

> Features of their system include (1) the selection of flat or gently sloping tracts, (2) the almost exclusive use of secondary growth, (3) small garden patch size and significant forest margins between gardens, (4) stunning of trees by scorching or ringing rather than total clearing, (5) planting in undisturbed forest litter without a general burn, (6) deferred completion of clearing until the crop is established, (7) polyvarietal planting of the staple crop, (8) a brief cropping period, and (9) long forest fallows.

A long forest fallow, generally at least twelve years but typically longer, provides for the restoration of soil fertility , especially organic matter. The combination of slash-and-burn and slash/mulch appear to bring several advantages to the Mountain Ok. Erosion is lessened, labor is reduced, and yields are increased.

Conclusions

Agricultural systems that combine the slash-and-burn and the slash/mulch systems are singularly important as they involve obtaining the benefits of both methods of agriculture. Thus, understanding the advantages provided by combing the two systems is important in the design of systems that need to move away from slash an burn practices for environmental, political, or socioeconomic reasons.

While some of the systems described have only reduced burning because it is too wet to burn, this is not universally true. There is an appreciation by farmers for the value of mulch itself in several instances described in the section above. In addition to gaining both short and long-term fertility benefits by both burning and mulching, there is also some evidence to suggest that disease control can be improved by a partial burn; as is the case with the Chinese "burnt earth" practice. The importance of the transitional partial burning systems is also underscored by the continual development of the more recently developed *E. inulifolium* slash/mulch and slash-and-burn systems by resource-poor farmers in Sumatra. Understanding older traditional and evolving agricultural systems that are either combining slash-and-burn and slash/mulch, but are headed towards slash/mulch, may provide many useful answers to increasing sustainability for farmers trying to find plausible alternatives to slash-and-burn.

7

Breeding Crops for Traditional Slash/Mulch Systems

There is little information to be found on varietal adaptation to slash/mulch systems. The development of cultivars for these systems has not been high on the list of priorities for plant breeders. Nonetheless, Smith (1994) reviewed the available literature and used the information on varietal performance from other agricultural production systems to speculate on the potential for genetic improvement which might increase the productivity of slash/mulch systems. Most of the cultivars developed for slash/mulch systems have been landraces developed over centuries or millennia by traditional farmers.

An analysis of the characteristics of the maize cultivar *chococito* or *chococeño*, which is used in slash/mulch systems on the Western coast of South America from Ecuador to Panama, gives insights into the traits useful under wet, warm conditions. Patiño 1956, Roberts et al. 1957, and Timothy 1963 list the following characteristics of *chococito* or *chococeño*: rapid plant development, tall plants with long internodes and thin strong stalks, unusually high ear placement, and the capacity to produce numerous tillers equal in size and productivity to the main stalk. For maize to prosper in one of the wettest areas of the world (for example a rainfall of over 10 meters has been recorded in Quibdo, Colombia, in one of the areas where *chococito* is grown), a cultivar must have the ability to withstand "wet feet" and prosper under extremely wet, warm conditions. Smith (1994) adds:

One can speculate that the rapid development and tall plant habit of Chococito allow it to establish well in the presence of a thick mulch, that its tall plants and high tillering capacity help in outcompeting weed regrowth in the plots, that the capacity to form productive tillers optimizes yield in a broadcast system where plant density may be low and erratic, and that highly placed ears may limit losses to pests and ear molds (the incidence of which would be favored by plant residues on the soil surface and high humidity conditions). Whether such traits are truly adaptive apparently has not been investigated.

One of the few slash/mulch systems in which variety evaluations have been made is the *frijol tapado* or covered bean system used in Central America. The varieties utilized in these systems are are highly competitive with weeds (De la Cruz 1994). Bean varieties are classified as indeterminate prostrate or indeterminate climbing. Smith (1994) reviewed the literature on comparisons of traditional and improved bean varieties used in the *frijol tapado* system and noted conflicting results. Two studies found no significant yield differences between improved or local varieties, whereas other studies found a yield advantage for the improved variety over the local bean variety.

In the early 1980s a collaborative project between CIAT and several Costa Rican organizations released two new bean varieties into Costa Rica (Pachico and Borbon 1987, Smith 1994). Talamanca 1 was a determinate erect bush bean and Brunca was a spreading indeterminate bush bean. The characteristics of the bean cultivars adapted to *frijol tapado* differed in important ways from those improved cultivars adapted to row planting systems. Smith wrote:

> The changes which have occurred in bean production practices in Costa Rica constitute one of very few documented cases where the nature of improved varieties has clearly affected crop management practices. Rarely is the linkage so clear and identifiable.

Farmers began to abandon *frijol tapado* and adopt row planting (*espequeado*), and there was widespread adoption of the new varieties and new practices. The improved bean varieties yielded more than old varieties in the *espequeado* system (1103 kg/ha compared to 719 kg/ha) while in the *frijol tapado* system little yield improvement occurred (586 kg/ha versus 488 kg/ha) (Pachico and Borbon 1987). The adoption of the *espequeado* system was attributed to the greater ease of fertilizer and pesticide application in row planting, combined with the fact that the new varieties performed best when these inputs were used. Also, credit was offered to farmers who used the *espequeado* system (Bellows, 1992). In addition, most *tapado* plantings used traditional varieties while 97% of row planted beans use improved varieties (Pachico and Borbon 1987). Although the above results appear to favor the used of the *espequeado* system and the introduction of improved cultivars, from the results of her studies in Costa Rica Bellows (1992) wrote:

> The use of agrochemicals in *frijol espeque* (*espequeado* system) allows farmers to use their land more intensively. Despite the potentially higher yields of *frijol espeque*, *frijol tapado* can provide almost three times the returns on capital investments compared to *frijol espeque* (income/cost=10.60 for tapado versus 3.76 for *espeque*) when the opportunity value for land is low. A high, competitive, opportunity value for labor during the period of bean growth also favors *frijol tapado* over *frijol espeque*. No labor inputs are used for *frijol tapado* during the period between planting and harvesting. It is, therefore, favored in areas where off-farm activities, particularly coffee harvest, provide farmers with a secure source of income during the period of bean growth.

Relative to genetic improvement Smith wrote:

> If the economic and ecological benefits of *tapado* production systems justify their continued or increased use, bean breeders must respond by identifying the distinct traits needed in varieties adapted to *tapado* and releasing improved, higher yielding varieties which, rather than encouraging use of row crop systems, will fit the *tapado* system and increase its productivity.

Smith (1994) concluded that if slash/mulch systems truly offer agronomic, economic, and ecological benefits that make their used worthwhile, then cultivars should be developed by plant breeders that will optimize the productivity of such systems. In summary Smith wrote:

> Descriptions of varieties which have traditionally been used in slash/ mulch systems provide clues to the types of traits which will be needed. Rapid plant development and tall plant habit seem generally desirable. These traits allow rapid establishment of a canopy above the mulch, thus taking maximal advantage of solar radiation and competing effectively with weeds. Highly tillered varieties of grasses or indeterminate types of broad-leaved crops also would contribute to rapid and complete canopy establishment. Resistance to specific diseases and insects which may be favored by the presence of a mulch layer will be important. The environments in which slash/mulch systems have a comparative advantage may be distinct from those in which other systems are more desirable.

Unfortunately, the economic incentives to work on crops of low input, low yielding traditional systems are poor within the institutions that are able to carry out long-term systematic breeding programs.

3.1 Close-up of beans and the mulch produced in the *frijol tapado* system. (Courtesy American Phytopathological Society)

3.2 Web blight control provided by mulching with rice husks (background) compared to severe web blight in non-mulched check (foreground). (Courtesy American Phytopathological Society)

3.3 Steep hillsides in San Ignacio de Acosta, Costa Rica, that have been farmed for over a century using the *frijol tapado* (covered bean) system without significant erosion. (Courtesy Ramiro de la Cruz)

5.1 Apparent disorder of a slash/mulch plot in Irian Jaya, Indonesia. (Courtesy Lucy Fisher)

8.1 The slashed foliage produced by velvetbean increases the organic matter content of the soil, leading to increased yields with little or no use of chemical fertilizer. (Courtesy Milton Flores CIDICCO)

8.2 A major contribution of velvetbean is the significant quantities of nitrogen produced on nodules found on the roots. (Courtesy Milton Flores CIDICCO)

8.3 Farmers illustrating the amount of slashed material produced by velvetbean in a Honduran maize field. (Courtesy Roland Bunch)

9.1 Alley cropping in Sumba, Indonesia, has shown promise in reducing shifting cultivation and the need for slash-and-burn agriculture. (Courtesy Lucy Fisher)

9.2 Slashed Leucaena from alley farming hedgerows in Sumba, Indonesia, yield fuelwood in addition to mulch and fodder. (Courtesy Lucy Fisher)

9.3 Trimmed poró, (Erythrina peoppigiana) trees commonly used as a shade in Costa Rican coffee plantings. The trimmed branches provice nutrients and organic matter and produce a mulch that suppresses weeds. (photo by H. David Thurston)

8

Cover Crops and Green
Manure Crops

The value of cover crops and green manure crops in agriculture has been known for centuries. Cato (1934), a Roman who lived 234-149 B.C., wrote that lupines, beans, and vetch fertilized the land. Varro (1934), writing between 116-27 B.C., suggested that some plants, although they gave no benefit the year they were ploughed under, gave benefits the following year. Varro wrote:

> Some crops are to be planted not so much for their immediate return as with a view to the year later, as when cut down and left on the ground they enrich it. Thus it is customary to plough under lupines as they begin to pod--and sometimes field beans before the pods have formed so far that it is profitable to harvest the beans - - in place of dung, if the soil is rather thin.

Many slash/mulch systems use plants planted as "cover crops" or for use as "green manures." Considerable confusion occurs relative to the use of these terms (cover crops and green manures), as they are used in different ways by different authors. The terms are often used interchangeably. Traditionally the term "green manures" has referred to plants which are turned under or incorporated into the soil while green, or soon after flowering, in order to enrich the soil. In recent years however, the term has been used more loosely, and green manure may sometimes refer to plants or plant vegetation which may be applied as a mulch to the soil, either slashed and fresh or after the plant has dried out. As long ago as 1927 Pieters, in his comprehensive treatment of green manures, stated that "Green manuring is the practice of enriching the soil by turning under undecomposed plant material (except crop residues) either in place or brought from a distance." He further stated "A cover crop is one planted for the purpose of covering and protecting the soil." The Soil Science Society of America (1987) defined green manure as plant material incorporated into the soil while green or at maturity, for soil improvement.

Cover crops are any crops grown to produce soil cover, regardless of whether they are later incorporated. They are used to cover and protect the soil surface, although they may be turned under as green manures. Further, the term cover crop also refers to crops grown between orchard trees or on fields between cropping seasons to protect the land from leaching and erosion (Martin 1975). Diver and Sullivan (1992) wrote: "Any field or forage crop grown to provide soil cover is a "cover crop." Since a crop grown as a cover crop may later be soil-incorporated as a green manure, the two practices are often referred to interchangeably.

Leguminous cover crops or green manures are especially valuable because of the nitrogen many can fix and are often referred to as "legume green manures." Lathwell (1990) noted:

> Under favorable conditions large quantities of N can be fixed by legume green manure crops. First, legumes must be adapted to prevailing climatic conditions. Genetic diversity ensures that some legume species will be adapted to existing climatic conditions. Second, suitable soil conditions favoring dry matter accumulation are required to achieve maximum N fixation.

A major benefit of cover crops and green manures is weed management. The space and light that cover crops occupy reduces weed growth. In plantings of primary crops, cover crops interplanted as living mulches function as "smother crops" to suppress weeds, as they compete with them for light, moisture, and nutrients. Some cover crops produce natural toxins or "allelochemicals" which are becoming important as a weed suppression management practice. In no-till systems, the mulch that results from mowing or chemically killing allelopathic cover crops can significantly suppress weeds. Cover crops can also aid insect pest management by serving as habitat for beneficial insects.

On the negative side, cover crops may reduce crop yields as they may compete with crops for light and nutrients. Individuals working in agricultural development should also keep in mind that a number of plants have been introduced in the past with the best of intentions by well meaning people, but later their introductions became environmental disasters and caused serious losses to agriculture. The introduction into the United States of kudzu, johnson grass, floating water hyacinth, and crabgrass comes to mind. The adaptation, invasiveness, and competitiveness of new introductions should be considered and tested before wide-scale introductions are made.

Cover Crops and Green Manures
Used in Developing Countries

Considerable information on the common and scientific names, sources, and performance of hundreds of cover crops is available (De Sornay 1916, Duke 1981, Evans et al. 1983, Flores 1994, Monegat 1991, Sarrantonio 1991, Rodale 1992). The use of cover crops and green manures is spreading rapidly, especially in tropical developing countries (Van der Heide and Hairiah 1989). For example, Roland Bunch (personal communication) noted in 1994 that "in the last few years, some fifty organizations in Mexico and Central America have begun working with green manures for villager use." There has been an explosion of interest in cover crops, green manures, and associated mulch-based agricultural systems in the last decade, not only among NGOs, but among scientists, environmentalists, and farmers.

In recent decades Latin American campesinos have been faced with rising prices for most petroleum based inputs and have turned to various green manures and cover crops for their agricultural systems, especially velvetbean (*Mucuna* spp. or *Stizolobium* spp.), the use of which has expanded rapidly in Mexico and Central America. Often the green manures and cover crops are slashed. The principles used in slash/mulch systems, which are used around the world, present valuable examples of sustainable agricultural practices which cause little or no damage to the environment when compared to slash-and-burn systems, and which can make significant contributions to increasing food production and reducing environmental degradation in developing countries without the intensive use of expensive external inputs. Buckles et al. (1992) noted that to date, the scientific investigation on the use and adoption of green manures such as velvetbean have not kept pace with the adoption of these systems by the campesinos of Mexico and Central America.

The hundreds of cover crops important in developing countries can not all be listed here. Rather, the reader is referred to the references given above. Before adoption, numerous characteristics of each plant need be considered such as: various botanical characteristics; whether the plant is an annual or perennial; growth habit, ability to withstand drought, excess moisture and cold; toxicity to man and animals; adaptation to different soils and environmental conditions; food, forage value and other uses; nutritional data; cultivation practices; yields, pest problems, and economic value. Bunch (1994) lists the following as the species most commonly used in Mexico and Central America: jack bean (*Canavalia ensiformis*), lablab bean (*Dolichos lablab* or *Lablab purpureus*), *Lathyrus nigrivalvis*, kudzu (*Pueraria phaseoloides*) and scarlet runner bean (*Phaseolus coccineus*) along with the most common species, the velvet bean (*Mucuna* spp. or *Stizolobium* spp.).

Although there are hundreds of plants used as cover crops or green manures in developing countries, in addition to those mentioned above, below are listed a few of the more promising species for the lower tropical areas of developing countries:

Arachis pintoi - wild peanut
Cajanus cajan - pigeon pea
Canavalia gladiata - sword bean
Crotalaria spp. - various species of crotalaria
Crotalaria juncea - sunhemp
Desmodium intortum - greenleaf
Glycine max - soybean
Vigna unguiculata - cowpea
Voandzeia subterranea - Bambarra groundnut

Although there are numerous cover crops or green manures appropriate for use in the lower elevations of the tropics, fewer are found in the higher elevations. According to Bunch (1990) few widely useful systems are available for areas in the tropics above about 1,800 meters elevation. In the South American Andes the legume *tarwi* (*Lupinus mutabilis*) has been grown as food by traditional farmers for centuries. The value of *tarwi* as a cover crop at elevations between 2,500 and 3,500 meters elevation is now being investigated (Beingolea Ochoa 1993, Ruddell 1995). The scarlet runner bean (*Phaseolus coccineus*), called *chinapopo* in Spanish, has been grown for thousands of years by indigenous groups of Mexico, Central America and parts of South America in areas between 1,400 to 2,800 meters elevation. León (1987) wrote that seeds of scarlet runner bean 7,000 years old were found in northeast Mexico. Its use, almost always in association with maize by traditional farmers in Honduras, is described in detail by Solomon and Flores (1994). *P. coccineus*, once established by seed, produces tubers which reestablish the plant for up to 12 years. The plant is seldom pruned (slashed), and, because of its often aggressive foliage, *P. coccineus* is usually grown with tall maize cultivars that may reach 3.5 meters in height.

Research is needed on the adaptability of the numerous cover crops and green manures used in temperate zones to the higher elevations of the tropics. Monegat (1991) describes an number of cover crops and green manures used extensively in the temperate areas of Brazil. Continuing attempts to identify and exploit species already existing in the tropical highlands should also remain a priority.

Advantages and Disadvantages
of Cover Crop/Green Manure Systems

The practice of slash-and-burn agriculture is a major environmental problem in forested areas worldwide. Cover crop/green manure systems can reduce the use of the practice in a wide range of elevations and climatic conditions. Because many cover crops and green manures produce high quality forage, livestock enterprises can be intensified and thus less pressure would be exerted on forest resources. Farmers have been so impressed by the value of some cover crop/green manure systems that diffusion has occurred spontaneously from farmer to farmer, and from village to village. The cover crop/green manure systems fulfill nearly all the criteria used to judge the appropriateness of a technology for small and medium-sized farmers given by Bunch (1982) in his book *Two Ears of Corn*. Some of the positive aspects of the cover crop/green manure systems (such as the velvetbean system) suggested by Bunch (1990, 1994) plus others are listed below:

1. Green manure systems fit well into numerous traditional maize and sorghum based farming systems in Central America and Mexico.
2. The use of cover crops and green manure systems can often eliminate the need to burn in traditional shifting cultivation systems. Substitution of burning with mulching can enrich the soil, reduce soil erosion, and reduce the risks to neighboring farms and forests.
3. Systems using leguminous green manures are capable of fixing significant amounts of nitrogen. If petroleum prices rise significantly in developing countries the use of chemical fertilizers could become even more uneconomic for small-scale farmers than they already are.
4. The organic matter content of soils can be significantly increased by leguminous green manures. Velvetbeans may produce up to 50 tons/hectare/year of organic matter.

5. Velvetbeans are moderately aluminum tolerant and can be planted on acid, aluminum toxic soils.

6. A velvetbean mulch, even on land with a 35% slope, can protect the soil from erosion.

7. Velvetbeans have been shown to reduce nematode populations and jack bean leaves are sometimes used to control leaf cutter ant colonies.

8. Weeds are suppressed by cover crops, especially vigorously growing species such as velvetbean. Even perennial weeds such as nut grass (*Cyprus rotundus*) and Imperata grass (*Imperata cylindrica*) can be eliminated over a 4-5 year period.

9. The systems generally have low labor costs. The reduction in the cost of weeding is especially evident.

10. In the case of velvetbean, once farmers have obtained their initial supply of seed, the system requires no additional expense.

11. Some green manures supply nutritious food for humans (ie. lab-lab beans, scarlet runner beans).

12. Plants such as velvetbeans and lablab beans provide good animal forage.

13. Crop damage by free-roaming livestock can be reduced by providing reliable sources of forage from cover crops and green manures, thereby allowing animals to be penned. Regarding the damage done by free-roaming animals Bunch (1994) wrote:

In some instances, the potential of cover crops that can be grown in the dry season has convinced entire communities to pen their animals during this time of year. It is no longer necessary to free the animals since the cover crops provide forage, and the elimination of free pasturing allows other practices such as hedges and perennial crops to be introduced which was not possible while livestock roamed free.

14. Because many cover crops and green manures produce high quality forage, livestock enterprises can be intensified and thus less pressure would be exerted on forest resources which are often burned to provide forage for animals.

Bunch (1990, 1994) also listed disadvantages:

1. Few widely useful cover crop/green manure systems are known for areas above 2,000 meters in elevation. Velvetbeans are useful up to about 1,500 meters elevation in Central

America. However, scarlet runner beans (*Phaseolus coccineus*) have been intercropped with maize by farmers in Central America (Flores 1994, Solomon 1993, Solomon and Flores 1994) at elevations up to 2,500 meters elevation and trials are underway on their value in cover crop systems. In the Andes *tarwi* (*Lupinus mutabilis*), has been grown by traditional-farmers for food for centuries, and its value in as cover crop at elevations between 2,500 and 3,500 meters elevation is also being investigated (Beingolea Ochoa 1993).

2. Few systems for highly arid conditions are available, although the use of jack bean appears promising (De Jesus Huz 1994).

3. Most present systems can only be used with tall crops such as maize and sorghum.

4. Some pest problems can increase when cover crop/green manure systems are used as a mulch. Crop damage by rats, mice, and slugs may increase. Rabbits and leaf-cutter ants may damage velvetbeans.

5. The diseases, insects, and other important pests of cover crops and green manures are not well known. For example, the psyllid *Heteropsylla cubana* caused serious damage to *Leucaena leucocephala* after its introduction into Asia and the Pacific Islands, and the use of *L. leucocephala* has been abandoned in many areas. Promoters of cover crop/green manures systems should be alert to the possibility of the introduction of a devastating pest which could wipe out a promising cover crop/green manure system, especially when the cover crop itself is introduced as a monoculture.

6. Poisonous snakes such as the fer-de-lance in Central America may inhabit mulches.

7. Although the velvetbean has been consumed by humans in products such as coffee, tortillas, and flour for baking, the dried beans contain L-dopa or levadopa, a chemical which can cause headaches, dizziness, and vomiting if ingested in large quantities. L-dopa has beneficial uses also as it is used to treat the symptoms of Parkinson's disease. Therefore, velvetbeans should be consumed sparingly and with caution. CIDICCO has written a report on the utilization of velvetbeans as food (CIDICCO 1993), but great care is needed in preparation of food products from velvetbeans. Osei- Bonsu et al. (1995) described the common use of canavalia as traditional foods in stews and soups in Ghana for at least a century. Velvetbeans were once of importance in Asia as a food, but they have been replaced as a

food by more suitable legumes (Burkill 1966). Research is needed on human toxicity in velvetbean.

Regarding the future for slash/mulch systems Bunch (1994) wrote: The impact that green manures, cover crops and slash/mulches can have on poverty and the ecology is encouraging. Mulch crops not only have great potential for improving the economy and ecology of Central America, they have great potential for being widely adopted. Certain limiting factors such as the lack of existing systems for some situations and problems with rabbits and leaf cutter ants may be eliminated through research. Prospects for cover crops seem to depend on three factors: 1) the number of extension programs and their effectiveness in diffusing these technologies; 2) the intensification of rural agriculture; and 3) the price of chemical fertilizers. Once the use of cover crops is widespread, their importance will depend largely on the balance between intensification of agriculture and the price of fertilizers. If the former occurs faster, the author believes that cover crops will lose their value. If the latter increases quicker, then these crops will gain even more importance.

Velvetbean Slash/Mulch Systems

Velvetbean is a vigorously growing leguminous green manure or cover crop widely used in warm, moist tropical areas (Skerman et al. 1988), generally at elevations from 0 to 1,500 meters above sea level (Bunch 1994). Velvetbeans are currently one of the most popular cover crops in the warm, humid tropics throughout the world. Buckles (1994) notes that at least 50 non-governmental organizations and research institutions feature this genus among the plants they research or promote. Many thousands of farmers in Latin America and Africa are using velvetbean for improving crop yields or controlling noxious weeds. The recent review article by Buckles (1994, 1995) summarizes the history of this interesting plant, how it has been popularized, and how its use has subsequently "waxed and waned in various parts of the globe."

The velvetbean originated in South Asia or Malaysia according to Duke (1981) or India or China according to Wilmont-Dear (1987). The taxonomy of velvetbeans appears somewhat confused. There are over 100 species in the tropical genus *Mucuna* which belongs to the *Fabaceae* family. The designation *Stizolobium* has often been used for velvetbean, but according to Buckles (1994) "the genus *Stizolobium* was used to distinguish velvetbeans from perennial *Mucuna* species, but this distinction is no longer maintained." Buckles (1994) lists the following as the most commonly cited species: *M. deeringiana, M. utilis, M. pruriens, M. cochichinensis, M. nivea, M. capitata, M. hassjoo, M. diabolica,* and *M. aterrima.* Duke (1981) wrote that five epithets are involved in velvetbean (*Mucuna puriens*): 1) *nivea*--the Lyon bean; 2) *hassjoo*--the Yokohama velvetbean; 3) *aterrima* or *mauritius* velvetbean; 4) *utilis*--the Bengal velvetbean; and 5) *deeringiana*--the Florida or Georgia velvetbean. In reading the literature I have found the above names, plus others, used for species and cultivars (varieties) of velvetbean and have concluded that confusion reigns. Because of the confusion about taxonomy, in the following discussions I will use whatever scientific or common name is given in any article cited without trying to make taxonomic judgements.

Writing about *Mucuna utilis* in 1916 De Sornay was enthusiastic about its use:

> From an agricultural point of view this plant gives splendid results. It is of very sturdy habit, and forms on the soil surface a regular blanket, thick and tufted, which prevents the growth of weeds. It is very easy to cultivate, all that requires doing being to sow two or three seeds together at intervals of a metre. In this way the growth of the plants is fairly well assured and the ground soon covered. Its leaf organs are very large, it is a great spreader, covers the ground for two years at least, and produces an abundant amount of seed. The great size of its leaf organs allows this plant to store up a large amount of nitrogen, and this, in addition to its great productivity and its content of fertilizing matter, places it in the front rank of cover peas.

Some of the early cultivars of velvetbean, such as certain *Mucuna* species known as *cowitch* or *cowhage,* caused a severe itching due to long stinging hairs on the pod. In Spanish these cultivars were known as *pica pica.* "Pica" in Spanish means to prick, pierce, or puncture. Thus the plant had a very bad reputation in some regions of the world, and farmers naturally disliked using it. In some areas, such as India, (personal communication--Roland Bunch) cultivars that cause itching are still being used. Fortunately, cultivars have been selected that do not cause itching, and today most farmers naturally prefer the non-stinging velvetbeans (*Mucuna* species that have appressed, silky hairs).

The plant is known by a number of names in Spanish such as *mucuna, nescafe, frijol terciopelo,* and *pica pica dulce. Pica pica dulce* designates a velvetbean cultivar that does not cause itching. There are numerous cultivars of velvetbean with different characteristics. Velvetbeans tolerate a wide variety of tropical soils and can grow on somewhat acid soils. According to Haririah (1992) velvetbean is moderately tolerant of aluminum, and thus is able to grow on aluminum toxic soils. The roots are rather shallow. Velvetbeans produce a "spectacular" amount of foliage (Figure 8.3), and the vines of vigorous plants may reach a length of 15 meters. Bunch (1994) noted that although figures varied widely, organic matter production (fresh biomass) of 50 tons/ha per year have been reported (Figure 8.1).

Neugebauer and Bunch (1991) wrote that thousands of small farm families in Central America and Mexico have adopted systems using velvetbean or other cover crops where previously slash-and-burn systems were practiced. Farmers in the humid tropics of Mexico and Central America have been developing and refining the *mucuna* technology for more than 40 years. This fascinating story is given in detail by Buckles (1992, 1994, 1995).

Velvetbeans in the Southern United States

Farmers and the scientific community throughout the world are rediscovering the value of velvetbeans. For example, in the southeastern United States velvetbeans were grown in association with maize on over 2,758,000 acres in 1921 (Piper and Morse 1922). These authors noted:

> The velvet bean first came into notice as a forage and fertilizing crop about 1890, at which time its cultivation was confined, on account of its lateness, almost wholly to Florida. With its introduction and development of early varieties its culture has now been extended northward to Virginia and Tennessee.

Florida acreage probably never exceeded 700,000 acres. The "Florida velvetbean" was the only variety grown until about 1906 when the U.S.D.A. introduced other varieties from Asia, some of which became widely grown. Farmers in Alabama and Georgia selected early maturing varieties with wider adaptation, and several of these became widely used. Once the early maturing varieties were found, the rapidity with which velvetbean culture increased was astounding and, to quote the enthusiastic Piper and Morse: "The whole story of the velvetbean is one of the most striking romances of American agriculture." Reasons for the rapid increase included not only early maturing varieties, but also the serious losses caused by the cotton boll weevil in the south which made it necessary to change southern farming methods.

As previously mentioned, in the Southern United States the velvetbean was used not only as a rotation crop, but also as a livestock feed. It was utilized as a grazing crop, silage was made by mixing velvetbeans with maize, and the beans were used as a high feeding value concentrated food. Yields of 1-2 tons/acre of beans in the pod were commonly obtained in the Southern United States. One ton of pods yielded 0.6 to 0.66 tons of shelled beans. Buckles (1994) noted: "The net cash value of velvetbean produced as an intercrop in maize in 1917 was estimated at more than $ 20,000,000."

Although valuable as a livestock feed, velvetbeans were usually planted with maize to improve soil fertility and were planted either in the same row as maize or in separate rows. Piper and Morse (1922) described the planting methods and a number of the varieties used by Southern farmers in the USA in the early part of this century. Two rows of maize and one of velvetbeans was the most popular method of planting. Although the yield of maize could be decreased slightly by the beans using this system, the value of the velvetbeans for green manure and animal feed more than offset the slight reduction in yield. The variety "Alabama" constituted 80% of the acreage planted to velvetbean in the southern USA during the 1920's. Engineers even developed a planter specifically for planting maize and velvetbeans in the same row in one operation.

The evidence indicates that the introduction of synthetic nitrogen fertilizers in the early 1940's accounted for the decline of velvetbean production in the southern United States (Rodriguez-Kabana et al. 1992a). Buckles (1994, 1995), who recently reviewed in detail the history of velvetbeans in the United States, added that, in addition to the sharp decreases in inorganic fertilizer prices, the increasing popularity of the soybean as a high-value commercial crop also helped to explain the decline in the use of velvetbean.

The experience and knowledge gained on the use of velvetbeans in the Southern United States during the early twentieth century should be re-examined and applied to the use of velvetbeans in developing countries.

Guatemalan Velvetbean Slash/Mulch Systems

One of the first reports found in the literature on the use of velvetbeans in a slash/mulch system in Central America was by William E. Carter (1969). He described the use of velvetbeans as a mulch in the lowlands of Guatemala near Lake Izabal by Kekchi Indians, a Maya group that migrated from the highlands of Guatemala. Buckles (1994) suggests that velvetbeans were probably introduced into Guatemala as a forage crop by the United Fruit Company in the 1920's. The use of velvetbeans was reaching its height in the U.S.A during this time. Carter cites elderly banana workers as reporting that "velvetbean was intercropped in maize grown by banana plantation workers on company land and grazed by mules used to transport bananas from plantations to the railway depots." Mules were replaced by tractors in the 1930s, but the plant retained its local name in the Maya language "*quenk mula*" or "mule bean" among the Kekchi Indians of Guatemala. Although most agriculture in this lowland region used the slash-and-burn system for their maize plantings (*milpas*), in the dry season fields were often planted to velvetbeans. Carter (1969) wrote:

> Velvet bean (*quenk caballo*) is planted either at the time of the first dry season *milpa* cleaning or, with wet season *milpa*, just after maize has broken through the ground. The technique is to dibble a shallow hole and drop seeds three at a time into it, spacing the hillocks some 4 varas apart. After two months of growth, velvet bean begins to have drastic effects on the *milpa*. Where weeds, grasses, and small trees have begun to take hold, it gradually covers them and chokes them out. Within six months, it yields a thick cover of dark green leaves that can reach up to 8 feet in height.

Once the luxurious growth of the velvetbeans reached a height of 2.5 meters the Kekchi slashed the growth with machetes and chopped it up finely. The result was a mulch 8-10 cm thick of the decayed velvetbean vegetation on the soil. Carter claimed that plots planted to velvetbean did not revert to grassland or forest, and that some plots had been used consecutively for 14 years of dry season farming with little indication of diminishing fertility. The above observations were an early indication of the possibility of sustaining soil fertility in the lowland tropics with the velvetbean or other cover crop systems for long periods of time with a minimum of inputs.

It is interesting that the initial use of velvetbean use in the Guatemala lowlands emphasized its value as a forage for animals in the banana plantations, whereas its value in weed control and soil fertility were later emphasized in the Kekchi farming system.

Honduran Velvetbean Systems

Honduras is an extremely poor country. Agriculture employs over 60% of the labor force, and produces two-thirds of its exports, but in general agricultural productivity remains low. Approximately 70% of the land in Honduras is mountainous with slopes of more than 25%.

Melara and del Rio (1994) wrote that due to pests, land distribution problems, and lack of knowledge about soil conservation, productivity of many traditional farmer's land in Honduras has declined. Farmers often abandon their slash-and-burn plots after every two or three harvests in search of virgin land. The once extensive tropical forests of Honduras have been seriously diminished. World Neighbors, an international NGO (non-governmental organization) has probably had the most impact on spreading the use of the velvetbean/maize system (called in Spanish the *abonera* system) in Honduras.

According to Milton Flores (1989), the director of CIDICCO (Centro Internacional de Información sobre Cultivos de Cobertura--International Cover Crops Clearinghouse): "the use of legumes to improve fertility conditions of agricultural soils is becoming one of the most popular ideas among the international community of rural development workers." He described the adoption of velvetbean by hundreds of resource-poor farmers on the Atlantic coast of Honduras living in hilly areas with high temperatures (28° C average) and high precipitation (over 3,000 mm/year) as follows:

> Farmers using velvetbean for the first time, plant the legume 1-2 months after planting corn, at the beginning of January. Later on, when corn is harvested, its stalks are bended over and left on the fields. Velvetbean starts covering these stalks and soon the legume will take over the whole corn field. By December the large amounts of velvetbean foliage (varying from 50-70 mt/ha) begin to dry out until it finally ends on top of the ground providing a cover that can be up to 20 cm thick. This means that the next corn crop is planted directly through the mulch. The mulch suppresses weeds and allows an adequate establishment of the corn. During the second year, velvetbean seeds will volunteer from last year and the cycle continues with the planting of a new corn.

Even without chemical fertilizers, maize yields of 2-4 tons per hectare were obtained using the above system, more than double the national average yields for Honduras. Hillside erosion was also reduced in the region. By adopting the velvetbean system, rather than plowing fields, farmers have essentially changed to a more sustainable no-till system.

Another major attraction of the system is its cost. Flores wrote: "The use of velvetbean has virtually zero financial cost. Even the original seed is passed out from one farmer to another."

World Neighbors, The Ford Foundation, and the Inter-American Foundation collaborated in establishing a green manure or cover crop clearinghouse (CIDICCO) in Tegucigalpa, Honduras, and their newsletters describe the practice in detail.

The 1991 CIDICCO newsletter reported that in the department of Cortes, Honduras, farmers had practiced the velvetbean/maize system for over 15 years, but the origin of the idea was unknown. Bunch (1994) noted that the velvetbean system is being used to reclaim abandoned land in Mexico and the north coast of Honduras.

The CIDICCO newsletters indicated that velvetbean foliage was slashed to plant a second crop of maize, and then incorporated or left as a mulch. Although incorporation would clearly reduce loss of nitrogen due to volatilization (Costa et al. 1990), peasant farmers in Honduras, primarily because of the high labor requirements of incorporation, preferred to mulch (personal communication--Roland Bunch). Where farmers have access to tractors or animal traction and labor costs are low, incorporation might be advantageous, although benefits would obviously vary according to soil and climatic conditions and tillage would seldom be selected on very steep slopes.

In 1990 personnel of the Honduran government and CIMMYT interviewed 188 farmers from 27 farming communities in the Atlantic Coast of Honduras relative to their use of velvetbean in maize culture (Buckles et al. 1991). Over 60% of the farmers in the region used velvetbeans, which had been used in the region for about 16 years. Advantages cited by farmers in respect to the use of velvetbean were better yields, a source of nutrients for maize, weed control, and ease of weeding. Control of erosion, moisture conservation, and cost reduction were mentioned by only a few farmers. Farmers mentioned that one problem found with the use of velvetbeans was the creation of a favorable environment for rats, rabbits, ants and grasshoppers. Different forms of velvetbean/maize management were found in the area.

In a later paper Buckles et al. (1994) described work documenting the use of the velvetbean technology (locally know as the *abonera* system) in the same Atlantic district and their efforts to identify factors influencing adoption. The study area had an average annual temperature of 28° C and between 2,000 to 3,300 mm of rain per year. Two ecological zones exist in the area; the costal plain with rich, alluvial soils and the steep hillsides of the *Nombre de Dios* mountain range with thin, nutrient-poor soils. Hillside slopes ranged from 10% to more than 100%. The costal plain is used primarily for plantation crops for export (bananas, pineapple, and oil palm) while the hillsides are used primarily for maize, beans, and pasture. The region was once covered by luxuriant rainforests, but these have disappeared dure to logging, slash-and-burn agriculture, and cattle ranching. According to Buckles et al. (1994) slash-and-burn cultivation was generally followed by the establishment of impoverished pastures that degenerated rapidly into secondary forest vegetation. The system that farmers in the region have evolved in recent years is the *abonera* system. The system is described Buckles et al. (1994) as follows:

> An abonera is a field of mucuna relayed into a sole-cropped maize field. An abonera is established for the first time in a field 40-55 days after dry season maize is planted (mid- to late February). Two to three seeds per hill are planted every meter or so between each row of maize. Dry season maize is harvested between March and April and the mucuna is allowed to develop as a sole crop throughout the wet season. Wet season maize is planted in a separate field using the conventional technology of shifting cultivation. Meanwhile the mucuna develops into a thick mat of luxuriant growth some 1.5 m deep. The legume reaches the end of its vegetation period by late November when seed is formed. Farmers slash the vegetation and a few weeks later stick-plant maize into the mat of decomposing leaves and vines.

The several values of the *abonera* system were described as follows by Buckles et al. (1994):

> The abonera is a multipurpose technology. Land clearing is greatly facilitated by this aggressive legume, because it smothers virtually all competing weeds and is very easy to cut. The mulch left on the field conserves soil moisture and protects the soil from erosion while the decaying leaves, stems, and roots provide nutrients to the subsequent maize crop. As one Honduran farmer put it, "cowardly land becomes brave" when managed with "the fertilizer bean."

Buckles et al. (1994) concluded:

> Perhaps the greatest lesson to be learned from the use and diffusion of mucuna in Atlántida is that green manures can be effective and adoptable components in hillside maize systems. The principles of green manuring employed by farmers, not the particular legume or management practice, are far reaching. Innovation by resource-poor farmers is pointing the way to a promising area of research too long neglected by research institutions.

Buckles (1994, 1995) described the spread of velvetbean technology in Central America and Mexico from the 1950s to the present and noted that diffusion of the technology has been primarily from farmer to farmer.

Acceptance of the technology was greatest among hillside farmers in Atlantic Honduras. Some use of velvetbean was found in the 1970s (10% of farmers), but its use increased significantly during the 1980s. By 1992 about 66% of the farmers in the Atlantic district used *mucuna* (Buckles et al. 1994). Introduced in the early 1970s, the *abonera* system spread slowly during the first 10 years, swiftly in the following 10 years, but recently the spread has leveled off. Farmers using the system cultivated, on the average, 40% more dry season maize than farmers not using the technology. Among the factors that helped to account for this rapid acceptance Buckles cites labor considerations, lower availability of land, worsening weed problems, and improvement of transportation networks and thus better access to markets. Sain et al. (1994) conducted a study in the Atlantic Coast of Honduras near La Ceiba to determine the profitability of the *abonera* system compared to traditional maize production systems and to determine which factors and mechanisms affect the *abonera* systems profitability.

Farmers occasionally noted problems with the use of the *abonera* system. On very steep slopes during heavy rainfalls landslides have occurred where *mucuna* had destroyed deep rooted vegetation and soil was loosened. Rats and snakes were more prevalent in the *abonera* system. Despite the many advantages of velvetbean use in Honduras cited by development professionals and academics (soil moisture conservation, weed control, nutrient management, reductions in costs and labor) Honduran farmers most often cited weed control and increased soil fertility as their primary reasons for adopting mucuna into their maize-based farming systems.

Triomphe (1996) recently studied the velvetbean/maize system in the Atlantic region of Honduras. Maize yields of three to four tons/hectare were common, with little need for and response to nitrogen fertilizer (Figure 8.2). His study analyzed of some of the major agroecological processes which shaped the system, including seasonal nitrogen cycling and long-term trends in soil chemical and physical properties.

Bunch (1990) summarizes the value of intercropped green manures in Honduras as follows:

These systems have proven themselves capable of fitting into numerous traditional maize and sorghum-based farming systems in climates varying from wet tropical to semi-arid, and from sea level to approximately 2,100 meters in elevation. They have, in most cases, controlled most or all weed pests naturally, used no land that had an opportunity cost, occasioned no out-of-pocket expenses greater than a one-time purchase of a handful of seed, increased soil fertility significantly, and increased organic matter content over periods of four to five years in soils as they were being cropped, even under rainforest conditions. In all cases where slash-and-burn agriculture has been practiced previously, it has been abandoned by virtually all farmers adopting one of the green manure systems.

Mexican Velvetbean Systems

A study of the adoption of velvetbean by colonists in the Valle de Uxpanapa, Mexico, was made by Arevalo and Jimenez (1988). The numerous problems of colonization in the Uxpanapa area were described in detail by Ewell and Poleman (1980). The Uxpanapa region has an annual rainfall of 2,000 to 3,000 mm. The two major problems colonists faced were diminishing soil fertility and weed control. The Comisión de Papaloapan, which was in charge of the colonization effort, first proposed the use of velvetbean in 1976, but since the recommendation was to incorporate it by plowing it under with a tractor, initially farmers were not convinced of its value. Nevertheless, the value of velvetbean for controlling weeds and grasses in the Valle de Uxpanapa was noted by Del Amo (cited by Arevalo and Jimenez 1988).

Velvetbeans were planted in the Uxpanapa region in December or January after a field had been cleared of weeds (Arevalo and Jimenez 1988). The beans were planted between the rows of maize at a distance of 3-4 meters, with 1-3 seeds deposited in each hole made by a digging stick. Initially farmers weeded their maize, but later they realized that weeding was unnecessary, as the velvetbean suppressed the weeds, and farmers noted that the maize yields were little affected by the weeds that did grow.

Arevalo and Jimenez (1988) calculated the labor needed to plant velvetbeans. Yields of 4-10 kilograms per hectare of velvetbean seed were commonly harvested, which were used for the next cycle of planting. The major value of velvetbeans in the area was perceived as a means of managing grasses that invaded maize plantings. In addition, velvetbeans grew without inputs and improved the diminishing soil fertility of fields in the area. Another use of the plant was as a food for animals such as cattle, horses, and burros. Local campesinos perceived the favorable characteristics of velvetbeans to be their rapid growth, their production of profuse foliage which smothered undesirable weeds and grasses, and the maintenance of soil fertility.

In 1986 a velvetbean/maize system was used on almost 5,000 ha in Tabasco, Mexico (Garcia Espinosa et al. 1994). Their description of the system follows:

> The rotation system consists of alternately sowing corn with the vigorously growing leguminous genus Stizolobium. When starting up the system for the first time, the farmer sows Stizolobium towards the end of the corn cycle (May) by planting seeds at variable distances, up to 2 m, depending on availability. The legume grows to cover the corn stalks and forms an immense green mass. At the end of November, when the plant

has set seed, it is cut by machete and left on the soil surface. It is not dug into the soil since the farmers do not use farm implements. After 3-5 days, corn associated with squash (*Cucurbita maxima*) is sown between the shoots using a *"macana"* (a sharpened stick used for digging holes) and without burning. Towards the end of April, after the corn has been bent over and the cobs and squash have been harvested, the velvet bean starts to grow up the corn stalks once again. Resowing the Stizolobium is unnecessary since seeds remain in the soil. The farmer sometimes prunes the shoots of the legume during the corn cycle to avoid competition. They use neither chemical fertilizers nor herbicides and have only recently started to use insecticides.

Buckles and Perales (1995) described in detail the adoption of the various velvetbean systems in Mexico. They also described their work with on-farm experimentation with farmers in the Sierra of Santa Marta region of Mexico.

African Velvetbean Slash/Mulch Systems

Early efforts in Africa to use velvetbean for improvement of soil fertility gave mixed results. For example, Vine (1953) reported that experiments on maintaining soil fertility with velvetbean were made at Moor Plantation in Ibadan, Nigeria, from 1922 to 1951. Crop yields were maintained for 12 years at Ibadan using incorporated velvetbeans and crop rotations without other inputs. At other locations with higher rainfall and lower pH velvetbeans didn't grow as well, and yields declined. Crop yields were maintained at a "good level" for considerable periods of continuous cultivation without fertilizer, but fertility was lost "rather slowly" if continuous cultivation was prolonged for more than 10 years.

In 1986 the International Institute of Tropical Agriculture (IITA) began on-farm research with farmers in Benin on methods to restore soil fertility (IITA 1991, 1993) One of the technologies that IITA tested was the use of velvetbean (*Mucuna pruriens* var. *utilis*) as a cover crop or live mulch. After three years of promotion "it has been reported that more than 3,000 farmers in the 5 southern provinces were using mucuna, either as a sole crop to control speargrass or as an intercrop to improve soil fertility" (IITA 1993). (Speargrass is *Imperata cylindrica.*). Subsequently, velvetbean has become so popular in Benin that the national extension agency has chosen it for use countrywide, and the Global 2000 project is using it for demonstration trials by 500 farmers in Benin. Trials have confirmed that velvetbean is effective in smothering the noxious weed *I. cylindrica*, a the major problem in many farmer's fields. The trials also showed that soil fertility was greatly improved: "the results of farmers who had chosen mucuna were dramatic. They recorded, on average, a tenfold increase in maize yield (from 200 to 2,000 kg per hectare)." The use of velvetbean was described as follows (IITA 1991):

> The mucuna was to be planted one month after sowing maize, during the first rainy season, and would grow to a dense cover during the second rainy season. Subsequently, during the dry season the mucuna would die and form a dry mulch, which would fertilize the next year's first-season maize crop. Mucuna would once again be "relay planted" in this manner, one month after that crop.

Thus, in Benin it was concluded that the velvetbean restored soil fertility and effectively managed Imperata grass. Although the use of velvetbean systems are not as widespread in West Africa as in Central America, it appears that their use could be of considerable value to many low-income farmers on the low fertility soils of West Africa.

Effects of Velvetbean on Weeds, Diseases, Insects, and Other Pests

Traditional farmers spend a formidable amount of time in weed control. Kasasian (1971) suggested that more human effort is devoted to weed control than any other single human activity. Farmers in Nigeria may spend up to half of their time in weed control (Moody 1975). Weeds are a major cause of the abandonment of slash-and-burn plots after a few years and are especially important in the humid tropics where they are most difficult to manage.

Holt-Gimenez (1992) and Holt-Gimenez and Pasos C. (1994) described the use of velvetbeans in Nicaragua by farmers of a grassroots organization called *Movemiento Campesino a Campesino*. One of the major benefits of the use of velvetbean by farmers of this group was control of the noxious weed *Imperata cylindrica*. Nut grass (*Cyprus rotundus*) is considered to be the world's worst weed and *I. cylindrica* (spear grass) is also among of the most difficult weeds to control in the tropics (Holm et al. 1977). Both weeds can be managed with the velvetbean (Bunch 1994). According to Akobundu (1983) many authors have reported on the ability of velvetbean to control *I. cylindrica* and other noxious weeds. In Mexico (Garcia Espinosa et al. 1994) noted the control of weeds such as *Cyperus* spp. and *Cynodon dactylon* in maize/velvetbean systems.

Another benefit of the velvetbean systems that may not be appreciated by many farmers and researchers is their value in nematode management. Nematodes are serious pests of many tropical crops. As early as 1922 velvetbeans were recommended for the control of root-knot nematodes in Florida (Watson 1922). Rodriguez-Kabana et al. (1992a) reported on the efficacy of Florida velvetbean (*Mucuna deeringiana*) for the management of root-knot nematodes (*Meloidogyne arenaria*). In their experiments velvetbean, in contrast to peanuts, did not support significant populations of the nematode in the soil. They wrote:

> The results indicate that velvetbean is an excellent rotation crop for the management of *M. arenaria* in peanut. This tropical legume is a non-host for this nematode and other *Meloidogyne* spp. Velvetbean exerts a suppressive effect on development of *Meloidogyne* populations and there is evidence that the effect may be due to the production of nematicidal root exudates.

Vicente and Acosta (1987) in Puerto Rico found lower populations of *M. incognita* on tomato in experimental plots which had been in rotation with *mucuna*. Greenhouse studies in Spain also confirmed the value of two velvetbean (*Mucuna deeringiana*) accessions for managing nematodes (Rodriguez-Kabana et al. 1992b). The legume was not a host for three species of root knot nematodes (*Meloidogyne arenaria, M. incognita* and *M. javanica.*) In Alabama velvetbeans were not hosts for *Heterodera glycines, M. arenaria,* or *M. incognita* (Rodriguez-Kabana et al. 1992a). Other studies (Dominguez-V. et al 1990, Marban-Mendoza et al. 1989, Marban-Mendoza et al. 1991, and Tapica 1971) have also reported the value of *mucuna* and other green manures and cover crops such as *Crotalaria* spp. for reducing nematode populations.

Velvetbeans may also suppress soil-borne fungus pathogens. Laboratory experiments in Costa Rica in the 1960s (Sequeira 1962) involving velvetbean and other organic amendments indicated that all "exerted a significant depressing effect on viability of the fungus." The fungus was *Fusarium oxysporum* f. *cubense,* the causal agent of banana wilt. However, field experiments were not as promising, as extremely large quantities of organic matter were needed to have a significant effect. Nevertheless, several organic amendments including velvetbean, lablab beans (*Lablab purpureus*), kudzu, crotalaria, sorghum, and especially sugarcane gave promising results in reducing the viability of the populations of the soil-borne fungus.

Describing the importance of slugs on beans (*P. vulgaris*) Rizzo et al. (1994) wrote:

Of the invertebrate pests which attack the common bean *Phaseolus vulgaris* L. in Central America, the slug *Sarasinula plebeia* Fischer stands out because of its voracious appetite and recent appearance. The slug has only reached major pest status in recent years. It belongs to the Veronicellidae, a family that is represented in all tropical and subtropical areas, with around 100 species, of which over half appear in the Americas. Moreover, *S. plebeia* is an intermediate host for parasites of humans and other vertebrates of which the most important is the nematode *Angiostrongylus costaricensis* Morera and Cespedes, which causes angiostrongilosis. Many farmers have stopped growing beans because of high slug populations that can defoliate the crop during the first weeks after sowing. Their attack is most severe during the second cropping cycle because of higher population densities and the presence of a second generation.

Slug control is difficult since the most common method recommended is the use of poisoned bait. This has often given poor results as slug populations are too high, the bait often is often not fresh, the chemical is expensive, and often is not available on the market when needed.

Rizzo et al. (1994) force fed the foliage of velvetbeans, common beans, and jack beans (*Canavalia ensiformis*) to slugs. They found that forced feeding of fresh leaves of velvetbean and jack bean drastically reduced slug survival and growth, compared to slugs fed on common beans or an artificial diet. Slugs fed on common bean foliage grew and reproduced. These results indicate that both velvetbeans and jack beans man have considerable potential for controlling slugs in farmers fields.

Beaver et al. (1984) describe especially tragic and painful infection (abdominal angiostronylosis) of young children caused by the nematode, *Angiostrongylus costaricensis*. Fatal cases have occurred in Costa Rica where adult nematodes are found in cotton rats and black rats. The nematode larvae are passed in rat feces. The infective-stage is found as larvae in tissues of the slug *Vaginulus plebeius*. Human infection occurs by accidental ingestion of slugs when small children eat leaves and/or dirt containing slugs.

Diseases, Insects, and Other Pests of Velvetbeans

Velvetbeans are attacked by numerous plant pathogens. Duke (1981) and the U.S.D.A (1960) listed the fungi *Cercospora stizolobii*, *Mycosphaerella cruenta*, *Phyllosticta mucunae*, *Phymatotrichum omnivorum*, *Phytophthora dreschsleri*, *Rhizoctonia solani*, *Sclerotium rolfsii*, and

Uromyces mucunae as velvetbean pathogens. Bacterial pathogens listed were *Pseudomonas stizolobiicola* and *Pseudomonas syringae*. Duke noted that velvetbeans were resistant, but not immune, to root-knot nematodes, and were attacked by *Meloidogyne hapla.*, *M. incognita*, and *M. javanica*. Other nematodes isolated from velvetbeans included *Belonolaimus gracilis*, *Pratylenchus brachyurus*, and *Rotylenchulus reniformis*. There are doubtless other pathogens of velvetbeans which have not been identified or reported.

In tropical Mexico Granados Alvarez and Garcia Espinosa (1992) listed these insect pests of velvetbeans: leaf cutter ants (*Acromyrmex* spp.), *Diabrotica* spp., leafhoppers (Family *Cicadellidae*), blister beetles (Family *Meloidae*), and the southern green stink bug (*Nezara viridula*). Melara and del Rio (1994) listed the aphid *Rhopalosiphum maidis*, the front leaf beetle (*Monomacra frontalis*), the gall midge (*Asphondylia websteri*), and the pod borer (*Melanagromyza* spp.) as insect pests of velvetbeans in Honduras. Metcalf and Flint (1939) included the white-fringed beetle (*Naupactus leucoloma*) as a serious insect pest on velvetbean in Southern USA.

Several authors listed the velvetbean caterpillar (*Anticarsia gemmatali*) as a serious insect pest. Watson (1916) issued a bulletin on the control of the velvetbean caterpillar and stated that it was the only serious pest of velvetbeans in Florida where damage was often severe and sometimes disastrous. It still commonly occurs as a pest of soybeans in Florida (Waddill et al. 1982). The susceptibility of different species and varieties of velvetbean to the velvetbean caterpillar varies considerably. The recommendation of lead arsenate powder for spraying (Watson 1916) would not be accepted today, but his recommendation to leave the many natural enemies of the velvetbean caterpillar unmolested would be timely and appropriate today. Birds, lizards, skunks, wasps, moles, turkeys, and various predaceous insects were cited as enemies giving natural control of the velvetbean caterpillar. Watson added:

> By far the most efficient check on the increase of this pest is a disease called "Cholera" by farmers. This is caused by the fungus (*Botrytis rileyi*). In October, 1914, and again in 1915, and also in previous years, this fungus almost exterminated the caterpillars in the fields around Gainesville. Less than one-tenth of one per cent escaped. On the Experiment Station grounds where they had been numerous enough to destroy much of the crop, the caterpillars became scarce in one week. This is not unusual, but occurs almost every year. Sooner or later the fungus appears and nearly exterminates the caterpillars, tho it is often too late to save the crop. After it becomes established in the field, the fungus seems to control the insect

for the remainder of the season. The fungus, to become epidemic, seems to require a cool, prolonged, rainy period, such as usually occurs in late September or October.

It is interesting that eighty years later biological control is "coming around again" as a preferred management practice for insects.

Lupine as a Slashed Green Manure in the High Andes

Pre-Incan people have used lupines (*Lupinus mutabilis*), called *tarwi* in Spanish, as food in the Andes for more than 1,500 years (National Research Council 1989). Lupine seeds have been used as human food for centuries in Rome, Egypt, the Sudan, Ecuador, Peru, and Bolivia after their toxic alkaloids have been leached out by soaking in water. Cato (1934), a Roman who lived 234-149 B.C., wrote that lupines, beans, and vetch fertilized the land. Varro (1934), writing between 116-27 B.C., cited lupines and broad beans as suitable for plowing under green.

Campesinos living in high elevations of the South American Andes are among some of the poorest people of the world. Ruddell (1995) states that incomes among the *campesinos* of Northern Potosi, Bolivia are estimated at US $ 300 per year. Potato yields in this area of Bolivia are among the lowest in the world because of poor soils and extremely high elevations. A suggestion made by Milton Flores of CIDICCO (Centro Internacional de Información Sobre Cultivos de Cobertura), Honduras encouraged World Neighbors to test local varieties of *tarwi* as a cover crop for potatoes in the Andean region. They were also encouraged by studies in California which found that a white lupine crop produced about 200 kg/n/ha when used as a green manure (Larsen et al. 1989). Ruddell (1995) and Beingolea (1993) described the work. Ruddell wrote:

> During the 1990 planting season, World Neighbors motivated UNICEF ProAndes to donate 2,300 kilos of the native seed purchased at the local markets. This was distributed in 37 communities. Each family received 4.4 kilograms which was planted at 60 kg/ha. The lupine was planted on fallow land with no additional fertilizer after the rainy season had begun in November. After broadcasting the seed, oxen covered it with a harrow. No other fertilizer or cultural practices were required until it reached the flowering stage four months later, in late February. At that point indigenous program leaders encouraged all farmers to turn the crop under as a green manure, but not every family did. So impressed were they with their crop, especially the women, that they preferred to produce it for the beans.

Before the *tarwi* was slashed and incorporated into the soil, samples were weighed, and it was found that 17,000 kg/ha of biomass was produced. In some cases the *tarwi* crops towered over the head of the farmers. Farmers cut swaths of *tarwi* which were laid in furrows and covered. Ruddell and Beingolea (1995) noted that peasants played an important role in conducting the research and describes this process in an article entitled "Towards farmer scientists." Experimental field trials were conducted which included lupine without chemical fertilizer and with chemical and sheep manure fertilizer. *Tarwi* is one of the few cover crops that will grow at elevations of 3,000-4,000 meters and above. In the first trial potatoes with traditional fertilization yielded only 1.69 tons/ha while potatoes planted where lupine had been incorporated into the soil yielded 7.5 tons/ha. The following year the trials were repeated with similar results. These encouraging results suggest that the use of cover crops/green manures such as *tarwi* in the high elevations of the Andes may be a feasible method of increasing yields of the basic food crops of this region. Further experimentation and confirmation of this work is needed. Little work has been done to date to determine the value of *tarwi* as a mulch, as most experiments to date have incorporated the material.

Conclusions

Clearly, cover crop and green manure use is growing worldwide, with much of the work being pioneered by formers themselves. However, much remains to be done, especially with regard to adapting cover crop and green manure systems to drier climates where the need is great, but where success has been limited. In drier climates, finding species that survive through the dry season or produce sufficient biomass is a major constraint to developing successful cover crop and green manure systems in the semi-arid tropics. Incorporation, the use of in-row tillage, or supplementing green manures with animal manures may provide better results in drier areas with poor soils.

9

Systems Using Slashed (Pollard, Pruned, or Coppiced) Shrubs or Trees

Farmers have been combining trees and agriculture for millennia. However, it appears that scientists have only "discovered" this combination in recent decades. Descriptions of the numerous agroforestry systems in the tropics are given in detail by Huxley (1983), MacDicken and Vergara (1990), Nair (1989), and Steppler and Nair (1987) among others. Agroforestry systems are considered by many to be sustainable and promising alternatives to the destructive aspects of the slash-and-burn system. A major question in today's world, as energy sources and fertilizer become prohibitively expensive, is the degree to which agroforestry systems can also improve soil physical properties, maintain soil organic matter, and promote nutrient cycling (Sanchez 1987).

Of interest in this book are the several agroforestry systems in the tropics in which farmers cut branches from trees or shrubs to produce a mulch. The branches and litter are then spread on the soil and subsequently the decomposing mulch serves as a source of nutrients for crops. The decomposition rate of slashed litter may be important in weed control, as slow decomposition rates would be most beneficial in weed management. Various terms are used in the literature (according to one's discipline) for cutting off branches such as slashing, pruning, lopping, coppicing, and pollarding. Slash/mulch systems such as alley cropping are seldom designated as such in the literature. Moreover, in some agroforestry systems slashed or coppiced material is not used as a mulch, but rather is incorporated into the soil or used as a fodder.

Nyerges (1989) noted that "vegetative reproduction" or "coppicing" from the stumps and root masses of felled trees" is a major form of tree reproduction in tropical forests, especially in seasonally dry tropics. Brewbaker (1990) listed a number of tree species that have provided nutrients to various plantation crops through the leaf litter they produce and/or through "lopping" (slashing or coppicing) of foliage:

> The production of green manure has long been exploited in plantation crops such as coffee, tea and cacao, where intercropped legume trees provide light shade and a significant leaf litter or felled foliage as a "nurse" crop. Significant nurse trees include species of Erythrina, Gliricidia, Inga, Leucaena, Mimosa, Robinia and Sesbania. Biannual lopping of seedless leucaena clones in coffee plantations of Bali result in nitrogen fertilization of 30-80 kg/ha.

Numerous references are found in the literature on the use of litter from trees as a source of nutrients by traditional farmers. As an example, the use of leaf litter by traditional farmers in Zimbabwe gives an idea of its value in agriculture. Bradley and Dewees (1991) questioned farmers in Zimbabwe and found that 68% of their respondents brought leaf litter to their fields to improve soil fertility, although other surveys suggested lower levels. Farmers noted that various trees found in fields and field boundaries produced "high quality" sources of leaf litter, and particular trees species were preferred as a source of litter. Sometimes tree litter was mixed with manure from animal pens and applied as a compost (Campbell et al. 1993).

Alley Cropping Systems

Alley cropping is generally a slash/mulch system. Alley cropping is a special type of agroforestry in which food or cash crops are grown between rows of woody shrubs or trees, usually legumes, and in which the woody species are pruned periodically (Figure 9.1). The alley cropping system has been evaluated in many different tropical areas under different names. According to Kang and Wilson (1987) it was called "hedgerow cropping" by ICRAF and "avenue cropping" in Sri Lanka. In the 1970s over 20,000 ha were planted on the island of Flores in eastern Indonesia to a system similar to alley cropping using *Leucaena leucocephala*. This system was promoted by church and extension agencies (Garrity 1993, Metzner 1982). Although alley cropping is clearly a slash/mulch system, in most cases it seldom is classified or described as such. Some believe a better name for alley cropping would be "hedgerow intercropping" (personal communication--Anthony Young).

There is a voluminous literature on the alley cropping system, whereas the literature on similar traditional agroforestry systems that have survived for centuries is sparse in comparison. Numerous descriptions and reviews of alley farming research have been published (Fernandes et al. 1993, Garrity 1993, Hawkins et al. 1990, Kang and Wilson 1987, Kang et al. 1989, Kang et al. 1990, Kang and Mulongoy 1992, Kass et al. 1991, Ong 1994, Ssekabembe 1985, Wilson et al. 1986). Some of the agronomic lessons and principles to be learned by a study of alley cropping systems are pertinent to traditional agroforestry systems, and thus a brief review of these findings is presented.

It was in 1981 that Kang et al. (1981) first published on an alley farming experiment which had been conducted for six years at IITA in Ibadan, Nigeria, using *L. leucocephala*. Since that time innumerable experiments have been reported from around the world on alley cropping (Fernandes 1993, Kang 1993, Kang et al. 1990, Kass et al. 1991, Ong 1994). In most of the alley cropping experiments reported rows of woody leguminous trees or shrubs are pruned (slashed) and the prunings are spread on the soil, discarded, or supplemented with various levels of nitrogen fertilizer. Prunings may be used either as a mulch or incorporated into the soil. Various crops, such as maize, rice, various grain legumes, and root and tuber crops are grown between the rows (alleys) of trees (Kang 1993). Alley width is important as the following illustrates (Karim et al. 1993):

Alleys of 2-4 m wide, planted no closer than 0.5 m within rows, resulted in more than twice the yields of maize than in the 8 m alley planted at 0.25 m within rows, once the hedgerows were well established and were being managed.

Kang (1993) listed the many species that have been tried in alley cropping experiments:

Various woody species have been tried, with varying degrees of success, in hedgerows in different agroecological zones. These include: *Acacia auriculiformis, Alchornea cordifolia, Cajanus cajan, Dactyladenia barteri* (syn. *Acioas barteria), Calliandra calothyrsus, Senna siamea* (syn. *Cassia siamea), Senna spectabilis* (syn. *Cassia spectabilis), Erythrina poeppigiana, Flemingia macrophylla, Inga edulis, Gliricidia sepium, Gmelina arborea, Leucaena leucocephala,* and *Paraserianthes falactaria* (syn. *Albizia falcataria*). Results of long-term observations carried out in the humid/subhumid zones of southwestern Nigeria have shown that at low altitude on high base status soils *Gliricidia sepium* and *Leucaena leucocephala* are the two species most suitable for use in alley cropping. These two species biologically fix N, can be established easily by direct seeding, withstand repeated prunings, produce large amounts of biomass and nutrients and are relatively long-lived.

Recently Fernandes et al. (1993), described their studies of alley cropping on an acid soil in the upper Amazon using the tree *Inga edulis*. There has been little diffusion of alley cropping to date in the Amazon region.

From a review of the literature on yields of various crops in alley cropping systems Petch and Mt. Pleasant (1991) concluded:

Alley cropping is unlikely to produce crop yields comparable to yields that can be obtained using optimum inorganic fertilizer applications with conventional cultivation. The main benefit of alley cropping to crop yield is provided by tree prunings; if these are removed, crop yields will be lower than if the prunings are retained. Crop yields may decline over time under alley cropping, but probably at a lesser rate than with conventional cultivation. Application of chemical fertilizer (notably phosphorus) and/or periodic fallowing may be necessary to maintain crop yields at acceptable levels.

In a recent discussion of alley cropping entitled "Alley cropping--ecological pie in the sky?" Ong (1994) suggested that alley cropping "is most suitable for food production on alfisols and other high-base soils in the humid and subhumid tropics." Also, the mulch produced when trees are slashed gave positive results in all sites except when there was no competition from trees. For example, mulched crops yielded 30-70% more than those without mulch in some cases. Ong noted that a major question was "why it was so difficult to reproduce the positive trial results in farmer's fields, even close to Ibadan (Nigeria) where these conditions are present, or elsewhere in the humid and subhumid tropics." He further noted that researchers have probably overestimated the capacity of the alley cropping technology to increase crop yield and suggested that small plot size is probably the most important reason.

Regarding Ong's pessimism about alley cropping's potential to increase crop yields, it is important to note that farmers may be alley cropping for other additional benefits such as fuelwood (Figure 9.2), fodder, microclimate effects, and even as a transition to cash tree crop systems.

Thus, the sole focus on cropping relationships to crop yields may not necessarily explain why farmers decide to adopt alley cropping into their farming systems or not.

Leucaena Leucocephala-*Based Agroforestry Systems*

The National Academy of Sciences (1977) and Brewbaker (1987, 1989) describe the multiple uses of *Leucaena leucocephala*, including its use for forage, human food, wood, fuel, soil improvement, land reclamation, erosion control, weed management, soil improvement, shade for plantation crops, wind breaks, and reforestation. The 1977 National Academy of Sciences advisory panel stated:

> only in the past two decades has a suggestion of its promise become apparent. During that brief period several significant factors emerged: researchers in Hawaii and tropical Australia have found that cattle feeding on leucaena may show weight gains comparable to those of cattle feeding on the best pastures anywhere; private firms in the Philippines have developed a sizable trade in processed animal feeds containing leucaena; researchers in the Philippines demonstrated leucaena's potential for reforesting eroded hillslopes, for use as firewood, for fueling industrial boilers, and for producing paper pulp; while in Mexico (leucaena's native habitat) researchers have located over 100 varieties for future testing.

Kang et al. (1981) noted some of the singular properties which makes the legume *L. leucocephala* valuable in association with other crops:

1. It can withstand repeated prunings and regenerates vigorously after pruning
2. The deep rooting habit of *L. leucocephala* reduces the level of root competition with the crop it is grown with such as maize. Also, plant nutrients are brought up of from the deeper soil horizons to the surface.
3. It produces large amounts of useful wood
4. The nitrogen composition of *L. leucocephala* prunings are well balanced.

There are about 12 species of leucaena and over 100 cultivars of *L. leucocephala* (Brewbaker 1987, National Academy of Sciences 1977). Leucaena is an evergreen nitrogen-fixing legume; however, in response to extreme drought it can shed its leaves. In English the plant is known as leucaena and also as cow tamarind. *L. leucocephala* originated in

Mexico and Central America. Various leucaena species were used by the Maya and Zapotecs of Central America thousands of years ago according to the National Academy of Sciences (1977). The Pre-Colombian word *"uaxin"* means the place where leucaena grows, and the word "Oaxaca" (a large city and state in Mexico) is derived from *uaxin*. The Spanish introduced *L. leucocephala* into southeast Asia centuries ago. Metzner (1982) wrote that leucaena has been known for several hundred years in Indonesia, and that it was brought to Indonesia by Spaniards from Central America. Leucaena has been part of slash/mulch systems long before the alley cropping system was suggested.

An enormous amount of literature has been written on leucaena in recent decades. Over 3,000 articles on leucaena research have been published in addition to books, bibliographies, several reviews, and the proceedings of several major conferences on leucaena (Brewbaker 1987). This flood of literature has continued into the 1990s.

It is interesting to contemplate what might have resulted if this immense effort had been focused on proven traditional practices instead of unproven "new, innovative" practices and a species that has resulted in what some (e.g. Oka 1990) have called a "disaster" in Asia and the Pacific when *L. leucocephala* was nearly wiped out by an infestation of the psyllid *Heterophylla cubana*.

Trees have been slashed and the resulting mulch used as a source of crop nutrients in Africa for millennia. For example Kang et al. (1990) wrote:

> The first author recently observed traditional fallow systems at Mbaise in Imo State of southeastern Nigeria and found that farmers have practiced some aspects of alley farming on acid ultisols for generations. They plant hedgerows of fast growing Acioa shrubs, which are spaced 2-3 m apart. The Acioa hedgerows are used for nutrient cycling and weed suppression, as a source of browse, and especially for staking material.

Much recent literature describes alley cropping or alley farming systems as one of the more recent innovations for agriculture in tropical developing countries. Nevertheless, similar systems have been used on the island of Cebu in the Philippines and in Indonesia for many decades. Lasco (1991) describes an indigenous system used in the Philippines for over 80 years. The Naalad system, practiced by a rural community on the island of Cebu on steep slopes, is a planned fallow system using *L. leucocephala*. Lasco writes "using native leucaena as a fallow crop, however, Naalad farmers reduce the fallow period to just five or six years, presumably due to the ability of leucaena to fix nitrogen." After the fallow the leucaena strips are cut (slashed) and the dead branches are piled along the contours to form fascine-like structures spaced 1-2 m apart called *babag*. The dead mulch of branches decays over time. Crops are planted in the alleys formed by the *babag*. Lasco continues:

> When asked why he didn't use live hedgerows, one farmer answered that by the time the *babag* decay, it is time again to fallow the area. Further more, dead branches require less maintenance than live hedgerows.

In 1977 the National Academy of Sciences also noted that in the Barrio Naalad, Cebu, Philippines innovative farmers had been using leucaena for erosion control, soil reclamation, and crop fertilization on extremely steep, rocky hillsides for over 50 years:

> They plant blocks of their land with leucaena to control erosion and provide soil improvement. Some of the leaves are harvested, dried, and sold as leaf meal to local feed millers; also, most households keep goats that are fed leucaena mixed with coconut and banana leaves. After 3-6 years the blocks with leucaena are cleared (large pieces of the wood are sold for fuel) while an equal number are seeded with leucaena and left fallow. Along the contour of the steepest slopes of the newly cleared blocks the farmers drive leucaena stakes into the ground, pile branches behind them, and scrape soil against the barrier so formed. This provides a terrace (varying from 0.15-1.5 m wide) in which tobacco and onions are interplanted. This creates arable land out of slopes as steep as 70° that are otherwise totally unusable.

A similar system, which was started in 1973 in Indonesia, has been described by Piggin and Parera (1985) as follows:

> Early establishment is slow and can be reduced by weeds and grazing. With reasonable management, thick hedges form within two years and collect soil washed from upper slopes by the rain and gradually form terraces. Once established hedges are generally cut each 6-8 weeks at a height of 75-80 cm during the rainy season and before formation of fruit. Cut material is thrown on the upper slope to fertilize the soil. In recent times several variations on this cutting system have been developed with farmers either breaking branches down, or girdling the leucaena trunk, and allowing the leaves to fall and fertilize the soil.

The above quote describes a slash/mulch system. Although the primary aim of the project was to control erosion, other benefits followed:

Established areas are now being cropped more intensively and are more productive. Unterraced fields can be cropped for 3-4 years and need a recovery period of 4-9 years because of loss of soil and soil fertility. Terraced slopes can be cropped continuously if leucaena herbage is used as green manure and cereal/legume rotations are used. Leucaena also discourages the build-up of the weed *Imperata cylindrica* that often causes abandonment of unterraced fields. Many terraced fields have been planted to permanent tree crops such as coconut, coffee, cacao, cloves, and pepper with the contour hedges of leucaena providing shade, soil stabilization, increased soil fertility, and improved moisture infiltration

Metzner (1982) and Parera (1986) suggested that *L. leucocephala* was forced on farmers in Indonesia by the Dutch during the 1930s for soil rehabilitation, but that the species did not gain acceptance because of poor management. Piggin and Parera (1985) described the Dutch attempts to introduce *L. leucocephala* plantings in West Timor near Baun:

> In the 1930s, experimental plantings of leucaena were made under the guidance of the Dutch administration on abandoned fields around Baun. The plant was then sown widely around Baun in response to an *adat* (traditional) regulation pronounced in 1932 by the local ruler (*raja*) in accordance with the local council, which obliged every farmer in Amarasi to plant contour rows of leucaena not more than 3 m apart on cropping areas before they were abandoned. Failure to comply carried the threat of a fine and/or jail.

Maize is probably the most commonly used crop in alley cropping. Results with maize yields in alley cropping have been variable. From six years of trials Lal (1989) found that maize yields averaged 10% lower than the control in alley cropping systems with *L. leucocephala* and *G. sepium* even though fertilizer was used. Kang et al. (1984, 1985) and Kang and Dugma (1985) maintained maize yields at 2 t/ha for six years with the *L. leucocephala* prunings even without fertilizer applications. Lal (1989) reported a decrease in cowpea yields under alley cropping.

Insects, Diseases, and Weed Pests of Leucaena Leucocephala

Since the early promise regarding leucaena severe disappointments regarding its future in alley cropping and agroforestry have taken place. A bitter blow to the use of leucaena was the arrival of the leucaena psyllid (*Heteropsylla cubana*) in Asia and the Pacific region (Napompeth and MacDicken 1990, Van Den Beldt and Napompeth 1992). It was first noted in Hawaii in April 1984, but by mid-1985, the insect had moved throughout the Pacific. In 1986 it was found in Australia, Indonesia, Malaysia, and Thailand and in 1988 reached Madras, India. The psyllid is a tiny homoterous insect native to Central and South America, which is also the native home of various leucaena species. It has caused devastating damage and abandonment of many leucaena plantings in almost all countries of Asia and the Pacific. Repeated and cumulative attacks by the insect can result in complete defoliation or milder damage. The use of leucaena has been abandoned or severely reduced in many countries such as the Indonesia and the Philippines. This caused tremendous losses to countries such as Indonesia which planted 1.2 million acres of leucaena (Oka 1990). A description of the impact of the psyllid in Indonesia, how rapidly it became a problem, and the magnitude of the loss was given by Oka:

> Prior to 1986, no economically significant pests attacked the leucaena trees. However, since April 1986, an exotic insect pest, *Heteropsylla cubana*, defoliated and killed the trees around Bogor. In July and August of 1986, the pest had spread throughout the whole archipelago. The conducive climate and the absence of significant natural enemies (parasitoids, predators, and diseases) of this pest in Indonesia allowed the psyllid populations to increase rapidly. During 1986, the economic loss was estimated at Rp 538 billion (more than US $316,000,000). The pest was declared a national disaster and a Ministerial Decree in 1986 established the National Task Force for Control of the Psyllid.

Leucaena is still widely used in the Americas and Africa where the damage caused by the psyllid is not so severe. Efforts are being used to utilize resistant cultivars, biological control, and other practices in order to manage the psyllid. Only time will tell whether these efforts will be effective in Asia and the Pacific in restoring leucaena as an important component of the alley cropping system. A number of other insects attack leucaena (Brewbaker 1987), but none are as serious as the psyllid. The devastation cause by the psyllid can be used an excellent example of development organizations "putting too many eggs in one basket."

Leucaena is subject to numerous diseases. Lenné (1990, 1991) has reviewed the literature on the diseases of leucaena. Over 60 fungi are reported to attack leucaena. According to Lenné (1991), the most important diseases of leucaena are Camptomeris leaf spot (*Camptomeris leucaenae*), gummosis (various pathogens), and various root and pod rots. Management strategies include the use of resistant cultivars, and cultural management through cutting and grazing. Over 2,000 leucaena accessions have been collected and include considerable diversity and a wide range of pest resistance (Brewbaker 1989).

Akobundu (1993) noted that weeds can be managed in alley cropping systems:

> Weed control in this system consists of weed suppression by the hedgerow canopy during the fallow period, smothering of weeds by the prunings left as mulch on the soil surface, and possible effects of leachates from the decaying mulch on growth of weed seedlings. This system not only controls weeds but reduces soil degradation through its beneficial effects on soil physical properties, organic matter maintenance, erosion control, and nutrient recycling.

Gliricidia Sepium

After *Leucaena leucocephala*, *Gliricidia sepium* is probably the most commonly used tree in alley cropping systems. The use of Gliricidia has increased significantly as a hedgerow species in Asia following the decline of *L. leucocephala* due to the psyllid infestation in the late 1980s and early 1990s.

G. sepium has numerous common names. In English it is most commonly known as "mother-of-cocoa" and in Spanish "*mata ratón*" (rat killer) or "*madre de cacao*" (mother of cacao). The Aztec Indians of Mexico named the tree "*cacahuanantl*", which also means mother-of-cacao (Little and Wadsworth 1964). The common name for *G. sepium* in Spanish, *mata ratón*, means "mouse killer." As the name suggests, the toxic seeds, bark, leaves, and roots of the plant are used to poison rats, mice, and other rodents. Fernandes (1991) noted that *G. sepium* was one of a few tree species not attacked by leaf-cutter ants in the Peruvian Amazon. The leaves seem to be nutritious to cattle, but poisonous to horses and dogs. The tree is commonly used for shade in coffee (CIDICCO 1995) and cacao plantings. *G. sepium* is also used in alley cropping systems as a green manure and for weed control. In Sri Lanka it is used for fencing, shade, vine support, and as a sheep and cattle feed (Chadhokar 1982). Gupta (1993) lists its use in India for timber, firewood, fences, and fodder. It is widely used in Latin America as a living fence, for firewood, as a slashed green manure for various crops, for weed control, as animal forage, and as a shade tree for crops such as coffee, cacao, tea, pepper, and vanilla (Sumberg 1986).

A Gliricidia bibliography by Sumberg lists fifteen references to insect pests found on Gliricidia, but no references to diseases or pests other than weeds were given.

Fernandes et al. (1993) cite van Eijk-Bos and Moreno (1986) as stating that alley cropping with *Gliricidia sepium* on slopes of 45 and 70% in Colombia under an annual rainfall of 4,000 mm reduced soil losses of 23 to 38 tons/ha per year under maize to 13 tons/ha per year. CIDICCO (1995) noted that farmers traditionally planted *G. sepium* simultaneously with maize in the state of Lempira, Honduras. After a few years the gliricidia provided a protective cover for hillsides. Farmers then pruned the *G. sepium* branches leaving a mulch over their fields. Bean seeds were then planted in the mulch produced by the *G. sepium* cuttings. In alley cropping experiments Kass and Araza (1987) found that a *G. sepium* mulch continually increased the yields of both beans and maize. Rippin et al. (1994) described eight years of alley cropping experiments with *G. sepium* at CATIE in Costa Rica.

Erythrina *Species*

One of the most promising trees for alley cropping in Latin America has been *Erythrina poeppigigiana*. Kass (1994) recently reviewed the botany, origins, and multiple uses of Erythrina. Ramírez et al. (1990) and Kass (1994) noted that the genus contains 112 pantropical species. Seventy species are found in the American tropics, 31 in Africa, and 12 in Asia. One species, *Erythrina fusca*, is found in both the New and Old Worlds. Ramírez et al. (1990) wrote:

> Some of the species have a wide altitudinal range and are adapted to different ecological and soil conditions. However, the genus is most abundantly represented at higher elevations (between 500 and 2,500 masl). A small number of species are found in lowlands areas especially along stream edges, marginal forest or swampy ground.

Erythrina spp. are commonly used as shade trees in coffee and cacao plantations. "As shade trees they are ideal because of their high growth rate, abundant litter production, good coppicing, relative ease of husbandry, ease of management of shade and ability to fix nitrogen" (Ramírez et al. 1990). They are also commonly used in alley cropping, as a forage for animals (in spite of a high alkaloid content), and as living fences. In Latin America the flowers of many species are eaten, and the seeds of *E. edulis* are ground into a flour to make various food products in Colombia (Kass 1994).

Long term alley cropping experiments using *E. poeppigigiana* have been conducted in Costa Rica by CATIE (Rippin et al. 1994). The trees were initially fertilized. A 20 t/ha mulch was produced after a six month interval or twice yearly prunings were made to produce a mulch. Biomass and nutrient content of the prunings increased over a five year period despite two yearly prunings (Ramírez et al. 1990). Kass (1994) noted that *Erythrina* spp. are commonly recognized for their high biomass production which involves frequent prunings. Nevertheless, despite its reputation for high biomass production *E. poeppigigiana* "produced less in alley farming experiments than other nitrogen fixing trees *(Gliricidia sepium* and *Inga edulis)."* Weed competition significantly reduced maize yield in all systems. *E. poeppigigiana* is usually pruned twice a year in Costa Rican coffee plantations, whereas *E. fusca* and *E. berteroana* are usually pruned only once per year.

Inga *species*

Various species of Inga are used as shade in coffee plantations (de Leon 1987), but *Inga edulis* (known in Spanish as *guamo*) is the most commonly used. Most Inga species are small trees, but some can reach up to 40 meters. The fruits of several Inga species, such as *I. feullei*, sometimes reach over a meter in length and contain large seeds surrounded by a white, succulent, sugar-rich pulp. The fruit is highly prized and is sometimes called "the ice cream bean". The Inca Emperor Atahualpa sent Francisco Pizzaro a basketful of Inga beans as a gift (National Research Council 1989). Inga trees are used for producing mulch fruit, animal forage, wood for construction, fuelwood, shade for coffee and cacao, and soil improvement.

Fernandes et al. (1993) studied alley cropping on an acid soil in the upper Amazon using the acid tolerant, leguminous tree *I. edulis*. Objectives of their study were the effects of mulch, fertilizer addition, and root pruning on crop yields, weeds, and production and nutrients of biomass in a hedgerow (alley cropping) system using Inga. The study was done in Yurimaguas in the Amazon basin of Peru which has a mean annual rainfall of 2,200 mm. The mulch produced by Inga decomposes very slowly in comparison to other leguminous trees. The Inga hedgerows were planted to rice and cowpeas using a digging stick. Fernandes et al. (1993) noted:

> Placing hedgerow prunings in the alleys (mulched plot) vs. at the base of the hedgerow (non-mulched plot) did not have a significant effect on hedgerow yields. Root pruning of hedgerows on mulched plots, however,

resulted in significantly lower hedgerow yields than for non-root pruned hedgerows suggesting that hedgerows compete strongly for the nutrients in prunings. Fertilizer application to alleys significantly increased the contents of N, P, K, Ca, and Mg and concentrations of N and P in hedgerow prunings relative to non-fertilized alleys providing more evidence of the ability of hedge row trees to capture and recycle nutrients at the expense of the crop in the alley. Although hedgerow prunings accumulated large quantities of nutrients, and application of the mulch to the alleys significantly reduced weed biomass, there was no significant improvement in crop yields relative to non-mulched plots probably due to asynchrony between nutrient release from decomposing prunings and nutrient demand by crops.

There has been little diffusion of alley cropping to date in the Amazon region (personal communication--Eric Fernandes).

Time and Method of Applying Prunings

Tree-pruning is a common feature of many agroforestry systems. Kass et al. (1991) noted that experimental results from Africa regarding alley cropping were generally more positive than from other places and attributed this to the more frequent prunings at lower heights than in other experiments. Frequency and timing of prunings are major considerations in evaluation of alley cropping results. Mulongoy and Akobundu (1992) state that hedgerow trees in alley cropping systems can yield prunings containing more than 300 kg of nitrogen/ha. Unfortunately, perhaps only 10% of the nitrogen in prunings ends up in the associated crop, especially in the immediately succeeding cropping cycle (Mulongoy and Sanginga 1990). Kass et al. (1991) noted that tree prunings generally had sufficient quantities of potassium, magnesium, and calcium to supply crop needs on most soils. They also noted that phosphorus levels were generally inadequate in these systems and that phosphorus might become a limiting factor in alley cropping systems.

Adoption

Although reliable statistics are difficult to obtain, the alley cropping system appears to have been most widely adopted in tropical Asia and Africa. Examples of the adoption of alley cropping in Latin America are few. Work in Costa Rica at CATIE on the potential of alley cropping has not been particularly encouraging. In Costa Rica the tree species

Erythrina poeppigigiana and *Gliricidia sepium* have been the main species used in alley cropping studies (Escobar Muñera et al. 1994, Ramírez et al. 1990). Although "there is a history of greater production" in alley cropping experiments, the yields generally have not been significantly greater than controls (Escobar Muñera et al. 1994). It is difficult to find evidence that the alley cropping practice has been adopted by more than a handful of farmers in Latin America.

Advantages

Possible benefits from alley cropping systems are:

1. as an alternative to slash-and-burn systems (Kang 1993, Kang et al. 1990, Kang and Reynolds 1989);
2. control of erosion on steep slopes (Akobundu 1993, Fernandes et al. (1993), Kang et al. 1981, Kang et al. 1984, Kang 1993, Piggin and Parera 1985, National Academy of Sciences 1977);
3. improvement of soil physical properties by addition of organic matter (Akobundu 1993, Fernandes et al. 1993, Kang 1993, Kang and Reynolds 1989);
4. provision of nutrients from the mulch provided by prunings and the N fixed by leguminous trees (Fernandes et al. (1993), Kang et al. 1984, Kang 1993, Kang and Reynolds, 1989, Kang and Mulongoy 1992, Mulongoy and Sanginga 1990, Szott and Kass 1994);
5. provides firewood, poles, and other wood products (Kang et al. 1981, Kang et al. 1984, National Academy Sciences 1977);
6. provides fodder for animals (Kang and Reynolds, 1989, National Academy Sciences 1977, Sumberg 1984);
7. weeds can be suppressed by shading and the mulch produced (Akobundu 1993, Kang et al. 1984, Kang 1993);
9. beneficial effects on soil physical properties (Akobundu 1993, Kang and Reynolds 1989).

Disadvantages

There are also numerous drawbacks or disadvantages to alley cropping systems:

1. the hedgerows compete with crops for moisture, sunlight, and nutrients;

2 the hedgerows take up valuable space that could be used for crops;

3. alley cropping requires high labor inputs, especially in the initial stages;

4. diseases and other pests may be more serious in alley cropping in comparison to conventional agriculture;

5. some tree species may become weeds in the alleys if large amounts of seed are produced;

6. the long term effects of alley cropping are unknown;

7. migrating animals may cause serious damage to trees in the system;

8. a high level of management is necessary for the system to succeed;

9. without land tenure few farmers will establish alley cropping systems.

Perhaps more serious than the various agronomic constraints to alley cropping are socio-economic constraints. Establishment and maintenance require high labor inputs and may be expensive. Alley cropping systems have had variable success in different parts of the world with limited adoption in Africa and Asia, but little adoption in Latin America. Francis and Atta-krah (1989) cited limited success in southeast Nigeria of alley cropping as due to sociological, institutional, and soil factors as follows:

> The limited success of the trials is traced to a number of related sociological, institutional and edaphic factors. These include poor soil fertility; the incompatibility of established cropping patterns and rotation practice with the planting of trees on farms; the division of labor and organization of decision making within the household; the land and tenure rules. It is argued the farmer-managed trials are necessary to reveal the importance of sociological and institutional factors in farmer decision-making and that such trials require a high level of farmer autonomy in their management.

Reviewing the literature on alley cropping Kass et al. (1991) concluded:

> However, in general, it can be stated that the responses to alley farming in the absence of fertilizer, if positive, were generally small and the application of at least nitrogen fertilizers to most alley cropping systems generally brought about considerable yield increases. Soil physical properties were generally improved by the alley farming systems.

Again, it is important to remember that crop yield increases alone are rarely the sole reason for the adoption of alley cropping. Rather it is often for a combination of advantages that include benefits such as the production of fuelwood, fodder, microclimate effects, and even as a transition to cash tree crop systems. The jury is still out on the future and potential of alley cropping systems.

Costa Rican *Erythrina*/Coffee Systems

In Costa Rica, different species of *Erythrina*, such as *poró (E. poeppigiana)* are commonly used shade trees for coffee (Kass 1994, Ramírez et al. 1990, Rippin et al. 1994, Russo and Budowski 1986). Trees are pruned or pollard (slashed) 1-3 times a year (Figure 9.3). The pruned branches produce a mulch or litter layer and return nitrogen to the soil. It has been estimated that this practice may return over 300 kg of N/ha to the soil per year (Glover and Beer 1986, Russo and Budowski 1986). Bornemisza (1982) wrote that 100 kg N/ha/yr was sufficient for low to medium density plantings of coffee, but not for high density plantings (i.e. > 5,000 plants/ha). Beer (1988) concluded that *E. poeppigiana*, when pruned 2-3 times per year, can return to the litter layer the same amount of nutrients applied to coffee plantations in Costa Rica via inorganic fertilizers, even at the highest recommended rates of 270 kg N, 60 kg P (phosphorus) and 150 kg K (potassium)/ha/yr. In addition, trees contribute 5,000 to 6,000 kg of organic matter/ha/yr. Although the nutrient contribution is important, Beer concluded that in fertilized plantations of cacao and coffee, litter productivity is a more important shade-tree contribution than nitrogen fixation, due to the beneficial effects of all that organic matter on soil physical and chemical properties.

In the mid 1980s, many growers in Latin America decided to grow coffee in full sunlight without shade to avoid coffee rust (caused by *Hemileia vastatrix*) and to increase yields per unit of land. Previously, most coffee in Costa Rica was grown under shade trees such as *poró (E. poeppigiana), Inga* spp., and some *Gliricidia sepium*. Budowski (1993) wrote:

> In this system, it was customary to drastically prune shade trees once or twice a year, either totally to a 3-m height or with 1-3 branches left intact to form what was locally known as a "chimney".

Budowski noted that modern techniques, such as improved cultivars, high rates of fertilization, and pesticide use, was officially encouraged in

Latin America. As a result, considerable increases in production per hectare was achieved, as generous credit from state banks was available and coffee extension program personnel were trained specifically for new program. However, these measures primarily benefitted large estate growers who had access to the credit and who benefited from the generally high coffee prices of the 1980s. Budowski (1993) added:

> Many small producers had financial difficulty acquiring herbicides. pesticides and fertilizer, and also had problems applying them (especially in the correct amounts). Furthermore the shade trees had traditionally provided fuelwood (especially Inga) and fruits (e.g., banana, citrus, avocado). Erosion increased, the useful life of a coffee bush decreased considerably, incidents of human poisoning from herbicides were reported, and several problems arose related to the coffee crop's exposure to the sun. Many farmers started to plant shade trees. Again, an easy task since they only had to plant stakes from shade trees that had always existed in the region. Despite all the incentives, many small coffee growers (and some big ones) returned to using shade trees, or what we now call agroforestry combination, arguing that this system requires less fertilizer and less weeding labor (or herbicide expense).

The density of crop cover, and the shade dense foliage produces, has important effects on disease incidence. Palti (1981) cited Waller's description of how the density of tree foliage can effect tropical plant diseases:

> In tropical plantation crops, density of plant cover may have a twofold effect. In the rainy season, when rain runs down limbs and trunks, wet soil and foliage will take longer to dry under dense cover, and prolonged periods will favour many diseases, such as the coffee berry disease (*Colletotrichum coffeanum*). Conversely, in seasons poor in rain but rich in dew, dense plant cover will shield lower organs from dew formation, and will thus reduce the proportion of shoot growth in danger of attack by pathogens requiring films of water for their development.

Numerous references report that shading reduces the severity of several coffee diseases (Thurston 1992). Fewer lesions due to brown leaf spot of coffee (*Cercospora coffeicola*) occur on shaded coffee. Wellman (1972) also found fewer lesions due to American leaf spot of coffee (*Mycena citricolor*), less algal attack (*Cephaleuros virescens*), and less pink disease (*Corticium salmonicolor*) on shaded coffee. However, it should be noted that in certain cases shade can increase the severity of some diseases.

Other Uses of *Erythrina* in Agricultural Systems

Erythrina burana is a leguminous tree found only in Ethiopia (Teketay 1990). The tree is commonly used as a shade for coffee plantations. In Ethiopia, when coffee trees show signs of nutrient deficiencies, leaves and branches of E. *burana* are cut and buried around the coffee bushes. Farmers claimed higher production for several years due to this practice. The foliage of E. *burana* was also reported to decompose faster than the foliage of most other species. In addition to the use described above, the trees also provide feed for livestock, fuelwood, construction material, living fence posts, and medicine.

In the South Pacific farmers use cut leaves of a different *Erythrina* spp. as a mulch. Weeraratna (1990) wrote that farmers there also used grass, weeds, banana leaves, and parts of the coconut palm--fronds, husks, wood chips, and shredded logs--as mulches for taro (*Colocasia esculenta*). The application of leaves of *Erythrina* spp. at the rate of 30 tons/ha as a mulch for taro increased yields by 65%.

Sudanese *Acacia* Coppicing System

Skerman et al. (1988) described a system used in the Kordofan Province of the Sudan where gum arabic was produced from the leguminous tree *Acacia senegal*. Trees were coppiced after a cycle of gum production, and subsequently peanuts, sorghum, bulrush millet, and sesame were grown on the land until soil fertility was exhausted. The A. *senegal* trees were then allowed to regenerate and fertility was slowly restored, so another cropping cycle could occur.

Tanzanian "Fodder Tree" Coppicing System

Ludwig (1968) describes the Wakara, a group who live on the small island of Ukara in Lake Victoria. They grow a wide variety of crops in the diverse environments and agroecosystems. Farmers add as much as ten to twelve tons per hectare per year of stable manure to some fields. In addition various leguminous green manures, household refuse, and human waste are added as fertilizer to fields. They also have an interesting practice which consists of slashing the leaves of certain trees for animal fodder. In addition, Ludwig noted that the leaves are used in their fields as green manure. Ludwig's (1968) article has an illustration of how the branches and leaves are cut off the so called "fodder trees." No specific identification of the "fodder trees" was given.

Guatemalan *Sauco* Coppicing System

Near Ostuncalco, Guatemala, farmers maintain *sauco* trees (*Sambucus mexicana*) in their potato, maize, and bean fields. Wilken (1987) noted that the volcanic soils in the Ostuncalco area are sandy, low in nitrogen and organic material, have a low moisture-retention capacity, and are easily eroded. The farmers of the area have evolved a fascinating system of using the coppiced or slashed vegetation of *sauco* trees as green manure. Wilken describes the system as follows:

> The sauco are not allowed to achieve tree stature but instead are pruned rigorously so that only small stumps are left to sprout new growth. Leaves and small branches are removed annually, spread carefully around individual plants or matas, then chopped and interred with broad hoes. Farmers claim that crop quality and yields depend on these annual applications of sauco leaves.

This sauco system is in only one of numerous systems which farmers have evolved around the world that incorporate the the slashed or coppiced vegetation of trees into the soil as a source of nutrients and organic material in order to improve crop yields.

Conclusions

The use of trees, as a mulch and for a variety of other benefits, is common in traditional agriculture systems. While integrating trees into existing agricultural systems has shown increases in crop yields, in most cases the results are rarely as spectacular as those produced by chemical fertilizer. The value of trees in agriculture, in most cases, should not be viewed simply according to their provision of mulch, biomass, or increasing yields. Agroforestry systems need to be evaluated and extended according to the sum of the numerous benefits they may provide to the entire system. For many emerging agricultural systems, mulch alone may not provide the only benefit.

10

Effects of Organic Mulches, Soil Amendments, and Cover Crops on Soil-borne Plant Pathogens and Their Root Diseases

H. David Thurston and George Abawi

In this chapter, organic materials left or spread on the soil surface are considered as mulches, whereas organic materials incorporated into the soil are considered as soil amendments. Slash/mulch production systems practiced by traditional farmers are varied, but most produce and maintain considerable amounts of organic matter on the soil. Thus, the abundant quantities of organic matter provided by the various slash/mulch systems creates a thick covering layer on the soil surface that undergoes decomposition at different rates. Many other forms of organic matter such as fresh or composted crop residues, mud from rivers and streams, human and animal wastes, and aquatic plants have been used by traditional farmers. The beneficial effects of organic materials in improving the availability of soil nutrients, reducing soil erosion, increasing water retention, and improving soil structure and other soil parameters are well known. It has also been shown that mulches and other forms of organic matter contribute to the establishment of soil conditions that are ideal for root growth, and thus generally result in increased vigor and yield of crop plants. However, phytotoxic metabolites may be produced during the decomposition of certain organic materials that might directly or indirectly exert an adverse effect on plant growth (Linderman and Gilbert 1975, Patrick et al. 1964).

Root diseases incited by fungal and nematodal soil-borne pathogens are of common occurrence on many crop species, especially food legumes, grown in Latin America. For example, six root rot diseases are considered to be of major importance on common beans (*Phaseolus vulgaris*) grown in the principal production areas in Latin America. These are Fusarium yellows (caused by *Fusarium oxysporum* f. sp. *phaseoli*), Fusarium root rot (caused by *F. solani* f. sp. *phaseoli*), charcoal rot (caused by *Macrophomina phaseolina*), Rhizoctonia root rot (caused by *Rhizoctonia solani*), southern blight (caused by *Sclerotium rolfsii*), and root-knot nematodes (*Meloidogyne* spp, principally *M. incognita* and *M. javanica*) (Abawi and Pastor-Corrales 1990, Mullin et al. 1991). One or more of these diseases may predominate in a production system and/or area. Root rot diseases are most severe when soil conditions are poor; this is particularly true of soils with low organic matter, poor structure, high compaction with inadequate drainage, and others. In addition, root diseases tend to become prevalent when susceptible crops are used in a sequence or intercropped in such a way that build-up of high population densities of soil-borne pathogens is permitted. Plant roots severely infected with soil-borne pathogens are less efficient in absorbing water and nutrients, especially if the plants are under physical or biological stress conditions.

The use of resistant crop cultivars is the most effective, economical, and practical control strategy against root disease pathogens; this is especially true for resource-poor farmers who cannot afford to purchase even modest inputs. However, this strategy requires the development of adapted cultivars with resistance to all the major soil-borne pathogens that prevail in a given production/ecological zone. Until such cultivars become available, effective control of root diseases is possible only through the use of a combination of compatible and appropriate control measures. For example, the lack or low level of resistance in an adapted cultivar to one or more of the major root disease pathogens in a production area may be managed by implementing a disease control measure that is cultural (organic mulches and composts, selecting an appropriate cropping sequence, intercropping, planting on raised ridges, adjusting planting time, planting density, etc.), biological (addition or enhancement of beneficial soil-borne microorganisms), chemicals (choice of herbicides and fertilizers, judicial use of chemicals where needed such as treatment of seeds and other planting materials), or any combination of these measures.

The direct and indirect role of crop residues and various other sources of organic matter on crop health and yield has been known for centuries (Cook et al. 1978, Cook and Baker 1983, Thurston 1992). Today, the major influence of organic matter on root pathogens is believed to be through the modification of soil microbial activities, especially by stimulation of antagonistic microorganisms (Cook et al. 1978, Cook and Baker 1983). A brief summary of available information on the effect of organic matters on soil-borne pathogens and their root diseases follows. However, only a few selected examples are presented, and therefore only a small number of the numerous available references are listed.

Organic Matter and the Incidence and Severity of Root Diseases

The majority of the information available in the literature indicates that maintaining a high level of organic matter on and in the soil is generally associated with reduced incidence and severity of root diseases (Cook & Baker 1983). Ancient Chinese, Greek, Roman, Arab, and Spanish writers have documented the importance and use of composted organic materials and several types of manures to improve crop production and for the management of plant diseases (Thurston 1992).

Traditional Chinese farmers have annually added large quantities of organic materials and home-made composted organic fertilizers to their land. Considering the nature of the intensive production systems practiced in China, such as their vegetable production systems, one expects to find a considerable number of root diseases impacting on crop production. However, several authors (Abawi and Thurston 1994, Cook and Baker 1983, Kelman and Cook 1977, Williams 1979, among others) have surprisingly reported only limited occurrence and impact of root diseases incited by fungal and nematodal soil-borne pathogens in China. It appears that the extensive addition of manures and composted organic fertilizers combined with flooding are major factors improving root health by suppressing or eliminating inoculum sources of soil-borne plant pathogens.

The *chinampa* production systems of Xochimilco, Mexico, which date back to the Aztec era, also annually receive large quantities of mud rich with nutrients from the bottom of the canals, aquatic plants, crop residues, weeds, animal manures, and other types of organic matter. No reports were found suggesting that root diseases were of importance on the *chinampas*. However, it was recently found (Lumsden et al. 1981, Zuckerman et al. 1989) that these soils contain low population densities of fungal and nematodal pathogens. Several biological control agents recovered from these soils suppressed the population and damage of *Pythium* spp. and the root-knot nematode (*Meloidogyne* spp.) to vegetable crops under experimental conditions.

In the humid lowlands of the tropics, web blight is the most destructive disease on beans planted under clean cultivation systems. The disease is caused by the soil-borne pathogen *Rhizoctonia solani* and its telemorph *Thanatephorus cucumeris*. The main source of inoculum of the pathogen, in hot and humid production areas, is sclerotia and mycelial fragments free in soil or in the form of colonized debris. Inoculations of beans occur mainly by splashing by rain drops containing infested soil. This disease was found to be of minor importance in growers fields under the traditional *frijol tapado* production system (Galindo et al. 1982, Galindo et al. 1983) because of the mulch produced by slashed vegetation. The disease was also effectively controlled by mulching with rice husks. Both practices were equally effective and superior to the fungicide treatments.

A wide variety of terraces are still in extensive use, mostly by traditional farmers, on hillside agricultural production systems in many regions of the world. Large quantities of organic matter in the form of weeds, grasses, crop residues, manures and other organic materials are incorporated into the soils of the terraces annually. This practice undoubtedly contributes to the suppression of soil-borne pathogens and the sustainability of these production systems that have lasted for centuries.

Root diseases are generally rare in undisturbed or natural ecosystems such as native forests and prairies, whereas soil-borne pathogens and resultant root diseases are severe and often a limiting production factor in conventional production systems (Cook et al. 1978, Cook and Baker 1983). Some authorities have suggested that the increase of root diseases in the conventional production systems may be due to the tillage practices used and the destruction of organic materials. Several authors have reviewed the literature and listed the numerous examples available where the management of crop residues or the addition of various types of organic amendments (either fresh, dried, or composted) had either increased or decreased the populations of plant pathogens and their diseases (Allarmas et al. 1988, Cook et al. 1978, Cook and Baker 1983, Hoitink and Fahy 1986, Lewis and Papavizas 1975, Palti 1981, Patrick et al. 1964, Sumner et al. 1981, Rodriguez-Kabana et al. 1987). Successful suppression of plant parasitic nematodes including the destructive root-knot nematodes (*Meloidogyne* spp.) have been documented with the use of cover crops, green manure crops, trap crops, cropping sequences, and the addition of organic amendments (Muller and Gooch 1982, Nusbaum and Ferris 1973, Rodriguez-Kabana 1987, 1992a, 1992b). In the southern USA the cropping of velvetbeans (*Mucuna deeringiana*) as a rotational crop was found to reduce the population of *Meloidogyne arenaria* and increase peanut yield more efficiently than the use of the nematicide aldicarb in a peanut monoculture crop production system (Rodriguez-Kabana 1992a).

There are numerous examples of the value of incorporating organic matter. For example, incorporation of dry oats, barley, and maize as well as green oat and maize amendments has been shown to reduce *Fusarium, Rhizoctonia,* and *Thielaviopsis* root rots of beans (Cook and Baker 1983, Lewis and Papavizas 1975). Damage to avocado caused by *Phytophthora cinnamoni* was reduced with organic mulches (Borst 1986, Coffey 1984). A classic example of the positive effects of adding organic matter to the soil is given by Baker and Cook (1974) and Shea and Broadbent (1983). In Australia, *P. cinnamoni* causes a severe root rot of avocados. Growers who add large quantities of chicken manure to the avocado soils have little problem with *P. cinnamoni*. Growers in the same area with little organic matter in their soils have severe problems with avocado root rot. Root rot diseases of ornamental crops caused by species of *Phytophthora, Pythium, Rhizoctonia,* and *Thielaviopsis* were reduced by composts prepared with tree barks and used as mulch or planting medium (Hoitink and Fahy 1986). Dollar spot on creeping bentgrass and annual bluegrass turf caused by *Sclerotinia homoecarpa* was highly suppressed with topdressings amended with selected commercial organic fertilizers composed of animal and plant meals (Nelson and Craft 1992). Dollar spot was also suppressed by a poultry litter compost and a 2.5 year old sludge compost from Endicott, New York.

In contrast to the above mentioned benefits of organic matter in suppressing root diseases, there are examples in the literature documenting the direct or indirect effects of the management of certain mulches and organic matter on the increased severity of root diseases (Cook and Baker 1983, Palti 1981, Sumner et al. 1981). Increased severity of root diseases on several crops caused by *Pythium* spp., *Phytophthora* spp., *Rhizoctonia solani*, and *Sclerotium rolfsii* have been attributed to specific management of soil organic matter. All these fungi are non-specialized pathogens having a wide host range, good saprophytic ability under certain conditions, and are generally favored by high moisture conditions. A straw mulch of apple trees caused a significant increase in *Phytophthora* crown and root rots (35% infection) caused by *P. cactorum, P. megasperma,* and *P. cambivora* (Merwin et al. 1992). Apple trees growing in the sod grass and crown vetch "living much" remained free of these diseases, whereas apple trees growing in the other five ground cover vegetation management systems had up to 6% infection incidence.

The severity of three root rot diseases of wheat was increased when wheat was planted into soil mulched with wheat straws of the previous crop (Cook and Haglund 1991). These root diseases were take-all, Rhizoctonia root rot, and Pythium root rot caused by *Gaeumannomyces graminis* var. *tritici, R. solani,* and *Pythium* spp., respectively. Rhizoctonia root rot of beans caused by *R. solani* was increased in minimum-tillage plots where considerable bean residues of the previous crop were maintained on and near the soil surface (Abawi 1992). In addition, root tissues of crop plants may be predisposed to infection by soil-borne pathogens by phytotoxic metabolites (volatile and non-volatile) that are produced during the decomposition of organic matter (Cook et al. 1987, Linderman and Gilbert 1975, Patrick et al. 1964). The use of certain mulches and organic soil amendments have also been reported to serve as sources for plant viruses, to increase survival of bacterial and foliar fungal pathogens, and to increase damage to crops by slugs, seed corn maggots and other insects (Andrews 1987, Cook et al. 1978).

Mechanisms of Suppression of Soil-borne Pathogens by Organic Matter

As noted above, there is a long history and numerous examples documenting the use of mulches and organic amendments (including composts) in the control of root diseases as well as other plant diseases and pests. Proper management of mulches and soil amendments can can result in efficient and ecologically compatible control measures for plant diseases--especially those caused by soil-borne plant pathogens. Considerable research efforts have been devoted to the elucidation of the mechanisms by which organic mulches and soil amendments suppress soil-borne pathogens and their root diseases. However, only a limited number of cases are available where the specific mechanism(s) for the suppression of soil-borne pathogens by certain mulches and organic amendments are known. The latter is due to the differences in the chemical composition, stage of maturity, and rate of decomposition of the mulches and organic amendments as well as the complexity and differences of the soil parameters (biological, chemical and physical), and the environment. There are various types and levels of interactions, especially microbial interactions, resulting from the use of mulches and other organic amendments. It is difficult to verify the mechanism(s) involved in the suppression of soil-borne pathogens or the predictability of the effectiveness of mulches and organic amendments on soil-borne pathogens and the diseases they cause in various environments.

Cook et al. (1978) in reviewing the literature indicated that crop residues left in the field affect plant diseases in at least the following categories:

1. For many plant pathogens, residues provide food and a place to live and reproduce.
2. Residues affect the physical environment occupied by the host and the pathogen.
3. As organic soil amendments, residues intensify the microbial activity of the soil and this, along with a variety of decomposition products (some phytotoxic or fungitoxic), may affect pathogens, susceptibility of the host, or both.

The above are also applicable to mulches and other sources of organic amendments. Another potential influence of mulches and crop residues left on the soil surface is to function as a physical barrier preventing splashing of infested soil onto plant tissues, and thus preventing or reducing primary inoculum of certain soil-borne pathogens (Burdon and Chivers 1982, Fitt and McCartney 1986, Galindo et al. 1983). According to Fitt and McCartney (1986): "Rain splash is the second most important natural agent, after wind, in the dispersal of spores of plant pathogenic fungi." Intercropping cassava with maize, melons, or other crops reduced soil splashing by rain and significantly decreased the severity of cassava bacterial blight (*Xanthomonas campestris* pv. *manihotis*) in Nigeria (Ene 1977). Mulches can serve about the same purpose as intercropping. Muimba-Kankolongo et al. (1989) found that mulches reduced the incidence of a cassava stem tip dieback of unknown etiology in Zaire. Mulches may prevent direct contact of the foliage, fruit, or vines with the soil and thus prevent diseases transmitted from the soil. A brief discussion of a number of the reported mechanisms by which mulches and organic soil amendments suppress soil-borne pathogens and root diseases follows.

Germination/Lysis Phenomenon of Propagules of Plant Pathogens

Many studies have shown that mulches and organic amendments stimulate germination of fungal propagules (such as conidia, sclerotia, chlamydospores, and others) of several soil-borne pathogens through the release of nutrients, volatile metabolites, and other compounds (Cook et al. 1978, Cook and Baker 1983, Lewis and Papavizas 1975). The germ tubes of germinating propagules are then lysed before they are capable of infecting the host, colonizing suitable substrates, or producing secondary spores or other structures. Thus, the germination and lysis process results in reduction of the inoculum density of soil-borne pathogens and subsequently lowers incidence of root diseases. Lysis of germ tubes may be caused by various types of antagonisms and competitions by the stimulated microbial activities by organic amendments. For example, various crop residues caused the germination and lysis of sclerotia of *Phymatotrichum omnivorum* resulting in the control of Phymatotrichum root rot of cotton, whereas the addition of oat straw, maize stover, or alfalfa hay caused 90% reduction in population of *Thielaviopsis basicola* and control of black root rot of beans (Cook et al. 1978, Cook and Baker 1983, Lewis and Papavizas 1975).

Competition for Nutrients

The addition of soil amendments and especially those with a high C/N ratio have been shown to result in extreme competitions for several nutrients and especially for nitrogen, iron, and others. The stimulated microbial organisms are better competitors in soil, and thus they immobilize these nutrients in their cells and starve the pathogens or impose a soil fungistasis condition. For example, decomposing mature maize tissues reduced the severity of Rhizoctonia root rot of beans by suppressing the growth of *R. solani* (Lewis and Papavizas 1975). Another example is the reduction of Fusarium root rot of beans by the incorporation of barley straw residues into soil and the reversal of this effect by the addition of inorganic nitrogen to the residues (Cook et al. 1978).

Production of Volatile and Non-Volatile Toxic Compounds

Numerous studies have dealt with the biological and chemical effect of decomposition products of mulches and organic amendments on soil microorganisms and crop plants (Linderman and Gilbert 1975, Patrick et al. 1964). Crucifer amendments (cabbage, Kale, turnip, mustard, etc.) reduced Aphanomyces root rot of peas through the production of sulfur-containing volatiles (such as dimethyl sulfide and others) which were toxic to *Aphanomyces euteiches*. Ammonia and ethylene produced by decomposing organic amendments are toxic to many soil-borne fungal and nematodal pathogens. Ammonia was reported to prevent germination of zoospores and to kill the mycelium of *Phytophthora cinnamoni* in vitro (Lewis and Papavizas 1975). Marigolds (*Tagetes* spp.) produce terthienyl and other polythienyl which are known to inhibit plant parasitic nematodes such as the root-knot and lesion nematodes. In addition, organic materials such as oil cakes of castor beans and neem are known to contain compounds toxic to nematodes (Rodriguez-Kabana et al. 1987).

Modification of the Soil Environment

Many crop mulches and organic amendments are known to effect several soil parameters, especially soil temperature and moisture (Cook et al. 1978). The increase of Phytophthora crown and root rot of apples by a straw mulch was significantly correlated to the prolonged soil saturation condition in the straw mulched plots (Merwin et al 1992). Similarly, the poor growth and yield of wheat planted in soil mulched with wheat straw was attributed to keeping the top 10-15 cm of soil ideally moist for the activities and damage of *R. solani*, *Pythium* spp., and *Gaeumannomyces graminis* var. *tritici* (Cook and Haglund 1991).

Interference with Inoculum Dissemination

Organic mulches, amendments, and cover crops are known to influence the survival, production, and dissemination of primary and secondary inocula of aerial and soil-borne plant pathogens. Several soil-borne pathogens, such as *Rhizoctonia solani* and its telemorph *Thanatephorus cucumeris*, also cause aerial infections. Soil amendments left on the soil surface or natural vegetation mulches in the traditional *frijol tapado* production system effectively controlled web blight of beans by providing a physical barrier for the dissemination of the primary inoculum of the pathogen (sclerotia and mycelial fragments of *T. cucumeris* in rain-splashed infested soil) (Galindo et al. 1982, 1983).

Stimulation of Specific Antagonistic, Parasitic, or Predacious Biological Control Agents

As discussed above, the main effect of mulches and organic amendments is through their effect in stimulating the total microbial activities to the detriment of plant pathogens. Thus, the use of mulches and other organic amendments have long been recognized and accepted as a form of biological control (Cook et al. 1978, Cook and Baker 1983). In addition, many examples are available showing that the addition or the management of mulches and organic amendments have resulted in the stimulation of activities of specific biological agents that directly affected the target pathogens. For example, the addition of chitin amendments to soil increased several fungal species with chitinolytic ability which were also colonizers of nematode eggs (Rodriguez-Kabana et al. 1987).

Conclusions and Future Research Needs

Historically, many sustainable agricultural systems incorporated large quantities of organic matter into the soil. In addition to the agronomic benefits, this incorporation of organic matter generally resulted in the reduced incidence and severity of root diseases incited by soil-borne pathogens as well as other diseases. Mulches and soil amendments (including cover crops and composts) suppress plant diseases, especially root diseases, by reducing soil/inoculum splashing, influencing soil parameters such as moisture and temperature, and enhancing microbial activities that are antagonistic to plant pathogens.

In the hot, humid tropics where plant growth is rapid and luxurious, the use of green manures and natural vegetation as mulches (as in the slash/mulch system) should be seriously considered as they provide, in addition to agronomic benefits, an effective management practice for some important diseases. However, there are cases where mulch and/or soil amendments can increase the incidence of certain diseases. There is a need to study the effect of the continued use of these organic manures and mulches on other diseases and pests in the different ecological zones and under the different production systems that prevail in the tropics. In addition, the mechanisms by which these organic mulches and amendments suppress plant pathogens warrant in-depth studies. Elucidation of the mechanism(s) of suppressiveness to soil-borne pathogens will aid in the enhancement of such activities and the adaptation to other ecological areas and soils. Research is also needed on the integration of the use of mulches and organic amendments with other disease and pest management measures that are needed in each production system. However, there is a critical need for the availability of more funding for research on mulches and organic amendments in order to carry out a truly useful, integrated research agenda. Unfortunately, only miniscule funds are now being spent on research in this area, especially in developing countries. However, huge sums of money are presently being spent on research in the areas of genetic engineering for the development of host plant resistance and new chemicals for the management of plant pathogens and pests. Although the latter is important, the benefits of research on mulches and organic amendments might produce equal or even far greater returns in sound pest management measures, a better environment, and applicability to the millions of resource-poor farmers throughout the world, than current research in biotechnology and chemical development.

11

Recommendations

1. The farmer-to-farmer, spontaneous diffusion of cover crop/green manuring mulching practices, especially that of the velvetbean practices in Mexico and Central America, without the help of outside groups, merits close examination and consideration by development entities. A thoughtful study of the nature of the technology which generated this diffusion is recommended to development workers and researchers alike.

2. Mulches can reduce plant diseases by reducing soil splashing, influencing the moisture content and temperature of the soil, and enhancing the microbiological activities that suppress plant pathogens. In the hot humid tropics, where plant growth is rapid and bountiful, the use of green manures and natural vegetation as mulches (eg. in the slash/mulch system) should be examined, as their use provides an effective management practice for some diseases.

3. The use of mulches to reduce erosion is becoming acknowledged as the most effective strategy for reducing soil erosion on steep hillsides. Therefore, the use of mulches that protect the soil should be considered for systems of agriculture on sloping land where sufficient biomass can be accumulated.

4. Recent research results in Costa Rica suggest that farmers in humid tropical regions can greatly increase the efficiency of phosphorus fertilizer by applying it to a mulch. This avoids the problem of fertilizer phosphorus adsorption by the soil and could have a significant impact on improving mulch-based systems around the world.

Utilization and further testing of this practice in different systems and environments by development workers and researchers alike is recommended.

5. Agricultural systems that combine the slash-and-burn and the slash/mulch systems may obtain the benefits of both methods of agriculture. Development practitioners concerned with crop improvement systems that need to move away from the exclusively slash-and-burn practices for environmental, political, or socioeconomic reasons should consider the advantages of combining the two management systems.

6. Much remains to be done with regard to adapting cover crop and green manure systems to drier climates where the need is great, but where success has been limited. In drier climates, finding species that survive through the dry season or produce sufficient biomass is a major constraint to developing successful cover crop and green manure systems in the semi-arid tropics. It should be noted that incorporation, the use of in-row tillage, the use of mulch from coppiced drought tolerant trees, or supplementing green manures with animal manures may provide better results than cover crops or mulch-based systems in drier areas with poor soils.

7. In drought-prone areas mulches can significantly decrease evaporation of soil moisture, thus conserving moisture. Mulches are thus recommended for dry areas, although living green mulches can exacerbate drought problems in some cases.

8. Cover crops, green manures, and mulches have been shown to increase the beneficial activity and populations of both large and small soil-inhabiting organisms. Their use is recommended to improve the beneficial soil microflora and fauna.

9. Lack of nitrogen is often a limiting factor in crop production. Studies on the use of leguminous cover crops and green manures to increase the availability of soil nutrients, especially nitrogen are recommended.

10. Mulches protect seedlings and young plants from the impact of rain, hail, the wind, and from damage by birds and other animals. Their use should be considered when these particular problems are present.

11. Most mulch-based systems use few outside inputs; thus, little if any capital for inputs such as fertilizer or pesticides is required. For farmers with little access to credit or capital the use of some mulch-based systems can often be recommended.

12. All the positive benefits of mulch-based systems are often not taken into account or even recognized. For example in Sumatra, *Eupatorium inulifolium*, which was found to be a reliable indication of soil fertility and is used as a shade or nurse plant for cinnamon tree seedlings, as an insecticide (some farmers sprayed a concoction of it onto onions and peppers to kill insects), as a living fence, for firewood, as poles for vine crops, for construction, for medicine, and finally for weaning children from breast feeding. A thorough study of other overlooked non-agricultural benefits is recommended when considering the total benefits of mulch-based systems.

13. The use of cover crops and green manure systems can often eliminate or reduce the need to burn in traditional shifting cultivation systems. In addition to enriching the soil, as burning does immediately, substitution of mulching for burning can also reduce soil erosion and the risks to neighboring farms and forests. Thus, mulching should be considered as an alternative to burning.

14. The organic matter content of soils can be significantly increased by cover crops and green manures. For example velvetbeans may produce up to 50 T/ha/year of biomass. Improving the organic matter content of soils, where practical and economically feasible, can be recommended as a valuable practice.

15. Many weeds are suppressed by mulches, cover crops, and green manures, especially vigorously growing species such as velvetbean. Even perennial weeds such as Imperata grass (*Imperata cylindrica*) and nut grass (*Cyprus rotundus*) can often be controlled. Researchers and practitioners should consider this non-chemical weed management practice.

16. Mulch-based agricultural systems, especially those using mulches developed *in situ*, often have low labor costs. A reduction in the cost of weeding is an especially common example. When labor costs reduce or inhibit crop production the use of mulch-based systems should be considered.

17. Green manure or cover crops that are nutritious and easily edible,

such as the scarlet runner bean or the lab-lab bean, are especially attractive to farmers as they produce food or income and thus are recommended over alternative green manure or cover crops.

18. Cover crops and green manures that produce high quality forage for livestock enterprises are recommended as their production can be intensified and pressure on forest resources which are often burned to provide forage for animals can be reduced.

19. Clean seed or healthy propagating material often has positive and dramatic effects on plant health and crop yields. Healthy planting materials should always be recommended for mulch-based agricultural systems.

20. Agricultural credit agencies in developing countries should consider changing their policies in order to allow farmers to obtain loans for mulch-based systems or for seasonal fallows in severely degraded land.

Bibliography

Abawi, G. S. 1992. *Influence of reduced tillage practices on root rot severity and yield of snap beans, 1991.* Am. Phytopathol. Soc., Biol. and Cultural Tests 7:9.

_____. and M. A. Pastor-Corrales. 1990. *Root rots of beans in Latin America and Africa: Diagnosis, research methodologies, and Management strategies.* CIAT Publ. No. 35. CIAT, Cali, Colombia. 114 pp.

_____. and H. D. Thurston. 1994. "Effects of organic mulches, soil amendments, and cover crops on soilborne plant pathogens and their root diseases," pp. 89-99. In: Thurston, H. D., M. Smith, G. Abawi, S. Kearl. (eds.) *Slash/Mulch: How Farmers Use It, and What Researchers Know About It.* CIIFAD and CATIE, Cornell Univ., Ithaca, NY.

Abdul-Baki, A., J. R. Teasdale, and C. Prince. 1992 pp. 184-186. *Winter annual legumes as mulches in vegetable production.* Proc. Mid-Atlantic Vegetable Workers' Conf., Univ. of Delaware.

_____. and J. R. Teasdale. 1993. *A no-tillage tomato production system using hairy vetch and subterranean clover mulches.* HortScience 28: 106-108.

_____. and J. R. Teasdale. 1994. *Sustainable production of fresh-market tomatoes with organic mulches.* U.S.D.A. Farmers' Bull. FB-2279. Washington, D.C. 10 pp.

_____. and J. R. Teasdale. 1995. pp. 111-118. *Establishment and yield of sweet corn and snap beans in a hairy vetch mulch.* Proc. Fourth Nat. Symposium on Stand Establishment of Hort. Crops. Dept. of Vegetable Crops, Davis, CA.

Acland, J. D. 1971. *East African Crops.* Longman, London. 252 pp.

Adams, J. E. 1966. *Influence of mulches on runoff, erosion and soil moisture depletion.* Soil Sci. Soc. Am. Proc. 30: 110-114.

Agboola, A. and G. E. Udom. 1967. *Effects of weeding and mulching on the response of late maize to fertilizer treatments.* Nigerian Agricultural J. 4: 69-72.

Akobundu, I. O. 1983. "No-tillage weed control in the tropics," pp. 32-44. In: Akobundu, I. O. and A. E. Deutsch, (ed.) *No-tillage Crop Production in the Tropics.* Proc. Symposium. Monrovia, Liberia.

164

August 1981. Intl. Plant Protec. Center, Oregon State Univ., OR.

_____. 1984. *Advances in live mulch crop production in the tropics.* Proc. Western Soc. Weed Sci. 37:51-57.

_____. 1993. *Integrated weed management techniques to reduce soil degradation.* IITA Res. 6: 11-16.

Alcorn, J. B. 1990. "Indigenous agroforestry strategies meeting farmer's needs," pp. 141-151. In: Anderson, A. B. (ed.) *Alternatives to deforestation: steps towards sustainable use of the Amazon rain forest.* Columbia University Press, New York., New York.

Alfaro Monge, R. 1994. "Improving the slash/mulch "frijol tapado" system," pp. 209-214. In: Thurston, H. D., M. Smith, G. Abawi, and S. Kearl (eds.) *Tapado. Slash/Mulch: How Farmers Use It, and What Researchers Know About It.* CIIFAD and CATIE, Cornell Univ., Ithaca, NY.

Alfaro, R. and H. Waaijenberg. 1991. *A time-proven way of growing beans.* ILEIA Newsletter 7(1&2): 33.

_____. and H. Waaijenberg. 1992. *El cultivo de frijol tapado en Costa Rica: un resumen de investigaciones, 1978-1991.* CATIE-MAG-UAW. Informe Tecnico CATIE No. 190. 12 pp.

Allarmas, R. P., J. M. Kraft and D. E. Miller. 1988. *Effects of soil compaction and incorporated crop residues on root health.* Ann. Rev. Phytopathol. 26:219-243.

Andrews, K. L. 1987. *La importancia de las babosas veronicéllidos en Centroamerica.* CEIBA 28:149-153.

Anon. 1982. *Colombia Indigena.* Ministerio Gobierno, Bogota. 229 pp.

_____. 1989. *A successful technology for small farmers.* Int. Agricultural Develop. 9: 18-19.

Araya V., R. and W. Gonzalez. 1987. *El Frijol Bajo el Sistema Tapado En Costa Rica.* Ciudad Univ. Rodrigo Facio, San José, Costa Rica. 272 pp.

_____. and W. Gonzalez M. 1994. "The history and future of the common bean (Phaseolus vulgaris L.) grown under the slash/mulch system ("tapado") in Costa Rica," pp. 11-17. In: Thurston, H. D., M. Smith, G. Abawi, and S. Kearl (eds.) *Tapado. Slash/Mulch: How Farmers Use It, and What Researchers Know About It.* CIIFAD and CATIE, Cornell Univ., Ithaca, NY.

Archer, W. A. 1937. *Exploration of the Chocó Intendancy of Colombia.* Sci. Monthly 44: 418-434.

Arevalo R., J. and J. J. Jimenez O. 1988. "Nescafe (Stizolobium pruriens (L.) Medic. var. utilis Wall ex Wight) como un ejemplo de experimentacion campesina en el tropico humedo Mexicano<" pp. 75-89 In: Del Amo R., Silvia. Cuatro estudios sobre sistemas tradicionales. Instituto Nacional Indigenista, Mexico, D.F., Mexico.

Arias, F. and M. Amador. 1991. "Frijol tapado, un sistema ventajoso para el pequeño agricultor.," pp. 13-17. In: M. Bolaños Arquin and I. Bolaños Arquin (eds.) *I Simposio Sobre Tecnologia Apropiada y Agricultura Biologica Para un Desarrollo Rural Alternativo.* CICDAA, COPROALDE, Univ. Costa Rica, San José, Costa Rica.

Ayanlaja, S. A. and J. O. Sanwo. 1991. *Management of soil organic matter in the farming systems of the low land humid tropics of West Africa. A review.* Soil Technol. 4(3): 265-277.

Baars, B. 1993. *Mycorrhizae. Beneficial or parasymbiont. Its relation to crop decline in shifting cultivation.* Foundation for Ecodevelopment, Amsterdam, Netherlands. 48 pp.

Bandy, D. E. & P. A. Sanchez. 1981. *Managed Kudzu fallow as an alternative to shifting cultivation in Yurimaguas, Peru.* Agron. Abstracts. p. 40.

Barreto, H. 1994. "Evaluation and utilization of different mulches and cover crops for maize production in Central America," pp. 157-167. In: Thurston, H. D., M. Smith, G. Abawi, S. Kearl. (eds.) *Tapado. Slash/Mulch: How Farmers Use It, and What Researchers Know About It.* CIIFAD and CATIE, Cornell Univ., Ithaca, NY.

Beaver, P. C., R. C. Jung and E. W. Cupp. 1984. *Clinical Parasitology.* 9th Ed. Lea and Febiger, Philadelphia. 825 pp.

Beckerman, S. 1987. " Swidden in Amazonia and the Amazon rim," pp. 55-94. In: Turner, B. L., II and S. B. Brush. *Comparative Farming Systems.* Guilford Press, New York. 428 pp.

Beer, J. 1988. *Litter production and nutrient cycling in coffee (Coffea arabica) or cacao (Theobroma cacao) plantations with shade trees.* Agroforestry Systems 7: 103-114.

Beingolea Ochoa, J. 1993. "Utilización de tarwi como abono verde en el programa de Chiroqasa del norte de Potosi, Bolivia," pp. 33-40. In: Buckles, D. (ed.) *Gorras y Sombreros: Caminos Hacia la Colaboración entre Technicos y Campesinos.* CIMMYT, Mexico.

Bellows, B. C. 1992. *Sustainability of Bean (Phaseolus vulgaris L.) Farming on Steep Lands in Costa Rica: An Agronomic and Socio-Economic Assessment.* Ph.D. Thesis. Univ. of Florida, Gainesville. 232 pp.

_____. 1994. "Frijol tapado, frijol espeque, and labranza zero: a socioeconomic and agroecological comparison of bean production methods in Costa Rica," pp. 115-128. In: Thurston, H. D., M. Smith, G. Abawi, and S. Kearl (eds.) *Tapado. Slash/Mulch: How Farmers Use It, and What Researchers Know About It.* CIIFAD and CATIE, Cornell Univ., Ithaca, NY.

Borel, E. and P. Pélegrin. 1951. *La culture du bananier au Cameroun.* Fruits 6: 421-427.

Bornemisza, E. 1982. *Nitrogen cycling in coffee plantations.* Plant and Soil 67: 241-246.

Borst, G. 1986. *Observations on a biological root rot control trial in the Fallbrook Area.* California Avocado Soc. 70: 107-110.

Bradley, P. and P. Dewees. 1991. "Indigenous woodlands, agricultural production and household economy in the communal areas," pp. 63-137. In: Bradley, P. and K. McNamara (eds.) *Living With Trees. Policies for Forestry Management in Zimbabwe*. World Bank Tech. Paper No. 210. World Bank, Washington, D. C.

Brewbaker, J. L. 1987. "Leucaena: a multipurpose tree genus for tropical agroforestry," pp. 290-323. In: Steppler, H. A. and P. K. R. Nair. (eds.) *Agroforestry: A Decade of Development*. ICRAF, Nairobi, Kenya.

_____. 1989. *Leucaena: can there be such a thing as a perfect tree?* Agroforestry Today 1(4) :4-7.

_____. 1990. "Nitrogen fixing trees," pp. 253-261 In: Werner, D. and P. Müller. (eds.) *Fast Growing Trees and Nitrogen Fixing Trees*. Gustav Fischer Verlag, Stuttgart.,

Buckles, D. 1992. *Hearing the mucuna story*. ILEIA Newsletter 8(3): 30-31.

_____. 1994. *Velvetbean: A "new" plant with a history*. CIMMYT Internal Document, Mexico. 21 pp.

_____. 1995. *Velvetbean: a "new" plant with a history*. Econ. Bot. 49(1): 13-25.

_____. and H. Perales. 1995. *Farmer-based experimentation with velvetbean: innovation within tradition*. CIMMYT Internal Document. CIMMYT, Mexico, D.F. 22 pp.

_____., I. Ponce, G. Sain and G. Medina 1994. "Cowardly land becomes brave. The use and diffusion of fertilizer bean (Mucuna deeringianum) on the hillsides of Atlantic Honduras," pp. 249-261. In: Thurston, H. D., M. Smith, G. Abawi, and S. Kearl (eds.) *Tapado. Slash/Mulch: How Farmers Use It, and What Researchers Know About It*. CIIFAD and CATIE, Cornell Univ., Ithaca, NY.

_____., J. Salgado, H. Bojorque, H. Antuñez, L. Mejia, H. Nolasco, L. de Ramos, G. Medina y R. Matute. 1991. "Resultados de la encuesta exploratoria sobre el uso de frijol de abono (Stizolobium deeringianum) en laderas del littoral Atlantico de Honduras," pp. 85-93. In: *Analysis de Los Ensayos Regionales de Agronomia, 1990*. Programa Regional de Maíz Para Centro America, Panamá y El Caribe. CIMMYT, Mexico. 137 pp.

Budowski, G. 1993 *The scope and potential of agroforestry in Central America*. Agroforestry Systems 23: 121-131.

Bunch, R. 1982. *Two Ears of Corn*. World Neighbors, Oklahoma City, OK. 250 pp.

_____. 1990. *The potential of intercropped green manures in Third World Villager agriculture*. Conference on the Socio-Economics of Organic Agriculture. Int. Fed. Organic Agric. Movements, Hamstead Marshall, UK. 6 pp.

_____. 1994. "The potential of slash/mulch for relieving poverty and environmental degradation," pp. 5-9. In: Thurston, H. D., M. Smith, G. Abawi, and S. Kearl (eds.) *Tapado. Slash/Mulch: How Farmers Use It, and*

What Researchers Know About It. CIIFAD and CATIE, Cornell Univ., Ithaca, NY.

———. 1995. *Principles of agriculture for the humid tropics. An odyssey of discovery*. ILEIA Newsletter. (October 1995).

Burdon, J. J. and G. A. Chivers. 1982. *Host density as a factor in plant disease ecology*. Ann. Rev. Phytopathol. 20:143-166.

Burkill, I. H. 1966. *A Dictionary of the Economic Products of the Malay Peninsula*. Crown Agents for the Colonies, London, UK.

Cairns, M. 1994. "Eupatorium inlilifolium: noxious weed or multi-purpose shrub?" pp. 209-288. In: Chapter 3. Stabilization of Upland Agroecosystems as a Strategy for Protection of National Park Buffer Zones: A Case Study of the Co-Evolution of Minangkabau Farming Systems and the Kerinci-Seblat National Park. MES Major Paper, York University. UK

Campbell, B., I. Grundy and F. Matose. 1993. "Tree and woodland resources-- the technical practices of small-scale farmers," pp 29-62. In: Bradley, P. N. and K. McNamara. (eds.) *Living With Trees. Policies for Forestry Management in Zimbabwe*. World Bank Tech. Paper No. 210. World Bank, Washington, D. C.

Campbell, G., et al. 1982. *Allelopathic properties of < terthienyl and phenylheptatrijne, naturally occurring compounds from species of Asteraceae*. J. Chem. Ecol. 8: 961-972.

Cardenas-Alonso, M. R. 1989. *Web blight of beans (Phaseolus vulgaris L.) incited by Thanatephorus cucumeris (Frank) Donk. in Colombia*. Ph.D. Thesis, Cornell Univ., Ithaca, NY.

Carter, W. E. 1969. *New Lands and Old Traditions. Kekchi Cultivators in the Guatemalan Lowlands*. Univ. of Florida Press, Gainesville, FL. 153 pp.

Cato, Marco Porcius. 1934. *On Agriculture*. W. D. Hooper and H. B. Ash (trans.) Harvard Univ. Press, Cambridge. pp. 1-157.

Cavallini, R. 1972. *Recommendaciones para aumentar la produción de frijol tapado*. Agroindustria (Costa Rica) 1(6): 18.

Ceron Solarte, B 1986. *Los Awa-Kwaiker*. Ediciones Abya-Yala, Quito, Ecuador. 304 pp.

CGIAR. 1995. Internet World Wide Web page of the The Consultative Group on International Agricultural Research (CGIAR). *CGIAR-mandated food crops. Beans*. URL: http://www.worldbank.org/html/cgiar/report2.html

Chacón, J. C. & S. R. Gliessman. 1982. *Use of the "non-weed" concept in traditional tropical agroecosystems of south-eastern Mexico*. Agro-Ecosystems 8: 1-11.

Chadhokar, P. A. 1982. *Gliricidia maculata: a promising legume fodder plant*. World Animal. Rev. 44: 36-43.

Christensen, C. M. and H. H. Kaufmann. 1969. *Grain storage. The Role of Fungi in Quality Loss*. Univ. of Minnesota Press, Minneapolis. 153 pp.

CIDICCO. 1991. *CIDICCO Cover Crops News Newsletter No. 1*. CIDICCO,

168

Tegucigalpa, Honduras. 4 pp.

_____. 1993. *The utilization of velvetbean as a source of food.* CIDICCO Technical Report No. 8. 4 pp.

_____. 1995. *The use of Gliricidia sepium as cover/shade-tree in coffee plantations (based on experiences of coffee growers in Copán, Honduras).* Cover Crop News 8: 1-8.

Clarke, W. D. 1966. *From extensive to intensive shifting cultivation.* Ethnology 5: 347-359.

Coe, M. D. and R. A. Diehl. 1980. *In the Land of the Olmec. The People and the River.* Vol. 2. Univ. of Texas Press, Austin, TX. 198 pp.

Coffey, M. D. 1984. *An integrated approach to the control of avocado root rot.* Calif. Avocado Soc. 68: 61-68.

Cook, R. J., M. G. Boosalis and B. Doupnik. 1978. :"Influence of crop residues on plant disease," pp 147-163. In: *Crop Residue Management Systems.* Am. Soc. Agron. Spec. Publ. 31. Madison, WI. 248 pp.

_____., and K. F. Baker. 1983. *The nature and practice of biological control of plant pathogens.* Am. Phytopathol. Soc. St. Paul, MN. 539 pp.

_____., and W. A. Haglund. 1991. *Wheat yield depression associated with conservation tillage caused by root pathogens in the soil not phytotoxins from the straw.* Soil Biol. Biochem. 23: 1125-1132.

Conklin, H C. 1957. *Hanunoo Agriculture: A report on an integral system of shifting cultivation in the Philippines.* FAO Forestry Develop. Paper No. 12, Rome.

_____. 1961. *The study of shifting cultivation.* Curr. Anthropol. 2(1): 27-61.

COPROALDE. CEDECO. 1991. *Memoria del I Encuentro Nacional Campesino de Frijol Tapado.* COPROALDE. CEDECO. Colegio Agropecuario San Ignacio de Acosta. 12-14 de Julio de 1991. 35 pp.

Costa, F. J. S. A., D. R. Bouldin, and A. R. Suhet. 1990. *Evaluation of N recovery from mucuna placed on the surface or incorporated in a Brazilian oxisol.* Plant and Soil 124: 91-96.

Crispin, A. and C. C. Gallegos. 1963. *Web blight -- a severe disease of beans and soybeans in Mexico.* Plant Dis. Reptr. 47: 1010-1011.

Crowe, T. J. 1964. *Coffee leaf miner in Kenya. II -- Causes of outbreaks.* Kenya Coffee. 29: 223-231.

De Balboa, Cabello. 1945. *Obras.* Vol. 1. Editorial Ecuatoriana, Quito. 451 pp.

De Jesus Huz, M. 1994. "The use of Canavalia ensiformis and other leguminous species as mulches for farming in the Yucatan," pp. 207-208. In: Thurston, H. D., M. Smith, G. Abawi, and S. Kearl (eds.) *Tapado. Slash/Mulch: How Farmers Use It, and What Researchers Know About It.* CIIFAD and CATIE, Cornell Univ., Ithaca, NY.

De la Cruz, R. 1994 "The usefulness of weed diversity in slash/mulch bean production: difficulties in herbicide use," pp. 233-237. In: Thurston, H. D., M. Smith, G. Abawi, and S. Kearl (eds.) *Tapado. Slash/Mulch: How Farmers Use It, and What Researchers Know About It*. CIIFAD and CATIE, Cornell Univ., Ithaca, NY.

Denoon, D. and C. Snowdon (eds.) 1980. *A Time to Plant and a Time to Uproot*. Inst. Papua New Guinea Studies, Papua New Guinea. 348 pp.

De Sornay, P. 1916. *Green Manures and Manuring in the Tropics*. John Bale, Sons and Danielsson, London. 466 pp.

DeWalt, B. R. and K. DeWalt. 1984. *Sistemas de cultivo en Pespire, sur de Honduras: un enfoque de agroecosistmas*. Instituto Hondureño de Antropologia e Historia y Programa Internacional de Sorgo y Mijo, INTSORMIL & Univ. of Kentucky, Lexington. 88 pp.

Dijkman, M. J. 1950. *Leucaena -- a promising soil-erosion-control plant*. Econ. Bot. 4: 337-349.

Diver, S. and P. Sullivan. 1992. *Cover Crops and Green Manures*. ATTRA (Appropriate Technol. Transfer for Rural Areas). Fayetteville, AR.

Dominguez-V., J. A., N. Marban-Mendoza, R. De la Cruz. 1990. *Leguminosas de cobertura asociados con tomate var. "Dina guayabo" y su efecto sobre Meloidogyne arabicida López y Salazar*. Turrialba 40: 217-221.

Dotson-Brooner, B. 1995. *Modifying a Traditional Farming System in the Highlands of Western Cameroon for Enhancement of Productivity and Sustainability*. M.P.S. Thesis, Cornell Univ., Ithaca, NY. 322 pp.

Dove, M.R. 1980. "The swamp rice swiddens of the Kantu' of West Kalimantan, Indonesia," pp. 953-956. In: Furtado, J. I. (ed.) *Tropical Ecology and Development*. Vol 2. Int. Soc. Trop.Ecol., Kuala Lumpur, Malaysia.

_____. 1983. *Theories of swidden agriculture, and the political economy of ignorance*. Agroforestry Systems 1: 85-99.

_____. 1985. *Swidden Agriculture in Indonesia: the Subsistence Strategies of the Kalimantan Kantu'*. Mouton Publ., New York. 515 pp.

Duke, J.A. 1981. *Handbook of Legumes of World Economic Importance*. Plenum, New York. 345 pp.

Echandi, E. 1965. *Basidiospore infection by Pellicularia filamentosa (= Corticum microsclerotia), the incitant of web blight of the common bean*. Phytopathology 55: 698-699.

Eder, H. M. 1963. *El Río y el Monte. A Geographical Reconnaissance of the Río Siguirisúa Valley, Chocó District, Colombia*. Department of Geograph., Univ. of Calif., Berkeley.

El-Swaify, S. A., W. C. Moldenhauer and A. Lo. 1982. (eds.) *Soil Erosion and Conservation in the Tropics*. American Soc. Agron. Spec. Publ. 43. ASA and SSSA, Madison, WI.

Ene, L. S. O. 1977. *Control of cassava bacterial blight (CBB)*. Tropical Root and Tuber Crops Newsletter 10: 30-31.

Escobar Muñera, M. L., C. Ramirez, and D. Kass. 1994. "Nitrogen in alley

170

cropping using Erythrina poeppigigiana and Gliricidia sepium with common beans (Phaseolus vulgaris)," pp. 133-147. In: Thurston, H. D., M. Smith, G. Abawi, and S. Kearl (eds.) *Tapado. Slash/Mulch: How Farmers Use It, and What Researchers Know About It*. CIIFAD and CATIE, Cornell Univ., Ithaca, NY.

Evans, D. O., R. S. Yost and G.W. Lundeen. 1983. *A Selected and Annotated Bibliography of Tropical Green Manures and Legume Covers*. Inst. Trop. Agric. and Human Resources, Univ. of Hawaii. 211 pp.

Ewell, P. T. and T. T. Poleman. 1980. *Uxpanapa: Agricultural Development in the Mexican Tropics*. Pergamon, New York. 207 pp.

FAO Staff. 1957. *Shifting cultivation. An appeal by FAO to governments, research centers, associations, and private persons who are in a position to help.* Unasylva 11: 9-11.

FAO. 1973 *Shifting Cultivation and Soil Conservation in Africa*. FAO Soils Bull. 24. FAO, Rome, Italy. 248 pp.

Fernandes, E. C. M. 1991. "Ensayo de providencias de Gliricidia sepium (Jacq.) Walp. en un ultisol de la Amazonia Peruana," pp. 275-281. In: J. T. Smith, W. R. Raun and F. Bertsch. (eds.) *Manejo de Suelos Tropicales in Latinoamerica*. Soil Sci. Dept., North Carolina State Univ., Raleigh, NC.

_____., C. B. Davey, and L. A. Nelson. 1993. "Alley cropping on an acid soil in the upper Amazon: Mulch, fertilizer and hedgerow root pruning effects," pp. 77-96. In: ASA Special Publication 56. *Technologies for Sustainable Agriculture in the Tropics*. Am. Soc. Agron., Madison, WI.,

Finegan, E. J. 1981. *The Use of Agri-silviculture as a Resource Conservation and Rural Community Development Method in the Tropical Wet Forest of Colombia*. Ph.D. Thesis, Cornell Univ., Ithaca, NY.

Fisher, R. B. 1910. *On the Borders of Pigmy Land*. Marshall Brothers, London. 215 pp.

Fitt, B. D. L. and H. A. McCartney. 1986. "Spore dispersal in splash droplets," pp. 87-104. In: Ayres, P. G. and L. Boddy. *Water, Fungi and Plants*. Cambridge Univ. Press, Cambridge, UK.

Flores, M. 1989. *Velvetbeans: an alternative to improve small farmer's agriculture*. ILEIA Newsletter 5(2): 8-9.

_____. 1994. "The utilization of leguminous cover crops in traditional systems of agriculture in Central America," pp. 149-155. In: Thurston, H. D., M. Smith, G. Abawi, and S. Kearl (eds.) *Tapado. Slash/Mulch: How Farmers Use It, and What Researchers Know About It*. CIIFAD and CATIE, Cornell Univ., Ithaca, NY.

Flynn, P. 1992. *Vanishing Homelands. A Chronicle of Change Across the Americas*. Homelands Productions, Tucson, AZ. Cassette No. 4.

Fragoso, C., I Barois, G. Gonzalez, C. Arteaga, and J. C. Patrón. 1993. "Relationship between earthworms and soil organic matter levels in natural and managed ecosystems in the Mexican tropics," pp. 231-239. In: Mulongoy, K. and R. Merckx (eds.) *Soil organic matter dynamics and sustainability of tropical agriculture*. Wiley, New York.

Francis, P. A. and A. N. Atta-krah. 1989. *Sociological and ecological factors in technology adoption: fodder trees in southeast Nigeria*. Exp. Agric. 25: 1-10.

Fultang, N. 1993. *Unpublished Manuscript on Kom Traditional Agriculture*. Mimeo.

Gale, W. J., R. W. McColl, and X. Fang. 1993. *Sandy fields traditional farming for water conservation in China*. J. Soil and Water Conservation. 48: 474-477.

Galindo, J. J. 1982. *Epidemiology and control of web blight of beans in Costa Rica*. Ph.D. Thesis. Cornell Univ., Ithaca, NY. 141 pp.

_____. 1987. "La moniliasis del cacao en centro America," pp. 7-16. In: Pinochet, J. (ed.) *Plagas y Enfermedades de Caracter Epidemico en Cultivos Frutales de la Region Centroamericana*. CATIE, Proyecto MIP, Panama. Informe Tecnico No. 110.

_____. 1994. "Incidence of web blight of beans grown under the the slash/mulch system in Costa Rica," pp. 101-107. In: Thurston, H. D., M. Smith, G. Abawi, and S. Kearl (eds.) Tapado. Slash/Mulch: How Farmers Use It, and What Researchers Know About It. CIIFAD and CATIE, Cornell Univ., Ithaca, NY.

_____., G. S. Abawi, H. D. Thurston and G. Galvez. 1982. *"Tapado", controlling web blight of beans on small farms in Central America*. NY Food and Life Sciences 14: 21-25.

_____, G. S. Abawi, H. D. Thurston and G. Galvez. 1983a. *Source of inoculum and development of bean web blight in Costa Rica*. Plant Dis. 67: 1016-1021.

_____. G. S. Abawi, H. D. Thurston and G. Galvez. 1983b. *Effect of mulching on web blight of beans in Costa Rica*. Phytopathology. 73: 610-615.

Gamble, J. F., H. I. Popenoe, and Associates. 1967. *Phase I. Final Report, Agricultural Ecology*. Battelle Mem. Inst., Columbus, Ohio.

Garcia Espinosa, R. 1980 *Incidencia de algunos fitopatógenos del suelo en maiz, con enfasis en Pythium sp. bajo dos tipos distinto de agroecosistemas en el tropico humedo*. Agricultura Trop. (CSAT) 2: 98-104.

_____ 1987. "Importancia de la fitopatologia tropical," pp. 1-17. In: *Taller de Fitopatologia Tropical*. 2nd Ed. Colegio de Postgraduados, Chapingo, Mexico.

_____., and L. Krishnamurthy. 1985. ":La teoria de los sistemas generales en el estudio y manejo de los problemas fitonematologicos," pp. 113-133 In: Marban M, N. y I. J. Thomason. (eds.) *Fitonematologia Advanzada I*. Editorial Colegio de Postgraduados: Mexico.

_____., Q. Madrigal, and N. G. Alvarez. 1994. "Agroecosystems for sustained maize production in the hot, wet regions of Mexico," pp. 61-74. In: Thurston, H. D., M. Smith, G. Abawi, and S. Kearl (eds.) *Tapado*.

172

Slash/Mulch: How Farmers Use It, and What Researchers Know About It. CIIFAD and CATIE, Cornell Univ., Ithaca, NY.

Garrity, D. P. 1993. "Sustainable land-use systems for sloping uplands in Southeast Asia," pp. 41-66. In: ASA Special Publication No. 56. *Technologies for Sustainable Agriculture in the Tropics*. Amer. Soc. Agron., Madison, WI.

_____. and A. Khan. 1994. *Alternatives to Slash-and-Burn. A Global Initiative*. ICRAF, Nairobi, Kenya. 73 pp.

Gindrat, D. 1979. "Biological soil disinfestation," pp. 253-287. In: Mulder, D. (ed.) *Soil Disinfestation*. Elseveir, Amsterdam.

Gliessman, S. R. 1990. "The ecology and management of traditional farming systems," pp. 13-17. In: Altieri, M. and S. Hecht (eds.) *Agroecology and small farm development*. CRC Press, Boca Raton, FL.

Glover, N. and J. Beer. 1986. *Nutrient cycling in two traditional Central American agroforestry systems*. Agroforestry Systems 4: 77-87.

Gogerty, R. 1994. *Cutting Back on Chemicals*. The Furrow 99(5): 10-13.

Gonzalez M., W. and R. Araya V. 1994. "Agroeconomic study of beans (Phaseolus vulgaris L.) grown under the "tapado" slash/mulch system in Costa Rica," pp. 263-282. In: Thurston, H. D., M. Smith, G. Abawi, and S. Kearl (eds.) *Tapado. Slash/Mulch: How Farmers Use It, and What Researchers Know About It*. CIIFAD and CATIE, Cornell Univ., Ithaca, NY.

Goodell, G. 1984. *Challenges to international pest management research and extension in the third world: do we really want IPM to work?* Bul. Ent. Soc. Am. 30: 18-26.

Granados Alvarez, N. and R. G. Espinosa. 1992. *La rotación nescafe-maíz, un sistema productivo, ecologico, y sostenible, sistema tradicional*. Serie Agroecologia Tropical. Folleto Tecnico No. 1. Colegio de Postgraduados. CEICADES., H. Cardenas, Tabasco, Mexico. 32 pp.

Greenland, D. J. 1975. *Bringing the green revolution to the shifting cultivator*. Science 190: 841-844.

Griggs, T. 1995. *Soil conservation starts at the grass roots*. Partners in Research for Development. No. 8: 16-21.

Gupta, R. K. 1993. *Multipurpose Trees for Agroforestry and Wastelands Utilization*. Int. Sci. Publisher, New York. 562 pp.

Haarer, A. E. 1962. *Modern Coffee Production*. Leonard Hill, London. 495 pp.

Haririah, K. 1992. *Aluminum tolerance of Mucuna, a tropical leguminous cover crop*. Univ. Groningen, Haren, The Netherlands. 152 pp.

Harris, D. R. 1972. *The origins of agriculture in the tropics*. American Scientist 60: 180-193.

Harwood, R. R. and D. L. Plucknett. 1981. "Vegetable cropping systems," In: Plucknett, D. L. and H. L. Beemer Jr. (eds.) *Vegetable Farming Systems in China*. Westview, Boulder, CO. 386 pp.

Hawkins, R., H. Sembiring, and D. L. Suwardjo. 1990. *The Potential of Alley*

Cropping in the Highlands of East and Central Java. Agency Agric. Res. and Develop. 71 pp.

Hiraoka, M. and S. Yamamoto. 1980. *Agricultural development in the Upper Amazon of Ecuador.* Geograph. Rev. 70: 423-445.

Hoitink, H. A. J. and P. C. Fahy. 1986. *Basis for the biological control of soilborne plant pathogens with composts.* Ann. Rev. Phytopathol. 24:93-114.

Holliday, P. 1989. *A Dictionary of Plant Pathology.* Cambridge Univ. Press, Cambridge. 369 pp.

_____. and W. P. Mowat. 1963. *Foot rot of Piper nigrum L. (Phytophthora palmivora).* Phytopathol. Paper No. 5. Commonwealth Mycol. Soc., Kew, England.

Holm, L., D. Plucknett, V. J. Pancho, and J. P. Herberger. 1977. *The World's Worst Weeds, Distribution and Biology.* Univ. Press Hawaii, Honolulu, Hawaii. 609 pp.

Holt-Gimenez, E. 1992. *Peasant to peasant.* ILEIA Newsletter 8:3-4.

_____. and R. Pasos C. 1994 "Farmer to farmer: The potential for technology generation and transfer for farmers in Rio San Juan, Nicaragua," pp. 75-84. In: Thurston, H. D., M. Smith, G. Abawi, S. Kearl (eds.) *Tapado. Slash/Mulch: How Farmers Use It, and What Researchers Know About It.* CIIFAD and CATIE, Cornell Univ., Ithaca, NY.

Huber, D. M. and R. D. Watson. 1970. *Effect of inorganic enrichment on soilborne plant pathogens.* Phytopathology 60:22-36.

Hudelson, J. E. 1987. *La Cultura Quichua de Transición: Su Expansión y Desarrollo en el Alto Amazonas.* Ediciones Abya-Yala, Quito, Ecuador. 221 pp.

Huxley, P. A. (ed.) 1983. *Plant Research and Agroforestry.* ICRAF, Nairobi. 617 pp.

IITA. 1991. "Mucuna. Farmers turn experimenters with a dual-purpose technology," pp. 36-37. In: IITA Annu. Rept. 1991. IITA, Ibadan, Nigeria. 64 pp.

_____. 1993. *IITA Annu. Rept. 1993.* IITA, Ibadan, Nigeria. 64 pp.

Isacsson, S. 1985. "Observations on Chocó Slash-Mulch Culture. Work diary and dietary of an Emberá domestic group in mid-eastern Chocó, Colombia," pp. 70-95. In: Carneiro, R. L., B. Cohen, R. A. Ibarra, Sven-Erik Isacsson, and C. E. Batt eds. *Anthropological Investigations in Amazonia.* Selec. Papers. Museum of Anthropol., Univ. N. Colorado, Greeley, CO. 115 pp.

Jimenez, S. E. 1978. *Comentarios sobre la produción de frijol comun (Phaseolus vulgaris L.) en Costa Rica.* Agron. Costarricense 2: 103-108.

Jordan, C. F. (ed.) 1989. *An Amazonian Rain Forest. The Structure and Function of a Nutrient Stressed Ecosystem and the Impact of Slash-and-Burn Agriculture.* Parthenon Pub. Group, Park Ridge, NJ. 176 pp.

Kang, B. T. 1993. *Alley cropping: past achievements and future directions.* Agroforestry Systems 23: 141-155.

174

_____. and B. Dugma 1985. "Nitrogen management in alley cropping systems.," pp. 269-283. In: Kang, B. T. and J. van der Heide (eds.) *Nitrogen management in farming systems in humid and subhumid tropics*. Inst. Soil Fertility and IITA. Haren, The Netherlands.

_____. H. Grimme, and T. L. Lawson. 1985. *Alley cropping sequentially cropped maize and cowpea with Leucaena on a sandy soil in southern Nigeria*. Plant and Soil 85: 267-277.

_____. and K. Mulongoy 1992. "Nitrogen contribution of woody legumes in alley cropping systems," pp. 367-375 In: Mulongoy, K., M. Gueye, and D. S. C. Spencer (eds.) 1992. *Biological Nitrogen Fixation and Sustainability of Tropical Agriculture*. Wiley, New York.

_____. and L. Reynolds. (eds.) 1989. *Alley Cropping in the Humid and Subhumid Tropics*. IDRC, Ibadan, Nigeria. 251 pp.

_____., L. Reynolds, and A. N. Attra-Krah 1990. *Alley farming*. Adv. Agron. 43: 315-359.

_____. G. T. Wilson, and L. Sipkens. 1981. *Alley cropping of maize (Zea mays L.) and Leucaena (Leucaena leucocephala Lam.) in southern Nigeria*. Plant Soil 63: 165-179.

_____. G. T. Wilson, and T. L. Lawson. 1984. *Alley cropping: a stable alternative to shifting cultivation*. IITA, Ibadan, Nigeria.

_____. and G. F. Wilson. 1987. "The development of alley cropping as a promising agroforestry technology," pp. 227-244. In: Steppler, H. A. and P. K. R. Nair. (eds.) *Agroforestry: A Decade of Development*. ICRAF, Nairobi, Kenya.

Karsten, R.. 1935. *The head-hunters of Western Amazonas; the life and culture of the Jibero Indians of eastern Ecuador and Peru*. Commentationes Humanarum Litterarum ; v. 7, no. 1., Helsingfors. 598 pp.

Kasasian, L. 1971. *Weed Control in the Tropics*. Leonard Hill, London. 307 pp.

Kass, D. L. 1994. "Erythrina species - Pantropical multipurpose tree legumes," pp. 84-95. In: Gutteridge, R. C. and H. M. Shelton (eds.) *Forage Tree Legumes in Tropical Agriculture*. CAB International, Wallingford, England. 389 pp.

_____ and J. F. Araza. 1987. "Alley cropping with Gliricidia sepium on farmer's fields in Costa Rica," In: *Gliricidia sepium (Jack) Walp. Management and improvement*. NFTA y CATIE, Turrialba, Costa Rica.

_____, I. Hernandez, and L. T. Szott. 1991. *Agroforestry as an alternative cropping system in developing countries and its implications for fertilizer use*. IFDC Training Program. CATIE, Turrialba, Costa Rica. 36 pp.

Karim, A. B., P. S. Savill, and E. R. Rhodes. 1993. *The effects of between-row (alley widths) and within-row spacings of Gliricidia sepium on alley-cropped maize in Sierra Leone*. Agroforestry Systems 24: 81-93.

Kelly, R. C. 1977. *Etoro Social Structure. A Study in Structural Contradiction*. Univ. Michigan Press, Ann Arbor. 329 pp.

Kelman, A. and R. J. Cook. 1977. *Plant pathology in the People's Republic of China*. Ann. Rev. Phytopathol. 15: 409-429.

Kemper, W. D., A. D. Nicks, and A. T. Corey 1994. *Accumulation of water in soils under gravel and sand mulches*. Soil Sci. Soc. Am. 58: 56-63.

Kloepper, J. W., R. Rodriguez-Kabana, J. A. McIntroy and D. J. Collins. 1991. *Analysis of populations of microorganisms in rhizospheres of plants with antagonistic properties to phytopathogenic nematodes*. Plant and Soil 136: 95-102.

Kramer, B. J. 1977. *Las implicaciones ecologicas de la agricultura de los Urarina*. Amazonia Peruana 1: 75-86.

Lal, R. 1975. *Role of mulching techniques in tropical soil and water management*. IITA Tech. Bull. No. 1. 38 pp.

_____. 1977 "Soil management systems and erosion control," pp. 93-97 In: Greenland, D. J. and R. Lal (eds.) *Soil Conservation and Management in the Humid Tropics*. Wiley, New York.

_____. 1981. "No-tillage farming in the tropics," pp. 103-151. In: Phillips, R. E., Thomas, G. W., Blevins, R. L. (eds.) *No-tillage Research: Research Reports and Reviews*. Univ. Kentucky, Lexington.

_____. 1982. "Effective conservation farming systems for the humid tropics.," pp. 57-76. In: El-Swaify, S. A., W. C. Moldenhauer and A. Lo. (eds.) *Soil Erosion and Conservation in the Tropics*. Am. Soc. Agron. Spec. Publ. 43. ASA and SSSA, Madison, WI.

_____. 1987. *Tropical Ecology and Physical Edaphology*. Wiley, New York. 732 pp.

_____. 1989. *Agroforestry systems and soil surface management of a tropical alfisol: I: Soil moisture and crop yields*. Agroforestry Systems 8:7-29.

_____. 1990. *Soil Erosion in the Tropics. Principles and Management*. Mcgraw-Hill, New York. 550 pp.

Larsen, K. J., K. G. Cassman, and D. A. Phillips. 1989. *Yield, dinitrogen fixation, and above ground nitrogen balance in irrigated white lupine in a Mediterranean climate*. Agronomy J. 81: 538-543.

Lasco, R. D. 1991. "MPTS in indigenous agroforestry systems: the Naalad case," pp. 19-23. In: D. A. Taylor and K. G. MacDicken (eds.) *Research on Multipurpose Tree Species in Asia*. Winrock Int. Inst. Agric. Develop., Morrilton, AR.

Lathwell, D. J. 1990. *Legume Green Manures. Principles for Management Based on Recent Research*. Tropsoils Bull. 90-01. North Carolina State Univ., Raleigh, NC. 30 pp.

Lenné, J. M. 1990. *A World List of Fungal Diseases of Tropical Pasture Species*. CAB Int. and CIAT, Wallingford, Oxon, UK. 162 pp.

_____. 1991. Diseases of Leucaena species. Trop. Pest Management 37: 281-289.

León, J. 1987. *Botanica de los Cultivos Tropicales*. IICA, San José, Cost Rica. 445 pp.

176

Lewis, J. A. and G. C. Papavizas. 1975. "Survival and multiplication of soil-borne plant pathogens as affected by plant tissue amendments," pp. 84-89. In: G. W. Bruehl (ed.) *Biology and Control of Soil-borne Plant Pathogens*. Am. Phytopathol. Soc., St. Paul, MN. 216 pp.

Linderman, R. G., and R. G. Gilbert. 1975. "Influence of volatiles of plant origin on soil-borne pathogens," pp. 90-99. In: G. W. Bruehl (ed.) *Biology and control of soil-borne plant pathogens*. Am. Phytopathol. Soc., St. Paul, MN. 216 pp.

Little, E. L. and F. H. Wadsworth. 1964. *Common Trees of Puerto Rico and the Virgin Islands*. USDA Forest Service. Agric. Handbook, No. 249. Washington, DC. 548 pp.

Lorenz, C. and A. Errington. 1991. *Achieving sustainability in cropping systems: the labour requirements of a mulch rotation system in Kalimantan, Indonesia*. Trop. Agric. (Trinidad) 68: 249-254.

Lotero Villa, L 1977. *Monografía de la Indigenista Noamama*. Univ. de Los Andes, Bogotá, Colombia

Ludwig, H. D. 1968. "Permanent farming on Ukara," pp. 87-135. In: Ruthenberg, H. (ed.) 1968. *Smallholder Farming and Smallholder Development in Tanzania: Ten Case Studies*. Weltforum Verlag, Munich.

Maass, A. 1902. *Bei Liebens Würdigen Wilden. Ein Beitrag zur Kenntnis der Mentawei-Insulaner*. Wilhem Süsserott, Berlin. 256 pp.

MacDicken, K. G. and N. T. Vergara (eds.). 1990. *Agroforestry Classification and Management*. Wiley, New York. 382 pp.

Marban-Mendoza, N., M. B. Dicklow, and B. M. Zuckerman. 1989. *Evaluation of Meloidogyne incognita and Nacobbus aberrans on tomato by two leguminous plants*. Revue Nematol. 12(4): 409-4112.

_____. 1992. *Control of Meloidogyne incognita on tomato by two leguminous plants*. Fundam. Appl. Nematology 15: 97-100.

Martin, J. H. 1975. *Principles of Field Crop Production*. Macmillan, New York. 1118 pp.

Massing, A. 1980. *The Economic Anthropology of the Kru (West Africa)*. Franz Steiner Verlag, Wiesbaden, Germany. 281 pp.

McCalla, T. M. and D. L. Plucknett. 1981. "Collecting, transporting, and processing organic fertilizers," In: Plucknett, D. L. and H. L. Beemer, Jr. (eds.) *Vegetable Farming Systems in China*. Westview Press, Boulder, CO.

Melara, W. and L. del. Río. 1994. "The use of minimum tillage and leguminous cover crops in Honduras," pp. 53-59. In: Thurston, H. D., M. Smith, G. Abawi, and S. Kearl (eds.) Tapado. *Slash/Mulch: How Farmers Use It, and What Researchers Know About It*. CIIFAD and CATIE, Cornell Univ., Ithaca, NY.

Mercado, J., F. Calderon, and H. Sosa. 1994. "Systems for sowing with mulches: Conservation tillage without burning, an alternative for sustainable

177

agriculture," pp. 43-52. In: Thurston, H. D., M. Smith, G. Abawi, and S. Kearl (eds.) *Tapado. Slash/Mulch: How Farmers Use It, and What Researchers Know About It*. CIIFAD and CATIE, Cornell Univ., Ithaca, NY.

Merwin, I. A., W. F. Wilcox and W. C. Stiles. 1992. *Influence of orchard ground management on the development of Phytophthora crown and root rots of apple*. Plant Disease 76: 199-205

Mestanza, I. and C. Alberto. 1994. "A traditional slash/mulch system for beans in Peru," pp. 85-87 In: Thurston, H. D., M. Smith, G. Abawi, and S. Kearl (eds.) *Tapado. Slash/Mulch: How Farmers Use It, and What Researchers Know About It*. CIIFAD and CATIE, Cornell Univ., Ithaca, NY.

Metzner, J. K. 1982. *Agriculture and population pressure in Sikka, Isle of Flores: a contribution to the study of the stability of agricultural systems in the wet and dry tropics*. Australian Nat. Univ., Canberra, Australia. 355 pp.

Monegat, C. 1991 *Plantas de Cobertura do Solo. Caracteristicas e Manejo em Pequenas Propiedades*. Chapecó, Santa Catarina, Brazil. 337 pp.

Moody, K. 1975. *Weeds and shifting cultivation*. Pest Articles and News Sum. (PANS) 21: 188-194.

Moreno, R. A. and L. E. Mora. 1984. *Cropping pattern and soil management influence on plant diseases. II. Bean rust epidemiology*. Turrialba 34: 41-45.

_____ and J. F. Sánchez. 1994. "The effect of using mulches with intercropping," pp. 191-205. In: Thurston, H. D., M. Smith, G. Abawi, and S. Kearl (eds.) *Tapado. Slash/Mulch: How Farmers Use It, and What Researchers Know About It*. CIIFAD and CATIE, Cornell Univ., Ithaca, NY.

Morren, G. and D. Hyndman. 1987. *The Taro Monoculture of Central New Guinea*. Human Ecology. 15: 301 - 315.

Muimba-Kankolongo, A., L. Simba, T. P. Singh, G. Muyolo. 1989. *Outbreak of an unusual stem tip dieback of cassava (Manihot esculenta Crantz) in western Zaire*. Agric. Ecosystems and Environment 25: 151-164.

Muller, R. and P. S. Gooch. 1982. *Organic amendments in nematode control: an examination of the literature*. Nematropica 12: 319-326.

Mullin, B. A., G. S. Abawi, M. A. Pastor-Corrales, and J. L. Kornegay. 1991. *Root-knot nematodes associated with beans in Colombia and Peru*. Plant Disease 75:1208-1211.

Mulongoy, K. and N. Sanginga. 1990. *Nitrogen contribution by Leucaena in alley cropping*. IITA Res. 1(1): 14-17.

_____. and I. O. Akobundu. 1992. *Agronomic and economic benefits of N contributed by legumes in live-mulch and alley cropping systems*. IITA Res. 4: 12-16

Myers, N. 1988. *News and Comment: Tropical forests: shifting cultivators in the Philippines*. Plants Today. January-February.

Nair, P. K. R. 1984. *Soil Productivity Aspects of Agroforestry*. Intl. Council Res. Agroforestry, Nairobi, Kenya. 85 pp.

_____. (ed.) 1989. *Agroforestry Systems in the Tropics*. Kluwer Academic and

178

ICRAF, Dordrecht, Netherlands. 664 pp.

Napompeth, B. and K. G. MacDicken (eds) 1990. *Leucaena Psyllid: Problems and Management*. Winrock Int. Inst. Agric. Develop., Morrilton, Ark. 208 pp.

National Academy of Sciences. 1977. *Leucaena. Promising Forage and Tree Crop for the Tropics*. Nat. Acad. Press, Washington, D.C. 115 pp.

_____. 1979. *Tropical Legumes: Resources for the Future*. Nat. Acad. Sci., Washington, D. C. 331 pp.

National Research Council. 1982. "Agriculture in the humid tropics," pp. 93-120. In: *Ecological Aspects of Development: Humid Tropics*. Nat. Acad. Press, Washington, DC.

_____. 1989. *Lost Crops of the Incas: Little Known Plants of the Andes with Promise for Worldwide Cultivation*. Nat. Acad. Press, Washington, D. C. 427 pp.

Nelson, E. B. and C. M. Craft. 1992. *Suppression of dollar spot on creeping bentgrass and annual bluegrass turf with compost-amended topdressing*. Plant Disease 76: 954-958.

Neugebauer, B. and R. Bunch. 1991. "Sustainable agriculture on Central American hillsides: Opportunities for interinstitutional collaboration," pp. 23-25. In: *Sustainable Agriculture on the Hillsides of Central America. Opportunities for Interinstitutional Collaboration*. CIAT, Cali, Colombia. 43 pp.

Nill, D. and E. Nill. 1993. "The efficient use of mulch layers to reduce runoff," pp. 367-375 In: Mulongoy, K. and R. Merckx. (eds.). *Soil organic matter dynamics and sustainability of tropical agriculture*. Wiley, New York.

Nusbaum, C. J. and H. Ferris. 1973. *The role of cropping systems in nematode population management*. Ann. Rev. Phytopathol. 11: 423-440.

Nye, P. H. and D. J. Greenland. 1960. *The Soil Under Shifting Cultivation*. Tech. Commun. 51. Commonw. Bur. Soils, Harpenden, England. 156 pp.

Nyerges, A. E. 1989. *Coppice swidden fallows in tropical deciduous forest: biological, technological , and sociocultural determinants of secondary forest successions*. Human Ecol. 17: 379-400.

Oka, I. N. 1990. 'Progress and future activities of the Leucaena psyllid research program in Indonesia," pp. 25-27 In: Napompeth, B. and K. G. MacDicken. (eds) 1990 *Leucaena Psyllid: Problems and Management*. Winrock Int. Inst. Agric. Develop., Morrilton, Ark.

Okigbo, B. N. and R. Lal. 1982. "Residue mulches, intercropping and agrisilviculture potential in tropical Africa," pp. 54-69. In: Hill, S. (ed.) *Basic Techniques in Ecological Farming*. Birkhäuser Verlag, Basel, Switzerland.

Ong, C. 1994. *Alley cropping -- ecological pie in the sky?* Agroforestry Today 6: 8-10.

Orozco-Segovia, A. D. L. and S. R. Gliessman. 1979. *The Marceño in flood-prone regions of Tabasco, Mexico*. Paper presented in Symposium on Mexican Agroecosystems, 43rd Int. Congr. of Americanists, Vancouver, Canada. 15 pp.

179

Osei-Bonsu, P., D. Buckles, F. R. Sosa, and J. Y. Asibuo. 1995. *Traditional uses of Mucuna puriens and Canavalia ensiformis in Ghana.* CIMMYT Internal Document. CIMMYT, Mexico, D. F.. 5 pp.

Pachico, D., and E. Borbon. 1987. *Technical change in traditional small farm agriculture: the case of beans in Costa Rica.* Agric. Admin. and Extension 26: 65-74.

Paganini, L. A. 1970. *The agricultural systems of the Chucuna/Tuira Basin in the Darien Province, Panama.* Ph.D Thesis. Univ. of Florida, Gainesville, FL. 244 pp.

Palti, J. 1981. *Cultural Practices and Infectious Crop Diseases.* Springer-Verlag,Berlin. 243 pp.

Patiño, V. M. 1956. *El maiz chococito. Noticia sobre su cultivo en America Ecuatorial.* America Indigena 16: 309-346.

_____ 1962. *El maiz chococito: Notas sobre su cultivo en America ecuatorial.* Rev. Interamericana de Ciencias Sociales 1(3): 358-388.

_____. 1965. *Historia de la Actividad Agropecuaria en America Equinoccia.* 1a Edición. Imprenta Departmental, Cali, Colombia. 601 pp.

Patrick, Z. A., T. A. Toussoun, and L. W. Koch. 1964. *Effect of crop-residue decomposition products on plant roots.* Ann. Rev. Phytopathol. 2:267-292.

Peck, R. B. 1990. "Promoting agroforestry practices among small producers: the case of the coca agroforestry project in Amazonian Ecuador," pp. 167-180. In: Anderson, A. B. (ed.) *Alternatives to Deforestation: Steps Toward Sustainable Use of the Amazon Rain Forest.* Colombia Univ. Press, New York.

Pereira, H. C. and P. A. Jones. 1954. *Field responses by Kenya coffee to fertilizers, manures, and mulches.* Empire J. Exp. Agric. 22:23-36.

Persoon, G.A. and F. Wiersum. 1991. "Anthropology in a forest environment," pp. 85-104. In: P. Kloos and H. J. M. Claessen (eds.) *Contemporary Anthropology in the Netherlands. The Use of Anthropological Ideas.* Vrije Univ. Press, Amsterdam.

Petch, B. and J. Mt. Pleasant. 1991. *Agronomic limitations of alley cropping: a review.* Dept. of Soil, Crop and Atmospheric Sci., Cornell Univ., Ithaca, NY. 28 pp.

Peters, W. J. and L. F. Neuenschwander. 1988. *Slash and Burn: Farming in the Third World Forest.* Univ. Idaho Press, Moscow, Idaho. 113 pp.

Phillips, R.E., R. L. Blevins, G. W. Thomas, W. W. Frye, S. H. Phillips. 1980. *No-tillage agriculture.* Science. 208:1108-1113.

Pieters, A. J. 1927. *Green manuring.* Principles and Practice. Wiley, New York. 356 pp.

Piggin, C. M. and V. Parera. 1985. "The use of Leucaena in Nusa Tenggara Timur," pp. 19-27. In: Caswell, E. T. and B. Tangendjaja (eds.) *Shrub Legume Research in Indonesia and Australia.* ACIAR., Canberra, Australia.

Posey, D. A. 1985. *Indigenous management of tropical forest ecosystems: the case of the Kayapó Indians of the Brazilian Amazon.* Agroforestry Systems

3: 139-159.

Powell, M. H. 1992. *Agroforestry project in Ecuador has multiplier effect*. NFTA News 14: 1-2.

Pruthi, J. S. 1993 *Major Spices of India: Crop Management and Post-harvest Technology*. Publ. Infor. Div., Indian Council Agric. Res., New Delhi, India. 514 pp.

Purseglove, J. W. 1968. *Tropical crops: Dicotyledons*. Wiley, NY. 719 pp.

———. 1972. *Tropical Crops, Monocotyledons*. Wiley, NY. 607 pp.

Ramamoorthy, M. and K. Paliwal. 1993. *Allelopathic compounds in leaves of Gliricidia sepium (Jacq.) Kunth ex. Walp. and its effect on Sorghum vulgare L.* J. Chem. Ecol. 19: 1691-1701.

Ramírez, C., G. Sanchez, D. Kass, E. Viquez, J. Sanchez, N. Vasquez, and G. Ramirez. 1990. "Advances in Erythrina research at CATIE.," pp. 96-105 In: Werner, D. and P. Müller. (eds) *Fast Growing Trees and Nitrogen Fixing Trees*. Gustav Fischer Verlag, Stuttgart.

Rava, C. A 1991. *Producción artesanal de semilla mejorado de frijol*. Proyecto FAO-TCP/NIC/8956(E) Agosto de 1991, Managua, Nicaragua.

Raver, A. 1991. *Now, for politically correct tomatoes: all hail the hairy vetch*. New York Times. December 8, 1991. p. 85.

Reed, C. A. (ed.) 1977. *Origins of Agriculture*. Mouton, The Hague. 1013 pp.

Reynolds, P. K. 1921. *The Story of the Banana*. United Fruit Co., Boston. 53 pp.

———. 1927. *The Banana*. Houghton Mifflin, Boston. 181 pp.

Ridley, H. N. 1912. *Spices*. Macmillan, London. 449 pp.

Rippin, M., J. P. Haggar, D. Kass and U. Köpke. 1994. *Alley cropping and mulching with Erythrina poeppigiana (Walp.) O. F. Cook and Gliricidia sepium (Jacq.) Walp.: effects on maize weed competition*. Agroforestry Systems 25: 119-134.

Rizzo Boesch, R., L. del Rio, A. Rueda, and A. Pitty. 1994. "The effect of two diets based on leguminous cover crops on weight gain and reproductive capacity of the slug Sarasinula plebeia Fischer," pp. 109-114. In: Thurston, H. D., M. Smith, G. Abawi, and S. Kearl (eds.) *Tapado. Slash/Mulch: How Farmers Use It, and What Researchers Know About It*. CIIFAD and CATIE, Cornell Univ., Ithaca, NY.

Roberts, L. M., U. J. Grant, R. Ramirez E., W. H. Hathaway y D. L. Smith. 1957. *Razas de Maiz en Colombia*. Ministerio de Agric. de Colombia. Oficina de Investigaciones Especiales, Bogota. Bol. Tecnico No. 2. 159 pp.

Rockefeller Foundation 1994. *The Rockefeller Foundation 1993 Annual Report*. Rockefeller Foundation, New York, NY. 139 pp.

Rockwood, W. G. and R. Lal. 1974. *Mulch-tillage: a technique for soil and water conservation in the tropics*. SPAN 17: 77-79.

Rodale Institute. 1992. *Legume Seed Source Directory*. Kutztown, PA. Rodale Inst. 23 pp.

Rodriguez-Kabana, R., G. Morgan-Jones and I. Chet. 1987. *Biological control of nematodes: soil amendments and microbial antagonists*. Plant and Soil 100: 237-247.

_____., R., J. W. Kloepper, D. G. Robertson, and L. W. 1992a. *Velvetbean for the management of root-knot and southern blight in peanut*. Nematropica. 22: 75-80.

_____, J. Pinochet, D. G. Robertson, and L. Wells. 1992b. *Crop rotation studies with velvetbean (Mucuna deeringiana) for the management of Meloidogyne spp*. J. Nematology 24(4S): 662-668.

Rosado-May, F. J., and R. Garcia Espinosa. 1986. *Estrategias empiricas para el control de la mustia hilachoza (Thanatephorus cucumeris Frank Donk) de frijol comun en la Chontalpa, Tabasco*. Rev. Mex. Fitopatologia 4: 109-113.

Rosado-May F., J., S. R. Gliessman, and M. Alejos Pedraza. 1986. *Potencial alelopatico del cadillo (Bidens pilosa L.) y su relacion con el ataque de algunas fitopatogenos del suelo al maiz*. Rev. Mexicana Fitopatología. 4: 124-132.

Rosemeyer, M. E. 1994. "Comparison of yields and formation of mycorrhiza and nodules of beans grown under the "frijol tapado" and "espequeado" systems with fertilizer," pp. 169-178. In: Thurston, H. D., M. Smith, G. Abawi, and S. Kearl (eds.) *Tapado. Slash/Mulch: How Farmers Use It, and What Researchers Know About It*. CIIFAD and CATIE, Cornell Univ., Ithaca, NY.

_____, R. Araya, and D. Cole. 1989. "Comparación de la produción de semillas, nodulación y mycorrizas en frijol tapado modificado y espequeado bajo varias dosis de fertilizantes en San Vito de Java, Coto Brus, Costa Rica," pp 27-33. In: Bolaños Arquin, M. and I. Bolaños Arquin. (eds.) *Memoria del I Simposio Nacional Sobre Tecnologia Apropiada y Agricultura Biologica para un Desarrollo Rural Alternativo*. COPROALDE, Univ. of Costa Rica, San José.

Rowe-Dutton, P. 1957. *The Mulching of Vegetables*. Commonw. Agric. Bur.,Farnham Royal, England. 169 pp.

Ruddell, E. D. 1995. *Empowering small peasant farmers to improve their food security through the use of green manures*. World Neighbors, Santiago, Chile. 11 pp.

_____. and J. Beingolea. 1995. *Towards farmer scientists*. ILEIA Newsletter. 11(1): 16-17.

Russell, E. W. 1973. *Soil Conditions and Plant Growth*. 10th ed. Longmans, London. 849 pp.

Russo, R. O., and G. Budowski. 1986. *Effect of pollarding frequency on biomass of Erythrina poeppigiana as a coffee shade tree*. Agroforestry Systems 4: 145-162.

Sain, G., I. Ponce, and E. Borbon. 1994. "Profitability of the abonera system practiced by farmers on the Atlantic Coast of Honduras," pp. 273-282. In: Thurston, H. D., M. Smith, G. Abawi, S. Kearl. (eds.) *Tapado. Slash/Mulch: How Farmers Use It, and What Researchers Know About It*. CIIFAD and

CATIE, Cornell Univ., Ithaca, NY.

Sanchez, P. A. 1976. *Properties and Management of Soils in the Tropics*. Wiley, New York. 618 pp.

_____. 1987. "Soil productivity and sustainability in agroforestry systems," pp. 206-223. In: Steppler, H. A. and P. K. R. Nair. (eds.) *Agroforestry: A Decade of Development*. ICRAF, Nairobi, Kenya.

_____ and J. R. Benites. 1987. *Low-input cropping for acid soils of the humid tropics*. Science. 238: 1521-1527.

Sarrantonio, M. 1991. *Soil-improving Legumes*. Rodale Institute, Kutztown, PA. 310 pp.

Schelhas Jr., J. W. 1991. *Socio-economic and Biological Aspects of Land Use Adjacent to Braulio Carrillo National Park, Costa Rica*. Ph.D. Thesis, Univ. Arizona. Tuscon, AZ.

Schiefflin, E. L. (1975). *Felling the trees on top of the crop; European contact and the subsistence ecology of the Great Papuan Plateau*. Oceania 46: 25-39.

Schlather, K.. 1996. Ph.D. Thesis, Cornell Univ., Ithaca, NY. (In Press)

Schwartz, H. F. and G. E. Galvez. 1980. *Bean Production Problems: Disease, Insect, Soil, and Climatic Constraints of Phaseolus vulgaris*. CIAT, Cali, Colombia. 424 pp.

_____. and M. A. Pastor-Corrales. 1989. *Bean Production Problems in the Tropics*. CIAT, Cali, Colombia. 654 pp.

Sequeira, L. 1962. *Influence of organic amendments on survival of Fusarium f. cubense in the soil*. Phytopathology 52: 976-982.

Sharp, W. F. 1976. *Slavery on the Spanish frontier: the Colombian Chocó, 1680-1810*. Univ. of Oklahoma Press, Norman, OK. 253 pp.

Shea, S. R. and P. Broadbent. 1983. "Developments in cultural and biological control of Phytophthora diseases," pp. 335-350. In: Erwin, D. C., S. Bartnicki-Garcia and P. Tsao. (eds.) *Phytophthora. Its Biology, Taxonomy, Ecology and Pathology*. Am. Phytopathol. Soc., St. Paul, MN.

Shenk, M. 1994. "Possible modifications of planting and mulch management schemes for frijol tapado," pp. 129-132. In: Thurston, H. D., M. Smith, G. Abawi, and S. Kearl (eds.) *Tapado. Slash/Mulch: How Farmers Use It, and What Researchers Know About It*. CIIFAD and CATIE, Cornell Univ., Ithaca, NY.

Simmonds, N. W. 1966. *Bananas*. Longman, London. 512 pp.

Skerman, P. J., D. G. Cameron, and F. Riveros. 1988. *Tropical Forage Legumes*. FAO, Rome. 692 pp.

Skutch, A. 1950. *Problems in milpa agriculture*. Turrialba 1: 4-6.

Smith, M. E. 1994. "Crop variety improvement for slash/mulch production systems," pp. 239-247. In: Thurston, H. D., M. Smith, G. Abawi, and S. Kearl (eds.) *Tapado. Slash/Mulch: How Farmers Use It, and What Researchers Know About It*. CIIFAD and CATIE, Cornell Univ., Ithaca, NY.

183

Snedaker, C. C., and J. F. Gamble. 1969. *Compositional analysis of selected second-growth species from lowland Guatemala and Panama*. BioScience 19: 536-538.

Soil Science Society of America. 1987. *Glossary of Soil Science Terms*. Soil Sci. Soc. America, Madison, WI. 44 pp.

Solomon, T. 1993. *El Chinapopo. Compañero de Maiz*. COMUNICA-CIDICCO. Tegucigalpa, Honduras. 36 pp.

_____. and M. Flores. 1994. *Intercropping corn and frijol chinapopo (Phaseolus coccineus)*. CIDICCO, Tegucigalpa, Honduras. 44 pp.

Spencer, J. E. 1966. *Shifting Cultivation in Southeast Asia*. Univ. Calif. Press, Berkeley. 247 pp.

Ssekabembe, C. K. 1985. *Perspectives on hedgerow intercropping*. Agroforestry Systems 3: 339-356.

Stauder, J. 1971. *The Majangir. Ecology and Society of a Southwest Ethiopian People*. Cambridge Univ. Press, Cambridge, UK. 200 pp.

Steppler, H. A. and P. K. R. Nair. (eds.) 1987. *Agroforestry: A Decade of Development*. ICRAF, Nairobi, Kenya.

Stevens, G. A. and C. S. Tang. 1987. *Inhibition of crop seedling growth by hydrophobic crop exudates of the weed Bidens pilosa*. J. Trop. Ecol. 3: 91-94.

Stevens, G. A. and C. S. Tang. 1991. *Inhibition of seedling growth of crop species by recirculating root exudates of Bidens pilosa L.* J. Chem. Ecol. 11: 1411-1425.

Stigter, C. J. 1984. *Examples of mulch use in microclimate management by traditional farmers in Tanzania*. Agric. Ecosystems Environ. 11: 173-176.

Stout, R. 1970. *Gardening Without Work for the Aging, the Busy and the Indolent*. Devin-Adair, Old Greenwich, CO. 214 pp.

Subler, S. and C. Uhl. 1990. "Japanese agroforestry in Amazonia: a case study in Tomé-Açu, Brazil," pp. 152-166. In: Anderson, A. B. (ed.) *Alternatives to Deforestation: Steps Toward Sustainable Use of the Amazon Rain Forest*. Colombia Univ. Press, New York. 281 pp.

Sumberg, J. E. 1984. *Alley farming in the humid zone: linking crop and livestock production*. ILCA Bull. 18: 2-6.

_____. 1986. *Gliricidia sepium (Jacq.) Steud. A Selected Bibliography*. Int. Livestock Centre for Africa, Addis Ababa, Ethiopia. 12 pp.

Sumner, D. R., B. Doupnik and M. G. Boosalis. 1981. *Effects of reduced tillage and multiple cropping on plant diseases*. Ann. Rev. Phytopathol. 19:167-187.

Sutcliffe, J. P. 1992. *Peoples and Natural Resources in the North and South Omo and Kefa Administrative Regions of Southwestern Ethiopia*. Nat. Conservation Strategy Secretariat, Ministry of Planning and Economic Development, Addis Ababa, Ethiopia. 91 pp.

Szott, L. T. and D. C. L. Kass. 1993. *Fertilizers in agroforestry systems*. Agroforestry Systems 23: 157-176.

Tapia Barquero, H. 1987. *Manejo de malas hierbas en plantaciones de frijol in*

184

Nicaragua. Inst. Superior de Ciencias Agropecuarias, Managua, Nicaragua.

_____. and A. Camacho Henriquez. 1988. *Manejo Integrado de la Produción de Frijol Basado en Labranza Cero*. Deutsche Gesellschaft für Technische Zusammenarbeit (GTZ), Eschborn, Germany. 181 pp.

Tapica, A. 1971. *Determinación de la susceptibilidad de especies de leguminosas forrajeras al ataque de nematodes del genera Meloidogyne*. Planta 159: 105-111.

Taylor, D. 1988. *Agricultural practices in Eastern Maputaland*. Develop. Southern Africa. 5: 465-481.

Teketay, D. 1990. *Erythrina burana. Promising multipurpose tree from Ethiopia*. Agroforestry Today 2(4): 13.

Thomsen, M. 1969. *Living Poor. A Peace Corps Chronicle*. Univ. Washington Press, Seattle, WA. 314 pp.

_____. 1978. *The Farm on the River of Emeralds*. Houghton Mifflin, Boston. 329 pp.

Thurston, H. D. 1984. *Tropical Plant Diseases*. Am. Phytopathol. Soc., St. Paul, MN. 208 pp.

_____. 1992. *Sustainable Practices for Plant Disease Management in Traditional Farming Systems*. Westview, Boulder, CO. 279 pp.

_____. M. Smith, G. Abawi, and S. Kearl (eds.) 1994 *Tapado. Slash/Mulch: How Farmers Use It, and What Researchers Know About It*. CIIFAD and CATIE, Cornell Univ., Ithaca, NY. 332 pp.

Timothy, D. H., W. H. Hathaway, U. J. Grant, M. Torregroza C., D. Sarria V. and D. Varela A. 1963. *Races of Maize in Ecuador*. Publ. 975. Nat. Acad. Sci., Washington, DC. 147 pp.

Todaro, M. P. 1977. *Economic Development in the Third World*. Longman, London. 588 pp.

Torres de Arauz, R. 1966. *Estudios etnologico y historico de la cultura Chocó*. Univ. Panama, Panama. 207 pp.

Triomphe, Bernard. 1996. *Seasonal nitrogen dynamics and long-term changes in soil properties under the mucuna/maize cropping system on the hillsides of Northern Honduras*. Ph.D. Thesis, Cornell Univ., Ithaca, NY. 272 p.

U.S.D.A. 1960. *Index of Plant Diseases in the United States*. Agric. Handbook No. 165. U.S.D.A., Washington, D. C. 531 pp.

Valencia-C., E. 1983. *Colonización en el Uraba chocoano*. Univ. Nac. Colombia, Bogotá. 97 pp.

Van Den Beldt, R. J. and B. Napompeth. 1992. *Leucaena psyllid comes to Africa. Time to learn some lessons*. Agroforestry Today 4(4): 11-12.

Van der Heide, J. and K. Hairiah. 1989. *The role of green manures in rainfed farming systems in the humid tropics*. ILEIA Newsletter. 5(2):11-13.

Van Eijk-Bos, C. and L. Moreno. 1986. *Barreras vivas de Gliricidia sepium (Jacq.) Steud. (mata raton) y su efecto sobre la perdida de suelo en terrenos de colinas bajas-Uraba (Colombia)*. Conif-Informa. Bogotá, Colombia.

Van Schoonhoven, A. and O. Voysest. 1989. "Common beans in Latin America and their constraints," pp. 33-57. In: Schwartz, H. F. and M. A. Pastor-Corrales. (eds.) *Bean Production Problems in the Tropics*. CIAT, Cali, Colombia. 654 pp.

Varro, Marcus Terentius. 1934. *On Agriculture*. W. D. Hooper and H. B. Ash (trans.) Harvard Univ. Press, Cambridge. pp. 161-543.

Vicente N., E. and N. Acosta. 1987. *Effects of Mucuna deeringiana on Meloidogyne incognita*. Nematropica 17: 99-102.

Vickers, W. T. 1978. "Native Amazonian subsistence in diverse habitats: The Siona-Secoya of Ecuador," pp. 6-36. In: Moran, E. R. (ed.) *Studies in Third World Societies*. Publ. No. 7. Dept. Anthropol., College of William and Mary, Williamsburg, VA.

_____. 1989. *Los Sionas y Secoyas. Su adaptación al ambiente amazónico*. Ediciones Abya-Yala, Quito, Ecuador. 374 pp.

Vine, H. 1953. *Experiments on the maintenance of soil fertility at Ibadan, Nigeria, 1922-51*. Empire J. Exp. Agric. 21: 65-85.

Von Platen, H., P. Rodriguez, and J. Lagemann. 1982. *Farming systems in Acosta-Puriscal, Costa Rica*. CATIE, Turrialba, Costa Rica. 146 pp.

_____. 1985. *Appropriate Land Use Systems of Smallholder Farms on Steep Slopes in Costa Rica. A Study on Situation and Development Possibilities*. Wissenschaftsverlag Vauk, Kiel, Germany. 187 pp.

Waddill, V. H., E. R. Mitchell, W. H. Denton, S. L. Poe and D. J. Schuster 1982. *Seasonal abundance of the fall armyworm and velvetbean caterpillar (Lepidoptera: Noctuidae) at four locations in Florida (Spodoptera frugiperda, Anticarsia gemmatalis)*. Florida Entomol. Soc. 65(3): 350-354.

Wardlaw, C. W. 1929. *Virgin soil deterioration*. Trop. Agric. (Trinidad) 6: 243-249.

_____. 1961. *Banana Diseases Including Plantains and Abaca*. Longman, London. 648 pp.

Watson, J. R. 1916. *Control of the velvet bean caterpillar*. Univ. Florida. Agr. Exp. Sta. Bull. No. 130. pp. 45-58.

_____. 1922. *Bunch velvet beans to control root-knot*. Univ. Florida. Agr. Exp. Sta. Bull. No. 163. pp. 55-59.

Weatherwax, P. 1954. *Indian Corn in Old America*. MacMillan, New York. 253 pp.

Weber, G. F. 1939. *Web-blight, a disease of beans caused by Corticum microsclerotia*. Phytopathology 29: 559-575.

Weeraratna, S. 1990. *External inputs for sustainable agriculture*. ILEIA Newsletter 6 (3): 20-21.

Weightman, B. 1989. *Agriculture in Vanuatu. A Historical Review*. British Friends of Vanuatu, Great Britain. 320 pp.

Wellman, F. L. 1961. *Coffee: Botany, Cultivation and Utilization*. Interscience, New York. 482 pp.

_____. 1972. *Tropical American Plant Diseases.* Scarecrow Press, Metuchen, N. J. 989 pp.

West, R. C. 1957. *The Pacific Lowland of Colombia: a Negroid Area of the American Tropics.* Louisiana State Univ. Studies. Social Sci. Ser. No. 8, La. State Univ. Press, Baton Rouge. 278 pp.

Whalen, J. 1990. *Adapting a traditional agroecosystem to current needs.* The Cultivar 8(1): 3-4 and 15.

Whitten Jr., N. E. 1974. *Black Frontiersmen. A South American Case.* Schenkman, New York. 221 pp.

_____. 1976. *Sacha Runa. Ethnicity and Adaptation of Ecuadorian Jungle Quichua.* Univ. Illinois Press, Urbana, IL. 348 pp.

Wilk, R. R. 1985. "Dry season agriculture among the Kekchi Maya and its implications for prehistory," pp. 47-57. In: Pohl, M. (ed.) *Prehistoric Lowland Maya Environment and Subsistence Economy.* Harvard Univ. Press, Cambridge, MA.

_____. 1991. *Household ecology: economic change and domestic life among the Kekchi Maya in Belize.* Univ. Arizona Press, Tucson, AZ. 280 pp.

Wilken, G. C. 1987. *Good Farmers. Traditional Agricultural Resource Management in Mexico and Central America.* Univ. Calif. Press, Berkeley, CA. 302 pp.

Williams, P. H. 1979. *Vegetable crop production in the People's Republic of China.* Annu. Rev. Phytopathol. 17: 311-324.

Wilmont-Dear, C. M. 1987 *A revision of Mucuna (Leguminosae - Phaseolaea) in the Indian subcontinent and Burma.* Kew Bulletin 42: 23-46.

Wilson, G. F. and K. L. Akapa. 1983. "Providing mulches for no-tillage in the tropics," pp. 51-65. In: Akobundu, I. O. and A. E. Deutsch. (eds.) *No-tillage Crop Production in the Tropics.* Symp. Monrovia, Liberia, August 1981. IPPC, Oregon State Univ., Corvallis, OR.

_____., B. T. Kang, and K. Mulongoy. 1986. *Alley cropping: Trees as sources of green-manure and mulch in the tropics.* Biol. Agric. Hortic. 3: 251-267.

Wolf, E. C. 1986. *Beyond The Green Revolution: New Approaches for Third World Agriculture.* Worldwatch Institute, Washington, DC. 46 pp.

Wood, D. and J. Lenné. 1993. "Dynamic management of domesticated biodiversity by farming communities," pp. 94-98. In: O.T. Sandlund and P.J. Schei. (eds.) *Norway/UNEP Expert Conference on Biodiversity.* Royal Garden Hotel, Trondheim, Norway. Norwegian Ministry of Environment and UNEP.

Yost, R. S., D. O. Evans, and N. A. Saidy. 1985. *Tropical legumes for N production: growth and N content in relation to soil pH.* Trop. Agric. (Trinidad) 62: 20-24.

Young, P. D. (ed.) 1991. *Fragile lands management in Latin America and the Caribbean: A synthesis.* DESFIL Tech. Rept.. Develop. Alternatives, Inc. , Bethesda, MD.

General Index

bean, common,
    crop, 15, 16, 27, 38-39, 42-61, 63,
      72, 94, 99-101, 103, 125, 137,
      145, 148
    diseases, 49, 55-58, 149-159
    seed, 45, 51, 58-59
    slugs, 27, 60, 122-123
    tapado (slash mulch), 16, 17, 44-
      61, 74-78, 100, 148
beer, 34, 63
beggar's tick (*Bidens pilosa*), 47, 77
Belem, Brazil, 22
Belize, 43
Belonolaimus gracilis, 124
Benin, 78, 120-121
Bidens pilosa (beggar's tick), 47, 77
biological control, 12, 95, 135, 149,
    155-156
birds, 26, 34, 43, 64, 95, 124, 160
black pepper, 89-90, 92, 134, 136
black polyethylene mulch, 61-72
blister beetles, 124
Bogor, Indonesia, 14, 90, 135
Bolas, Costa Rica, 63
Botrytis rileyi, 124
Braulio Carrillo Park,
    Costa Rica, 48
Bribri Indians, 62-63
broad beans (*Vicia faba*), 125
brown leaf spot of coffee,
    (Cercospora coffeicola), 143
Buenaventura, Colombia, 31, 33
bulrush millet, 144
burnt earth system, 89-90, 98
bush fallow, 23
bushmaster, 39

Cabello de Balboa, 31
cacao, 22, 41, 128, 134-138, 142
calcium, 16, 21, 55, 139
Calinguero grass (*Melinis minutiflora*), 63
Callejón de Huayla, 15
Cameroon, 24, 62, 70-75, 78

Campesinos, 53, 105, 119, 125
Camptomeris leaf spot,
    (*Camptomeris leucaenae*), 135
Canavalia ensiformis, 24, 67, 84, 106,
    109, 123
cassava, 12, 23, 34, 36-42, 63, 88-89
    diseases, 153
      cassava bacterial blight
      (*Xanthomonas campestris* pv.
      manihotis), 153
      cassava stem tip dieback, 153
castor beans, 155
caterpillars, 28, 124
Cato, 100, 122
cattle, 41-42, 66, 91, 116, 119, 131, 136
Cebu, Philippines, 132-133
Cecropia spp., 16, 55
Cephaleuros virescens, 143
Cercospora stizolobii, 123
CGIAR (Consultative Group in
    International Agricultural
    Research), 60
chagra, 39-40
charcoal rot (caused by
    Macrophomina phaseolina), 148
cherry tomatoes, 40
chicha, 63
chicken manure, 151
China, 7, 21, 28, 110, 149
chinampa, 149
chirimoya (*Annona squamosa*), 39
chitin amendments, 156
chitinolytic ability, 152
chlamydospores, 153
choclo, 35-36
Choco, Colombia, 31-38, 55, 87
chococito maize, 34-38, 99
Choluteca, Honduras, 65
CIAT (Centro Internacional de
    Agricultura Tropical), 51-100
CIDICCO (International Cover
    Crops Clearinghouse), 65, 109,
    115-116, 125, 136-137
Cieza de León, 31
CIMMYT (Centro Internacional
    de Mejoramiento de Maiz y

suppressiveness, 26, 90, 95, 156
soilborne pathogens, 26, 28, 95, 122,
   147-158
sorghum, 54, 64-67, 77, 107, 109, 118,
   122, 144
southern blight (caused by
   Sclerotium rolfsii), 95, 123, 148,
   151
southern green stink bug
   (*Nezara viridula*), 124
soybean, (*Glycine max*), 106, 113, 124
Spain, 122
Spanish, 31-34, 44-45, 132, 149
Spanish chroniclers, 31-34
Spanish moss, 21
squash, 62, 88, 94, 120
Sri Lanka, 128, 136
Stizolobium spp., 105-106, 110, 119-
   120
stone mulch, 21
storage practices, 35, 54, 58, 95
straw mulch, 21-22, 151, 154-155
subsistence agriculture, 2-4, 38, 76
subterranean clover (*Trifolium
   subterraneum*), 71
Sudan, 76, 125, 144
sugar cane, 22, 36, 38, 43, 83, 88, 122
sulfur, 21, 154
Sumatra, 14, 90-91, 98, 161
sunhemp *Crotalaria
   ochroleuca*), 77, 106
suppressive soils, 26, 90, 95, 156
swamp rice system, 81
sweet corn, 72
sweet potatoes, 12, 38, 40-41, 76, 88-
   89
swidden, 12, 81-82, 84, 89, 96
sword bean (*Canavalia
   gladiata*), 106

taboos, 89
Tagetes spp., 155
tannier (*Xanthosoma* spp.), 38
Tanzania, 21, 77, 144
taro (*Colocasia esculenta*), 12, 38, 40,

79, 83-84, 89, 97, 14
tarwi (*Lupinus mutabilis*), 106, 109,
   125-126
Tegucigalpa, Honduras, 9-10, 115
Tembe-Thonga system, 96
Tenochtitlán, Mexico, 68
tenure, 3-4, 43, 53-54, 141
Tennessee, 112
termites, 92
terraces, 133-134, 150
terthienyl, 154
Thalia geniculata
   (Popal grass), 15, 94-95
Thanatephorus cucumeris, 55, 95, 123,
   148-151, 154-155
Theobroma cacao (cacao), 22, 41, 128,
   134, 136-138, 142
Thielaviopsis basicola, 154
Thielaviopsis spp., 151, 154
Tingo Maria, Peru, 70-71
titepati (*Artemisia vulgaris*), 26
tobacco, 40, 133
tomatoes, 40, 71-72, 122
tortillas, 109
Tripsacum spp., 35
tumba y pudre, 38
Tumaco, Colombia, 38
turkeys, 124
turnip, 154

Ucayali, Peru, 16, 55
Ukara, Lake Victoria, Tanzania, 144
ultisols, 63, 132
United Fruit Company, 113
Uromyces mucunae, 124
Uxpanapa, 116

Vaginulus plebeius, 119
Valle de Uxpanapa, Mexico, 119
vanilla, 89, 136
Varro, 103, 125
vector, 27
vegetables, 20, 26, 71, 92, 94, 149

velvetbean caterpillar,
(*Anticarsia gemmatali*), 124
velvetbeans, 103-126
Venezuela, 17, 42, 89
vetch,
hairy, 71-72
Vigna unguiculata (cowpea), 106, 134,
138
vine support, 136
Virginia, 36, 112
Virginia colony, 36
volatile metabolites, 153
volatilization, 28, 116

Wakara tribe, 144
wasps, 124
water,
erosion, 3, 17, 19, 22-25, 27, 67,
93, 107, 147, 159, 161
pollution, 8
retention, 8, 20, 25, 57, 84, 94, 147,
148
runoff, 6, 23, 25, 66
water hyacinth, 9, 22, 104
watersheds, 6
web blight, 49, 55-61, 149, 155

weeds, 1, 3, 7-8, 13, 20-22, 26, 33, 35,
37, 51, 55, 58-59, 61-62, 64-65, 68-
71, 76-77, 82, 90-95, 99-104, 108-
121, 127, 131-144, 149-150, 161
West Kalimantan, Indonesia, 80
West Sumatra, Indonesia, 14, 90-91
West Timor, Indonesia, 134
white-fringed beetle,
(*Naupactus leucoloma*), 124
wild peanut (*Arachis pintoi*), 106
wind breaks, 131
World Neighbors, 115, 125

Xochimilco, Mexico, 149

yam beans (*Pachrrhizus erosus*), 40
yams, 12, 38, 41, 62
Yucatán, 67

zacate camalote (*Paspalum
fasciculatum*), 68
Zaire, 76, 153
Zapotecs, 132
Zimbabwe, 128
zoospores, 155

www.ingramcontent.com/pod-product-compliance
Lightning Source LLC
Chambersburg PA
CBHW060039030426
42334CB00019B/2397